MAD

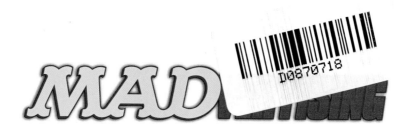

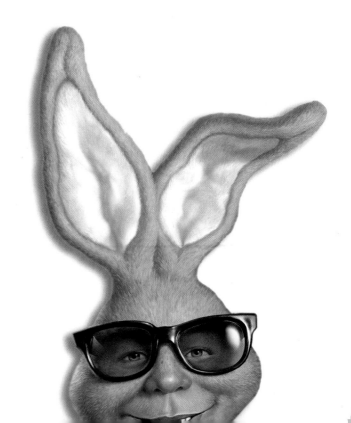

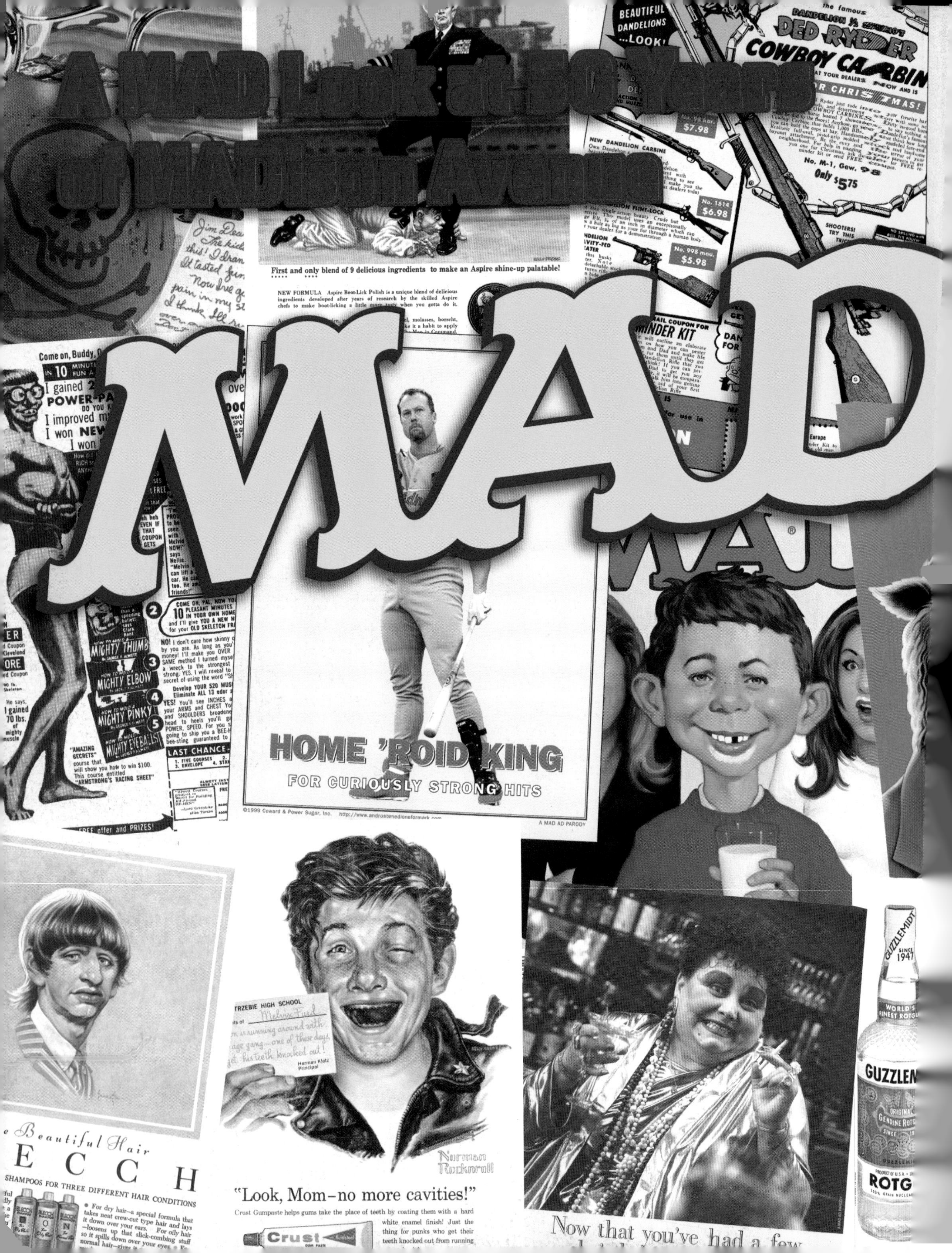
A MAD Look at 50 Years of MADison Avenue
MAD
BEAUTIFUL DANDELIONS ...LOOK!
the famous DANDELION ½ Ded Ryder COWBOY CARBINE
NEW DANDELION CARBINE
$7.98
$6.98
$5.98
Only $5.75
First and only blend of 9 delicious ingredients to make an Aspire shine-up palatable!
NEW FORMULA Aspire Boot-Lick Polish is a unique blend of delicious ingredients developed after years of research by the skilled Aspire chefs to make boot-licking a little more tasty when you gotta do it.
Come on, Buddy,
I gained
POWER-PA
I improved
I won
MIGHTY THUMB
MIGHTY ELBOW
MIGHTY PINKY
MIGHTY EYEBALLS
LAST CHANCE
"AMAZING SECRETS" course that will show you how to win $100. This course entitled "ARMSTRONG'S RACING SHEET"
FREE offer and PRIZES!
HOME 'ROID KING
FOR CURIOUSLY STRONG HITS
©1999 Coward & Power Sugar, Inc. http://www.androstenedioneformark.com
A MAD AD PARODY
Beautiful Hair
ECCH
SHAMPOOS FOR THREE DIFFERENT HAIR CONDITIONS
"Look, Mom–no more cavities!"
Crust Gumpaste helps gums take the place of teeth by coating them with a hard white enamel finish! Just the thing for punks who get their teeth knocked out from running
Crust
Norman Rockanroll
Herman Klotz Principal
GUZZLEMIDT
SINCE 1947
WORLD'S FINEST ROTGUT
ROTG
Now that you've had a few

VERTISING

by David Shayne

ABSOLUT WINTER.

iPot
New 1/4 oz.
and 1/2 oz. bags.
Perfect for
all your hits.

We don't try very hard!

Watson-Guptill Publications
New York

ACKNOWLEDGMENTS

Lenny Brenner, Dick DeBartolo, John Ficarra, Al Feldstein, Kelly Freas (and his wife Laura), Al Jaffee, Charlie Kadau, Arie Kaplan, Scott Maiko, Nick Meglin, Joe Raiola, Irving Schild and Sam Viviano generously shared their thoughts and memories about creating *MAD* ad parodies. Without their stories, my running commentary would have consisted entirely of "Um, here's another one that shows that smoking isn't good for you," and without their talent—and the talent of every other member of the Usual Gang of Idiots whose work appears in this volume—there would be no *MADvertising*.

At DC Comics, Paul Kupperberg shepherded this project from start to finish, never getting on me too much about word count or deadlines.

Dave Croatto and Amy Vozeolas at *MAD* always handled my requests for materials and information with far greater speed than I deserved. Grant Geissman offered up several contacts, and Lee Aronsohn (foolishly) entrusted me with his collection of original ads, many of which appear in the book.

Stuart Elliott of the *New York Times*, Randall Rothenberg of *Advertising Age*, and David Kennedy of Wieden + Kennedy were kind enough to share their thoughts about *MAD*'s influence on MADison Avenue.

I used several books for information and inspiration while compiling this volume. Specifically, *Completely MAD* by Maria Redielbach; *The MAD World of William M. Gaines* by Frank Jacobs; and *MAD About the Fifties*, *MAD About the Sixties*, and *MAD About the Seventies*, all with commentary by Grant Geissman. Warren Berger's *Advertising Today* and Randall Rothenberg's *Where the Suckers Moon: The Life and Death of an Advertising Campaign* filled my gaps in knowledge about the world of advertising, as did *The Milk Mustache Book* by Jay Schulberg.

Finally, I would like to dedicate this book to my late father, Herbert M. Shayne, who got his start some forty years ago as an ad man and was a guy who loved a good laugh as much as anyone.

DAVID SHAYNE
Los Angeles, California
February 2005

First published in 2005 by Watson-Guptill Publications
A division of BPI Communications, Inc.
770 Broadway, New York, NY 10003
www.wgpub.com

Library of Congress Control Number: 2005931068

ISBN 0-8230-3081-4

Printed in the United States of America

First printing 2005
1 2 3 4 5 6 7 8 9 / 13 12 11 10 09 08 07 06 05

For Watson-Guptill Publications:
Senior Acquisitions Editor: Candace Raney
Editors: Cathy Hennessy and Audrey Walen
Senior Production Manager: Ellen Greene

Front cover design: Patricia Dwyer
Page design: Jay Anning, Thumb Print, and Eric Mueller, Element Group

For E. C. Publications:
Editor: John Ficarra
Art Director: Sam Viviano

CONTENTS

INTRODUCTION

Spend any time in New York City and you quickly learn that the names of certain streets are synonymous with different industries.

Wall Street is shorthand for finance and banking.

Seventh Avenue is home to the nation's fashion designers.

The theater district is known simply as *Broadway*.

And *Madison Avenue* means advertising.

MAD Magazine has had offices in several locations around Manhattan, but for much of the magazine's fifty-plus years, its staff worked out of a tiny group of rooms located on the thirteenth floor of a building at 485 Madison Avenue. Not only did the Madison Avenue address give the magazine's editors an opportunity to include a visual pun in their stationery—the return address on the envelopes read "485 MADison Avenue"—but their home base in midtown Manhattan was just down the block from all the folks who were churning out the radio, TV, and print advertisements that enticed American consumers to purchase everything from Amana ovens to Zenith televisions.

In other words, the guys at *MAD* sure didn't have to travel very far to get a bead on one of their favorite targets.

IN THE BEGINNING...

MAD began its life as a 10¢ comic book in 1952, a boom time for the United States. The end of rationing, increased government spending, and overall economic growth following World War II meant that American consumers found themselves with more money than they had had in a long time, and they were looking for places to spend it. American industry was more than happy to oblige, stepping up production on goods and bombarding the public with ads to sell their wares.

From its start, *MAD* spoofed many aspects of popular culture, particularly comic books, movies, and television shows. But with the language of Madison Avenue permeating the vernacular, it was only a matter of time before *MAD* turned its eye on the world of advertising, with its first advertising parody appearing in *MAD* #17, a one-page ad for a product called Potgold Beer.

From 1942 to 1964, the beer company Rheingold had been running a campaign asking readers to vote in its annual Miss Rheingold contest, so in its parody *MAD* offered a ballot to choose the imaginary Miss Potgold of 1955. She would succeed Hester Shvester, Miss Potgold of 1954, who drunkenly slurred, "My beer ish Potgold—zha dry beer!"

Seeing the ad spoof today, one can't help but realize that it looks, well . . . a little dated. For one thing, you'd be hard-pressed to find anyone who drinks (or even remembers) Rheingold beer, and rather than make a comment about Rheingold or the dangers of drinking, the jokes are little more than a list of silly names for Miss Potgold candidates—Miss Bedney Flunt, Miss Fludney Bent, Miss Flentney Bunt, etc. Not exactly subversive stuff.

But context is key. Today, when pop culture oozes irony and post-modernism, *MAD*'s approach may not seem so cutting-edge. In the '50s, it was downright radical.

Corporations were promoting themselves as benevolent entities that contributed to the greater good of society. After all, American industry, which had churned out munitions and aircraft and chemicals, was viewed as a key component of America's success in World War II. It was an era when a corporation like DuPont would promote the idea of "Better Things for Better Living . . . Through Chemistry," or the head of GM would announce, "What is good for the country is good for General Motors, and vice versa."

Even so, not everyone was swallowing the corporate line. There were films like *Sweet Smell of Success* and *A Face in the Crowd* that looked at the public relations industry and its role in manipulating the American public, though they were heavy dramas. *MAD*, acting as the nation's court jester, was just about the only one to take on Madison Avenue with humor.

In this light, "Potgold" is *MAD* Magazine to its core—poking fun at a powerful corporate entity (like a major beer company) that will do anything (like run a lame beauty contest) to sell you its product. And, while not hitting anyone too hard, "Potgold" at least *hints* at the darker side of drinking.

Thus, "Potgold" is in many ways the quintessential *MAD* ad parody, establishing a style, format, and point of view that *MAD* would use throughout its history.

This book is a look at what followed.

MAD #17
November 1954
Artist: Basil Wolverton
Writer: Harvey Kurtzman

THE MAKING OF A CLASSIC (M)AD CAMPAIGN

What makes a great *MAD* ad parody? It takes a combination of things, but most of all it starts with a popular campaign.

"If it's not well known, we don't do it," says editor John Ficarra. After all, what fun is it to do a spoof if no one knows what you're spoofing?

In *MAD*'s earliest days, those well known campaigns were the print ads that ran in magazines like *Look*, *Life*, *Collier's*, and *The Saturday Evening Post*, all of which had large bases of faithful readers. As television caught on, *MAD* began spoofing TV ads too, but even today, *MAD* is much more likely to spoof print ads for the simple fact that they look the best on the printed page.

Why is this important? Because the most successful ad parodies, Ficarra says, are the ones that at first glance trick readers into thinking they're looking at an actual ad.

This process starts with the writer, who carefully breaks down the elements of an ad by asking questions—How do the headlines read? Is there body copy? Are there disclaimers in small type? What does the logo look like?—and then writes lines and gags that parody every element of the original. The writer will also come up with art notes to create an image or images that will both suggest and twist the original. The *MAD* editors then hone the piece before handing it over to the art department, which designs a layout based on the existing ad's look. Then, unless the piece stays in-house, a *MAD* artist or photographer gets the assignment and, when the final art is rendered, all of the elements are assembled back at *MAD*'s art department. Depending on deadlines and difficulty in re-creating a look, this process can take place in a matter of days or over the course of several months.

In *MAD*'s early years, art director John Putnam worked closely with the editors to get the look of the ad spoofs just right. Although notoriously sloppy in his personal habits, Putnam was meticulous in his *MAD* work, perfectly matching the typefaces and layouts of the original ads so that, at first blush, readers would think they were looking at the real thing. In fact, associate editor Jerry De Fuccio would often field angry letters from parents who couldn't believe that a magazine like *MAD*, with so many children among its readers, would accept tobacco advertising (more on *MAD*'s ad policies below). It was clear they had only caught a quick glimpse of a *MAD* cigarette parody, prompting De Fuccio to write back that one of the joys of reading *MAD* was actually *reading* it.

Lenny Brenner followed in Putnam's footsteps, and today Sam Viviano heads *MAD*'s talented art department. Viviano explains that when *MAD* spoofs an existing ad campaign, the design challenges are easier than creating a layout for other types of *MAD* articles, since the art director of the original ad has worked out the design issues, but there is still the tricky part of "creating a visual that is convincing within that design framework." Simply put, the *MAD* ad has to look like it belongs in the real ad's campaign, yet at the same time the reader has to realize that there's something not quite right going on. Hopefully, that something makes you laugh.

MAD ad parodies are also at their best when the writer figures out a way to hoist a product or company on its own petard. That's a shift from *MAD*'s earliest days, when the laugh was more important than any message.

As former co-editor Nick Meglin, who was with *MAD* almost from its start, puts it, "[Early on] we tried to have fun. Any gag that anyone thought of that made fun of the ad, as silly as it may have been, was acceptable as long as it was funny."

But over time, especially as *MAD* began doing more and more cigarette ad spoofs, the *MAD* ad parodies became as pointed as they were funny. And while

MAD still runs ad spoofs that are more silly than satirical, for the most part what passed muster in the early '50s and '60s probably wouldn't make the magazine today, because the commentary is just too soft.

The editors say *MAD* ad parodies have gotten harder to do over the years. As consumers have become more aware of the fact that they're being sold to, advertisers have started employing *MAD*-style humor, frequently making fun of themselves to beat everyone, including the Usual Gang of Idiots, to the punch. By the '60s, firms like Doyle Dane Bernbach were shaking up the staid Madison Avenue mentality with creative, humorous ads (such as its famous Volkswagen campaign) that actually poked fun at the very product it was selling, and the guys at *MAD* realized that they just might have become victims of their own success.

"[Advertisers'] pretentiousness was always a tremendous starting point for us, and when we lost that it became difficult," explains Meglin.

There are others who aren't so sure that *MAD* was entirely responsible for Madison Avenue's newfound self-awareness, but believe the magazine was undoubtedly a factor.

"How could it not be?" asks Stuart Elliott, who covers the advertising industry for the *New York Times*. "[*MAD*] was the only place to get that kind of sensibility back then."

Certainly by the '70s and '80s several generations of adults who had grown up on that *MAD* sensibility had begun working on Madison Avenue. But during their formative years *MAD* had taught them to question the hard sell, so, as *Advertising Age* columnist Randall Rothenberg explains it, they had to reconcile themselves by using "advertising as a palette to be subversive. You're taking your clients' money and you're selling your clients' goods, but you're doing it in a way that is incredibly entertaining." Those now-adult *MAD* readers had made advertising "completely self-referential and an ironic commentary on the culture of advertising."

Besides, if nothing else, all that self-referential humor is probably just smart business sense.

"That's what all good advertising people do. They co-opt it and absorb it and half the advertising you see now makes fun of advertising," says the *Times*'s Elliott.

The good news is, there are still plenty of companies that take themselves too seriously, and *MAD* will always be the first to point this out. Even when a company employs humor, there're still plenty of opportunities for *MAD* to get in its shots. Remember those revolutionary Volkswagen campaigns mentioned above? They're parodied on page 84. Fortunately, when the bottom line is selling, there's almost always something *MAD* can hit.

Just as a real advertisement will take one of many tones—from straightforward to offbeat to image-raising—a *MAD* ad parody usually falls into one of several categories. There are the ones that do the aforementioned petard-hoisting, pointing out the hypocrisy and deception inherent in the hard sell; the majority of the cigarette and alcohol parodies fall into this category. Other spoofs are more about old-fashioned silliness, taking a familiar ad campaign and spinning it into something new. That was more common in the '50s, but the tradition continues today with articles like "Cents-less Coupons" (page 182). And sometimes *MAD* will use an ad campaign not to parody a specific product, but to comment on a current event like the O. J. Simpson trial ("Absolut O. J." page 214) or steroid abuse in baseball ("Altoids" page 168).

WOULD YOU BUY A
MAGAZINE FROM THIS BOY?

It should come as no surprise that Madison Avenue is one of *MAD*'s most frequent targets, since even *MAD*'s mascot, Alfred E. Neuman, has his own ties to the world of advertising. After all, Alfred really isn't all that different from the Jolly Green Giant, Ronald McDonald, or Snap, Crackle, and Pop—he's the cartoon face of a familiar product.

Just as Tony the Tiger instantly makes you think of Frosted Flakes, Alfred's gap-toothed grin can only mean *MAD*. And like Tony's call of "They're great!" Alfred has his own slogan: "What—me worry?"

Alfred actually pre-dates *MAD*, with illustrations of an unnamed smiling gap-toothed boy appearing as early as the 19th century to advertise everything from painless dentists and patent medicines to barbecues and Broadway shows. *MAD*'s first editor, Harvey Kurtzman, incorporated small black-and-white versions of that boy (who was yet to be named Alfred) in various spots around the comic and, later, the magazine. After a few years, Kurtzman's successor Al Feldstein and then-associate editor Nick Meglin realized they might have something big on their hands, and went in search of an artist to create the fully rendered Alfred who went on to grace just about every cover of *MAD* since 1956.

They placed an ad in the *New York Times*, which found the attention of illustrator Norman Mingo. Mingo, who was sixty when he created the gold-standard Alfred, had retired after a career as an illustrator in . . . advertising.

Mingo's not the only *MAD*man who's worked on Madison Avenue. Not only did many of the magazine's artists get their start in commercial illustration, but as the *MAD*men became famous for their work in *MAD*, artists like Bob Clarke, Sergio Aragonés, Mort Drucker, and Jack Davis found themselves being hired to illustrate advertisements for everything from Hollywood films to Gen-X sodas. And why not? If you're trying to sell something, why not hire the best artist you can?

Besides, for some ad execs, hiring a *MAD* artist is a chance to work with a childhood idol. David Kennedy, founder of the Portland, Oregon-based ad firm Wieden + Kennedy (creator of many of Nike's and ESPN's most famous campaigns) grew up on the old E.C. comics and *MAD* and says that hiring Jack Davis to work on a campaign was "a dream come true."

Norman Mingo

Early advertisements featuring the unnamed boy who was the inspiration for Alfred E. Neuman.

MAD #35
October 1957
Artist: Norman Mingo
Writer: Staff

Alfred celebrates the magazine's fifth birthday with all of the popular advertising characters of the day in this cover illustrated by Norman Mingo. Rumor has it that Betty Crocker didn't actually bring a gift, but just signed her name to Aunt Jemima's card.

MAD AND ADVERTISING

As the legend goes, *MAD*'s publisher, William M. Gaines, refused on principle and under any circumstances to accept advertising, making *MAD* an extremely rare magazine among mainstream publications.

The actual story is a bit more complicated.

In its early comic book days, *MAD* indeed accepted advertising, running the same ads for novelties that appeared in the typical comic book. Gaines also used pages to promote other comics published by *MAD*'s parent company, EC Publications.

By the time *MAD* #21 arrived, editor Harvey Kurtzman had spoofed just about every comic book on the stands, from *Superman* and *Batman* to EC's own horror and sci-fi lines. So Kurtzman decided to lampoon the only thing that was left—the ads that ran in comic books, including *MAD* itself. Of course, this was *MAD*, so instead of running the piece on the back cover, Kurtzman put *MAD*'s spoof of Johnson Smith and Co.'s mail-order smorgasbord front and center.

MAD #21
March 1955
Writer: Harvey Kurtzman

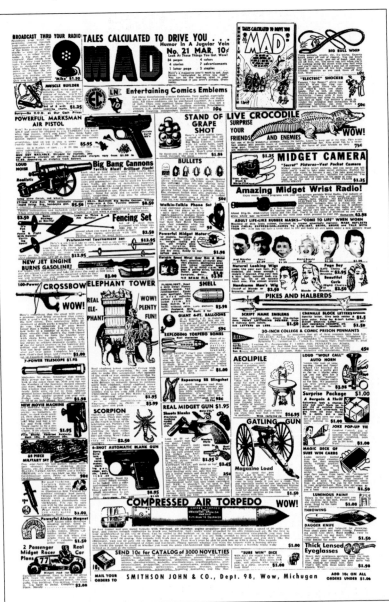

In *MAD About the Fifties*, author Grant Geissman recalls Kurtzman's comment to John Benson: "About a year's writing went into that cover. It's sort of like reading the Lord's Prayer on the head of a pin."

Gaines told author Maria Reidelbach in 1991 that *MAD*'s advertisers were "very upset"; not that Gaines cared very much, since most of *MAD*'s revenue came from newsstand sales, not advertising. Soon, Gaines decided to drop ads from *MAD* altogether.

Gaines's rationale was simple—*MAD* could spoof everyone if it was beholden to no one. Or, as he once told Mike Wallace on *60 Minutes*, "We long ago decided we couldn't take money from Pepsi-Cola and make fun of Coca-Cola." (To which *MAD* contributor Dick DeBartolo, recognizing the potential fortune lost, responded, "Can we do it the other way? Think, Bill, think!")

It was this same "beholden to no one" logic that also kept Gaines from ever taking a readership survey. Gaines was worried that if writers and artists knew who was reading the magazine, they would subconsciously (or consciously) pander to their readership. Although Gaines may have never mentioned it, there was probably another reason he didn't survey his readers: magazines take surveys primarily to help them lure advertisers with the promise of reaching a specific, quantifiable demographic—to convince, say, a beer company that your magazine appeals to their target audience of males ages 21–34. In an ad-free magazine, there are no advertisers to woo, so why would Gaines, a notorious cheapskate, want to waste his money on a survey?

MAD #21

March 1955
Artist: Will Elder
Writer: Harvey
Kurtzman

Gaines certainly feared that advertising would force *MAD* to improve its packaging. As he told author Frank Jacobs in 1972, "Most advertisers want to appear in a magazine that's loaded with color and has super-slick paper. So you find yourself being pushed into a more expensive package. You get bigger and fancier and attract advertisers. Then you find you're losing some of your advertisers. Your readers still expect the fancy package, so you keep putting it out, but now you don't have your advertising income, which is why it got fancier in the first place—and now you're sunk."

So *MAD* carried on, ad-free for over four decades.

But in the late '90s, the editors began to worry that the magazine looked dated. *MAD* was still printing in black and white while every other publication on the newsstand boasted color—even the *New York Times*, nicknamed "The Old Gray Lady" for its color-free front page, had introduced color. *MAD*'s printing felt more and more like it was from another era, so that when *MAD* spoofed the latest movie or newest trend there was an inherently out-of-date feel. As senior editor Joe Raiola would frequently lament, the magazine itself "looked like it was published in Mexico in 1958."

Problem is, printing in color is far more expensive than printing in black and white. Instead of one ink, color printing requires four, and demands the slicker and heavier (and more expensive) paper that Gaines had complained about to Frank Jacobs three decades earlier. The only way *MAD* could afford color was to increase the magazine's revenues, and that meant either a significant price increase, making the magazine prohibitively expensive, or adding several pages of advertising.

The main argument against accepting ads was that Gaines had never run them. But then, Gaines, who passed away in 1992, had the luxury of being a publisher in a different era, an era when black-and-white pages were still common in magazines, and an era when there were far fewer outlets competing for a reader's attention—no cable, no Internet, no video games—which meant a much wider circulation. *MAD*'s choice was to admit that the magazine needed a look that was as contemporary as its written material—or to press on in black and white, knowing full well that this would eventually mean the death of *MAD*.

This wasn't the first time the *MAD* editorial staff had considered using advertising to pay for color pages. Former editor Al Feldstein recalls approaching Gaines in the early '70s with the same idea, even mocking up a version of *MAD* #67 with ads tipped in.

Under Feldstein's plan, *MAD* would protect its integrity by refusing to spoof an advertiser's competitor (taking care of Gaines's problem of making fun of Coke while taking money from Pepsi), and would require a release from its advertisers that would allow *MAD* to make fun of their products. Feldstein also suggested establishing a *MAD* ad agency that would work in conjunction with a company's own agency to create humorous ads that would run exclusively in *MAD*. Whether any company would have agreed to such demands is unknown; Feldstein made his presentation, but found that "Bill would have no part of it."

Some twenty-five years later, and after much soul-searching, the editorial staff (including myself, an associate editor at the time) reached a conclusion: the magazine needed color pages. To improve the package was not, as Gaines had worried, something to make the advertisers happy; it had to be done to make the *readers* happy.

So we went upstairs to the "suits" and asked for a radical change. We wanted *MAD* to take ads.

We took comfort in the fact that in this day and age, perhaps Gaines's beholden-to-no-one logic, while admirable, doesn't quite carry the weight it once did. Ad parodies are a staple of other comedy outlets like *Saturday Night Live* and *MADtv* and no one has ever accused them of holding back for the sake of their advertisers.

Besides, from those earliest comic book ad spoofs, *MAD* has never been afraid to bite the hands that feed it. In 1961, Gaines sold *MAD* to the company that eventually became Warner Bros., yet the magazine has never dulled its comedic blade when cutting apart the latest dreck from Warner Bros.' movie and TV divisions. When *MAD* was folded under the DC Comics division in 1995 the magazine continued to spoof Superman and Batman, as it had from practically its first issue. And when AOL and Time Warner merged a few years ago, *MAD* still made fun of AOL's frequently buggy service and falling stock price. Just because *MAD* was changing its advertising policy didn't mean it was changing its editorial policy.

So, with this note from the editors on the index page of issue #403, *MAD* heralded a new era of color and, yes, advertising.

As of press time, an informal survey of *Time, Newsweek, Sports Illustrated*, and *Rolling Stone* reveals that all of those publications indeed accept advertising and have color pages.

The editors' prediction has come true.

ENOUGH WITH THE INTRO ALREADY...

You hold in your hands 224 pages of *MAD*'s greatest ad parodies, as well as several articles that spoof what Warren Berger, author of *Advertising Today*, estimates is a $400 billion industry.

This is only a small sampling of *MAD*'s shots at MADison Avenue from the magazine's fifty-plus year history, but if you take away one message from this tome, it's *caveat emptor*—"buyer beware." Folks will do whatever they can to separate you from your money, trying to sell you something you probably don't need, and which probably isn't all that good for you either.

Then again, you already bought this book, so it's probably too late for you.

MAD
Editor's Note

Dear MAD Reader:
As you know, MAD has long been an innovator in the magazine industry and now, beginning with this very issue you hold in your hands, we offer two exciting new concepts that are sure to revolutionize the magazine business: color and advertising. That's right, for the first time in history, a major publication will offer both full-color editorial pages and advertisements from important international companies. We are sure it's only a matter of time before other publications will do what they've always done — follow our bold lead and offer their own color pages and advertisements. But you, dear reader, will be able to tell your friends that you saw MAD do it first!
Onward to a new era in publishing!
MAD-ly,
The Editors

A NOTE ABOUT THE WRITING CREDITS

Pieces credited as written by "House" were done collaboratively in brainstorming sessions by the *MAD* staff, which included *MAD* editor Al Feldstein, associate editors Jerry De Fuccio and Nick Meglin, and art director John Putnam; the finished articles were put together by Feldstein. Pieces credited as "Staff" were done in collaboration by the more current *MAD* staff, including Nick Meglin, John Ficarra, Charlie Kadau, Joe Raiola, Dick DeBartolo, and art directors Leonard Brenner, Nadina Simon, and Sam Viviano.

MAD ADS

MAD #24
July 1955
Artist: Will Elder
Writer: Harvey Kurtzman

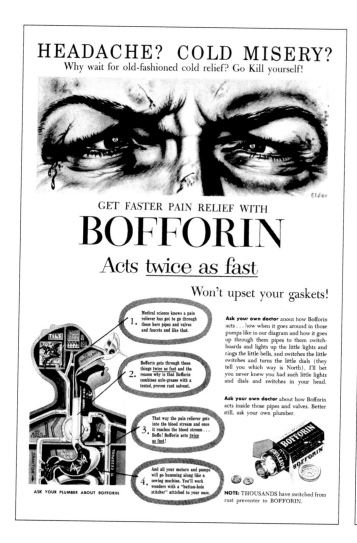

HEADACHE? COLD MISERY?
Why wait for old-fashioned cold relief? Go Kill yourself!

GET FASTER PAIN RELIEF WITH

BOFFORIN

Acts twice as fast

Won't upset your gaskets!

1. Medical science knows a pain reliever has got to go through these here pipes and valves and faucets and like that.

2. Bofforin gets through these things twice as fast and the reason why is that Bofforin combines axle-grease with a tested, proven rust solvent.

3. That way the pain reliever gets into the blood stream and once it reaches the blood stream . . . Boffo! Bofforin acts twice as fast!

4. And all your motors and pumps will go humming along like a sewing machine. You'll work wonders with a "button-hole stitcher" atttched to your nose.

Ask your own doctor about how Bofforin acts . . . how when it goes around in those pumps like in our diagram and how it goes up through them pipes to them switchboards and lights up the little lights and rings the little bells, and switches the little switches and turns the little dials (they tell you which way is North), I'll bet you never knew you had such little lights and dials and switches in your head.

Ask your own doctor about how Bofforin acts inside those pipes and valves. Better still, ask your own plumber.

ASK YOUR PLUMBER ABOUT BOFFORIN

NOTE: THOUSANDS have switched from rust preventer to BOFFORIN.

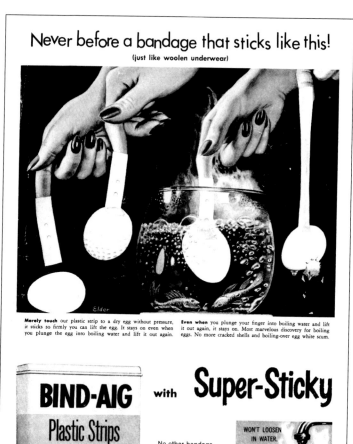

Never before a bandage that sticks like this!
(just like woolen underwear)

Merely touch our plastic strip to a dry egg without pressure, it sticks so firmly you can lift the egg. It stays on even when you plunge the egg into boiling water and lift it out again.

Even when you plunge your finger into boiling water and lift it out again, it stays on. Most marvelous discovery for boiling eggs. No more cracked shells and boiling-over egg white scum.

BIND-AIG
Plastic Strips

Stickier & Stickier

with **Super-Sticky**

No other bandage sticks to dry eggs so well.

WON'T LOOSEN IN WATER

Issue #24 marked *MAD*'s transition from a 10¢ comic book to a 25¢ magazine, and while the page size increased and the interior color was lost in favor of more inexpensive black and white, publisher William M. Gaines's no-ad policy remained in place. This meant that while *MAD* might advertise its own books and licensed products, any or all of the four covers (front, inside front, inside back, and back) could be dedicated to editorial, like this spoof of Bufferin, illustrated (as many of *MAD*'s early ad spoofs were) by legendary artist Will Elder.

  MAD #24 made it clear that ad parodies would be a staple of the new magazine, and this issue featured no fewer than eight, including the three ads shown here.

▼ (overleaf) **MAD #29**
September 1956
Artist: Wallace Wood
Writer: Al Feldstein

The New Expandable SEVEROLET

Seats a whol

THE BLAIR "CHECKMATE"—*no doors, 2 passengers . . . interior finish in black and red squares.*

. . .

THE TWO-PIECE "MALLETTE"—*2 doors, 3 passengers . . . interior finish in luxurious 3" deep Bermuda lawn grass.*

THE FOUR-PART "TOUCHDOWN"—*8 doors, 11 passengers, waterboy . . . interior finish in surgical gauze and absorbent co*

THE EIGHT-SECTION "OLYMPIAD"—*16 doors, 32 passengers, officials, time keepers, trainers, coaches, scorers . . . inte*

hecker team

hole croquet team

In place of checker players or Olympic players, of course, it could be other people. Like paying passengers, for instance. You could muscle in on the local bus franchise, run your own route, and recover the purchase price. Anyway, there's always enough room to meet your needs. Just add a section to fit. (A separate section is provided to house spare sections.) You can easily create space for an 8 man racing shell, a pair of hockey goals, or a boxing ring.

If you're joining the fast-expanding station wagon family, be sure to look over the fast-expandable Severolet. It's good looking, as you can see. It's practical, as you can see. It can be stretched out as far as you can see. Expanded, it packs Severolet's special brand of perform-ance which sheers off telegraph poles going around sharp corners, and makes anything but straightaway driving virtually impossible. Colors and interior choices are unusual. In fact, the whole idea is unusual. Ask your Severolet dealer about it. He still doesn't believe it himself.

Severolet Division of Generous Motors, Detour 2, Mishing.

SEVEROLET

The car you slice to fit your needs!

...a whole football team

...a whole Olympic team...*beautifully!*

laid trim.

shed in sawdust and cinders, laurel leaf trim.

Wood

MAD #42
November 1958
Artist: Kelly Freas
Writer: House

Does she...or doesn't she
...ever go out with fellows her own age?

Why only young boys? Only her psychiatrist knows for sure!

You can clearly see that this girl has lots of problems. Just one look at her obviously dyed hair is a good indication. Now, if she wants to dye her hair to attract attention, that's *her* business. But this compulsion she has for running around with young boys instead of men her own age—that's our business! Mainly, we can help her avoid embarrassment until she's worked this problem out with her analyst. All she has to do is buy a Miss Clairold Date-Ager Kit. With Miss Clairold, it takes *only* minutes to add those grey streaks to his temples, those little bags under his eyes, that five-o-clock shadow, that moustache,—all the other little things that will make him look as old as she is. And, when you think about it, why *should* you suffer one more day of embarrassment if you have a problem like this girl! Try a Miss Clairold Date-Ager Kit on that boy in your life—*today!* Then, all you'll have to do is figure out how to stretch him so it don't look like you're out with an old midget!

MISS CLAIROLD® DATE-AGER KIT

© 1958 CLAIROLD INCORPORATED. AVAILABLE ALSO FOR NEUROTICS IN CANADA

MORE CRADLE-ROBBERS USE MISS CLAIROLD THAN ANY OTHER DATE-DISGUISER

Miss Clairol pitched its hair-coloring line with the provocative-for-its-days headline, "Does she . . . or doesn't she?" and saw its sales skyrocket. *MAD* wondered for whom, exactly, she was dyeing her hair.

MAD #43
December 1958
Artist: Kelly Freas
Writer: House

"Look, Mom—no more cavities!"

Crust Gumpaste helps gums take the place of teeth by coating them with a hard white enamel finish! Just the thing for punks who get their teeth knocked out from running around with teen-age gangs.

Fluidsteel is a trademark for Proctor & Rumble's exclusive liquid metal gum-coater.

© 1958, The Proctor & Rumble Co.

The original artwork to this piece hangs in the home of the late artist Kelly Freas, whose visitors were always impressed that he owned an original Norman Rockwell . . . until, on closer inspection, they realized it's an original Norman Rocknroll . . . which is to say, an original Kelly Freas.

Like many of the *MAD* artists, Freas, who painted dozens of *MAD*'s early ad parodies, was a master at aping any style. Freas said one of the keys to successful mimicry is to paint in a different medium than the original; in the case of Rockwell, who used oils, Freas chose acrylics.

MAD #41
September 1958
Artist: Wallace Wood
Writer: House

It's Fun to Phone!

** "Smokers Who Know"...give it up!

A minute from now you can be having a happy time.
Just phone someone who means a lot to you.
Like your bookie. Place a bet with him today.
And nothing helps you do that so easily as
your telephone. Yes, "It's fun to phone!"
Providing the nag you pick don't run last!

Bet Telephone System

MAD #49
September 1959
Artist: Kelly Freas
Writer: House

"Stop pushing—you'll all get a chance to talk to Grandma"

How long has it been since you enjoyed a Long Distance visit?

CELL TELEPHONE SYSTEM Remember..."It's Fun to Phone!"

HUBERT THUMB

KELLY FREAS

PRESENTING THE BILL—reproduced here, is one of a series of original oil paintings,
"Practising Medicine For Fun and Profit", commissioned by Park-David.

Great
Moments
in
Medicine

Once the crisis has passed . . . once the patient has regained his strength . . . once the family is relieved and grateful . . . that's the time when the physician experiences one of the great moments in medicine. In fact, the *greatest moment* in medicine! Mainly, the moment when he presents his bill! That's the time when all of the years of training and study and work seem worthwhile. And there's always the chance that the shock might mean more business for him!

Park-David scientists are proud of their place in the history of practicing medicine for fun and profit, helping to provide doctors with the materials that mean higher fees and bigger incomes. For example, our latest development . . . tranquilizer-impregnated bill paper . . . designed to eliminate the shock and hysteria that comes when the patient gets a look at your bill. Not only will he remain calm when he sees what you've charged . . . now he won't even *care!*

PARK-DAVID   *. . . Pioneers in bigger medical bills*

◀ **MAD #48**
July 1959
Artist: Kelly Freas
Writer: House

Along with his painting for "Rummie Walker" (page 208), artist Kelly Freas listed "Great Moments in Medicine" as his personal favorite. Pharmaceutical giant Parke-Davis (known today as Pfizer) had commissioned artist Robert Thom to create two series of paintings entitled "A History of Medicine in Pictures" and "A History of Pharmacy in Pictures." The paintings were self-aggrandizing celebrations of the medical profession that were used as magazine ads, and also turned into prints that were sent to doctors and pharmacists to hang in their offices.

To make sure he got the look right, Freas studied all ninety of the prints and even honored Thom's work, in a manner of speaking, by including the signature of "Hubert Thumb."

Freas also filled the scene with visual gags. Look carefully on the table and amidst the doctor's tools of the trade you'll see an item that Freas managed to slip past the *MAD* editors—a penile splint (we'll leave it to you to figure out which one it is). And the man fanning the old woman in the background is modeled on German rocket scientist Wernher von Braun.

According to Freas's wife Laura, so many people, especially members of the medical profession, requested a copy of this painting that Bill Gaines granted Freas permission to sell a limited-edition print of this work.

MAD #46
April 1959
Artist: Kelly Freas
Writer: Al Jaffee

MAD couldn't understand why anyone would want to waste their money on the "extravagance" of color television. Ironically, *MAD* had to run this spoof on the back cover, since publisher Bill Gaines wouldn't waste his money on the "extravagance" of color interior pages.

Nothing stops it - not even power brakes-

THE "CRASH PROOF" BODY BY FISHEY

You buy *safety* when you buy a new Body by Fishey—safety that can be measured in *rate of climb*.

For only a Fishey body gives you the exclusive accident-prevention feature of *flight*.

The secret? Balsa wood bolts hold the Fishey Body to the chassis!

Yes, when you're out driving your new car with its Fishey Body, and an accident becomes suddenly imminent, all you have to do is apply them power brakes!

The chassis stops on a dime, but your "Crash Proof" Fishey Body takes off, sails into space, and keeps on going.

You avoid the problem of replacing crushed grilles and dented fenders. You avoid the problem of paying costly repair bills. And you avoid the problem created by the accident itself.

The only thing you can't avoid is the problem of getting back down to the ground.

We haven't been able to figure out this one yet ourselves!

Only the "G·M*Five" give you the Breakaway BODY BY FISHEY

THE FINISHING TOUCH

You may have thought all along that this is our trademark. Well it is not! This is the magnificent 18th Century coach we've got waiting for the first driver who avoided an accident in a Fishey Body to come back to Earth.

SEVROLET
PONTIARC
UPSMOBILE
BUCKIT
CADILJAC

*Gravity Masters

MAD #51
December 1959
Artist: Kelly Freas
Writer: Larry Siegel

One kind of husband...<u>two</u> kinds of underwear

Why do you suppose so much Hames underwear for all kinds of husbands is bought by their wives? Because women have an uncanny knack of picking out designs men wouldn't be caught dead in, no less buy themselves! That's why we run these ads which encourage wives to buy their husbands' underwear for them. Mainly, we're trying to get rid of all these shorts with ridiculous designs we're stuck with!

Hames Knitting Co, Wemus-Sellum, N.C. • European: Macht Schnell Undzell, Dershtripeses, Germany • Russian: Pusha Pohka, Dotz, U.S.S.R.

underwear for men and boys

MAD hits two of its favorite targets—lame ad campaigns and misbehaving celebrities—in this Hanes underwear spoof commenting on the 1958 affair between crooner Eddie Fisher and actress Elizabeth Taylor. Shortly after Taylor's third husband died in a plane crash, Fisher left his wife, Debbie Reynolds (with whom he had two children, including Carrie Fisher of *Star Wars* fame) to marry Taylor. That marriage lasted four years, before Taylor left Fisher for Richard Burton.

TV ADS
WE'D LIKE TO SEE
The Schleppe's Commercial

Tell me, Dahling! Whar did we meet? Whas it Cay-roh? Bay-root? Lohn-dohn?

You whar having a cocktail, Commandah Whytehead . . . and I remembah you telling the way-tah to make jolly-well sure that he mayde it with Schleppe's!

ART—JOE ORLANDO

But that could have bean any-whar! I ahlways mayke jolly-well sure my cocktails are mayde with Schleppe's Quinine Wahtah! Thar's no other mixah so jolly-well full of effervescence!

Effervescence? You used to call it "Schleppervescence"!

Schleppervescence! Ohv cawss! Those remahkable little bobbles that lahst the whole drink through!

**I FALL IN LOVE TOO EASILY—Mickey Rooney

But I say, Dahling, stohp trying to slip your bar check under my hahnd, and tell me! Whar did we meet? Whas it Pah-riss? Rhohm? Ind-yah?

THE ELBO ROOM
5.00
1.00
1.50

TAX
TOTAL 51.50

Silly boy! We met at the Berlitz School of Languages . . . whar we lahrned these ridiculous English accents no-whon cahn understahnd!

◀ *MAD* #51
December 1959
Artist: Joe Orlando
Writer: House

The Usual Gang of Idiots generally have an easier time spoofing print ads than they do TV campaigns. Why? Because *MAD*'s readers are used to seeing similar ads in other magazines, so it's relatively easy to trick them into thinking, that at least momentarily, they are looking at a genuine advertisement. But as Americans became addicted to their television sets, the *MAD*men found the boob tube an irresistable source of inspiration, such as this early parody of a Schweppes commercial.

MAD #51
December 1959
Artist: Kelly Freas
Writer: House

Memories . . . painted for all De Beers he could drink by Frank Kelly Freas

Memories . . . forever gleaming

In fleeting moments sweetly shared, the world is filled with joy for lovers, their way is bright with dreams. It is a magic time, and they may recall it always in the enchanting lights of her wedding diamond . . . sparkling behind the window pane of the pawn shop where they were forced to hock it when things got bad. That's one thing you can do when it seems like . . .

FACTS ABOUT DIAMONDS: When choosing a diamond it is wise to seek the counsel of a trusted jeweler, if you can find one. He will explain how color, clarity and cutting are important, but it's the size that's impressive. In other words, you can get a much bigger diamond for your money if it's got a little flaw or two. After all, who's gonna know? Mainly, who goes around with a jeweler's eyepiece, anyway?

1 carat $500 to $3000
2 carats $3000 to $5000
3 carats $5000 to $9000
1 carats $200 to $210

The prices quoted above are based on buying the three smaller stones from a reputable jeweler, and buying the larger ''hot'' rock from a disreputable fence. If you got half a brain, you can figure which is the better deal!

. . . PAYING FOR A DIAMOND IS FOREVER

MAD #52
January 1960
Artist: Kelly Freas
Writer: Larry Siegel

Got it!

And you know you've got it. Hubby out with that other woman. A once-in-a-lifetime shot you and your lawyer can't afford to miss. And you won't with the Parloraid Land Camera. Because just 60 seconds after you snap the shutter, you have your finished picture. And 60 seconds after that, you're in a Divorce Court with an air-tight case against your two-timing husband. Parloraid Land Cameras, from $74.95 or $1.50 weekly. Alimony payments from $10,000 or $200 weekly (in pennies, if hubby's the spiteful type).

MAD #53
March 1960
Artist: Kelly Freas
Writer: House

"*On our trip across the U.S.A.* I posed Mama against interesting backgrounds like this, and got 11-by-14 blowups for detailed study!"

Nikita Khrushchev says: "It was <u>easy as borscht</u>
taking Kossacolor pictures like these!"

Russia's Beloved Premier uses Kossacolor Film ... and shows the NKVD boys how easy it is to take pictures of <u>interest!</u>

"It's natural for a tourist to carry a camera," chuckles Premier Nikita Khrushchev, "which made it *easy* for me to take wonderful pictures during my tour of the United States. And Kossacolor Film insured clear, sharp backgrounds for close scrutiny by our Intelligence Service. Yes, sir, Kossacolor made my trip to America *profitable!*"

"*Here's Rada*, my daughter, standing beside a secret atomic pile. Kossacolor gave me the picture. The pile gave Rada blood-poisoning!"

"*I shot Alexei*, my son-in-law, looking over Admiral Rickover's shoulder. I shot him again when we got home for covering the blueprints!"

"*This is Julia*, my other daughter. She moved when I took this picture, but the Radar Installation didn't!"

See Kossak's "What's My Party Line?" and "I've Got The Secrets"

EASTZONE KOSSAK COMPANY, Moscow 4, U. S. S. R.

Kossak
Trade Mark

Cold War humor from the Usual Gang of Idiots, using a Kodak film ad to reimagine Soviet premier Nikita Khrushchev's eleven-day visit to the United States in the fall of 1959.

How we retired at the age of 11 with $800 a month

"Like many other 11-year-olds, my twin sister Rhoda and I had been dreaming of retiring for a long time. After all, we weren't getting any younger. We'd begun to notice that running up and down the two flights of stairs in our grammar school sometimes made us puff. And very often, when jumping off our front porch, we got like drawing pains in our ankles. Both of these, we knew, were sure signs of advancing age.

"So we thought about retiring. We figured out that if we saved half our combined weekly allowances, we would eventually have $500. Which isn't bad money. However, we wanted to retire at 11, not 101!

"Then, one day, while thumbing through a magazine, we came across an ad for the Phonyex Mutual Retirement Income Plan. It pointed out that any forty-year-old could retire in 15 years with $300 a month for life.

"Well, although we were only 11, Rhoda and I were so anxious to retire that we decided to look into this exciting and unusual plan anyway. And,

as you might well imagine, we discovered an exciting and unusual loophole. Namely that any forty-year-old could retire in 15 years with $300 a month, providing he first shelled out exciting and unusual premium payments. Something like $2000 a year for those 15 exciting and unusual years.

"So Rhoda and I went up to the Phonyex Mutual Offices, and we told the people there what we had discovered about their exciting and unusual retirement income plan. Mainly, that the only ones who could afford it were people who were so rich they had retired already!

"Naturally, the folks at Phonyex Mutual begged us to keep our little secret to ourselves, and we told them we would think about it.

"So now Rhoda and I are living on a huge estate in Florida, enjoying life. We like it so much, we intend to spend the remainder of our twilight years—say another 80, give or take 10—right here.

"And on the first of every month, like clock-work, we get our check for

$800 for Phonyex Mutual—in one of the most exciting and unusual blackmail deals cooked up this century.

"We heartily recommend similar retirement plans to all 11-year-olds thinking of retiring. Just remember this: go find other companies with exciting and unusual loopholes. The suckers at Phonyex Mutual are all ours!"

Send for Free Booklet

The preceding story is not typical at all. Our lawyers are working on this case right now, and one of these days we'll have those two fresh, blackmailing brats in jail. However, we assure you that you can retire in 15 years with wonderful monthly checks from us. Our payment plans are simple, and *any* millionaire can afford them. But even if you know you *can't*, why not fill in the coupon below and mail it off anyway? We've got tons of regular insurance literature here in our offices, and we're dying to find people to send it to. When you get right down to it—sly little sneaks that we are—this is the *real* reason we place these ads!

- -

PHONYEX MUTUAL

Retirement Income Plan

GUARANTEES OUR FUTURE

OVER 100 YEARS
OF COME-ON ADS FOR SUCKERS
LOOKING FOR THE SOFT LIFE

PHONYEX MUTUAL LIFE INSURANCE CO.
815 Security Street, Peace-of-Mind, Conn.

Please mail me, with plenty of obligation, your free 28-page booklet showing new requirement income plans I can't afford.

Also send me one ton of insurance literature ☐   Two tons ☐
Three tons ☐   Your whole office-full ☐
Your whole warehouse-full ☐
Name
Address
Names and Addresses of friends who like to receive insurance mail

◄ *MAD #54*
April 1960
Artist: Kelly Freas
Writer: Larry Siegel

MAD #54
April 1960
Artist: Kelly Freas
Writer: House

THE MAN IN COMMAND

Pompous . . . Pig-headed . . . Pathological — a sucker for an ASPIRE shine-up

The Man in Command
COMDR. FENWICK STERNWALLOW
The Destroyer U.S.S. Queeg
The Navy's chickenest ship

KELLY FREAS

First and only blend of 9 delicious ingredients to make an Aspire shine-up palatable!

NEW FORMULA Aspire Boot-Lick Polish is a unique blend of delicious ingredients developed after years of research by the skilled Aspire chefs to make boot-licking a little more tasty when you gotta do it.

Aspire contains licorice, caviar, chocolate, caramel, molasses, borscht, halavah and Moxie in a base of chicken fat. So make it a habit to apply Aspire Boot-Lick Polish next time you shine up to The Man in Command.

ASPIRE BOOT-LICK POLISH

To many, being lampooned in the pages of *MAD* is a sign that you've made it, and the makers of Esquire shoe polish sent several shoeshine kits to the *MAD* offices to show their pleasure with the "Aspire" spoof. Although the gifts were sent *after* the parody ran, Bill Gaines, who notoriously detested even the appearance of a payoff, confiscated the kits from his staff and sent them back.

A few years later, Gaines was furious to discover that several *MAD*men had received custom lighters for a Zippo spoof. Having learned from the "Aspire" incident, the *MAD*men hid their lighters before Gaines got wind of the gift, so no one had to return anything.

Now that Gaines is deceased, you have to wonder why *MAD* hasn't taken to spoofing ads for 48-inch plasma TVs and luxury sports sedans.

"My Fair Ad-Man" has earned its place in the *MAD* pantheon because up until its appearance in *MAD* #54, the magazine's song parodies were simply one-page song spoofs. "Ad-Man" marks the first time *MAD* created an actual musical, using songs to tell a continuous story, illustrated here by Mort Drucker.

Nick Meglin, who had left the *MAD* editorial staff after being drafted into the military, wrote this article freelance to supplement his $71/month Army salary. In it, he took the story of *My Fair Lady* (which itself was a musical version of George Bernard Shaw's *Pygmalion*) and replaced snobbish professor Henry Higgins with ad man Henry Higgenbottom.

And, just as Higgins accepted the wager that he could teach a young waif to join high society, Higgenbottom ("played" here by Cary Grant) accepted the challenge to teach a beatnik (Frank Sinatra) the language of Madison Avenue, which by 1960 had become a major voice in American culture.

The result is a *MAD* classic which has been reprinted on many occasions over the years, but here it is for the first time . . . um, on high-quality paper.

MAD #54
April 1960
Artist: Mort Drucker
Writer: Nick Meglin

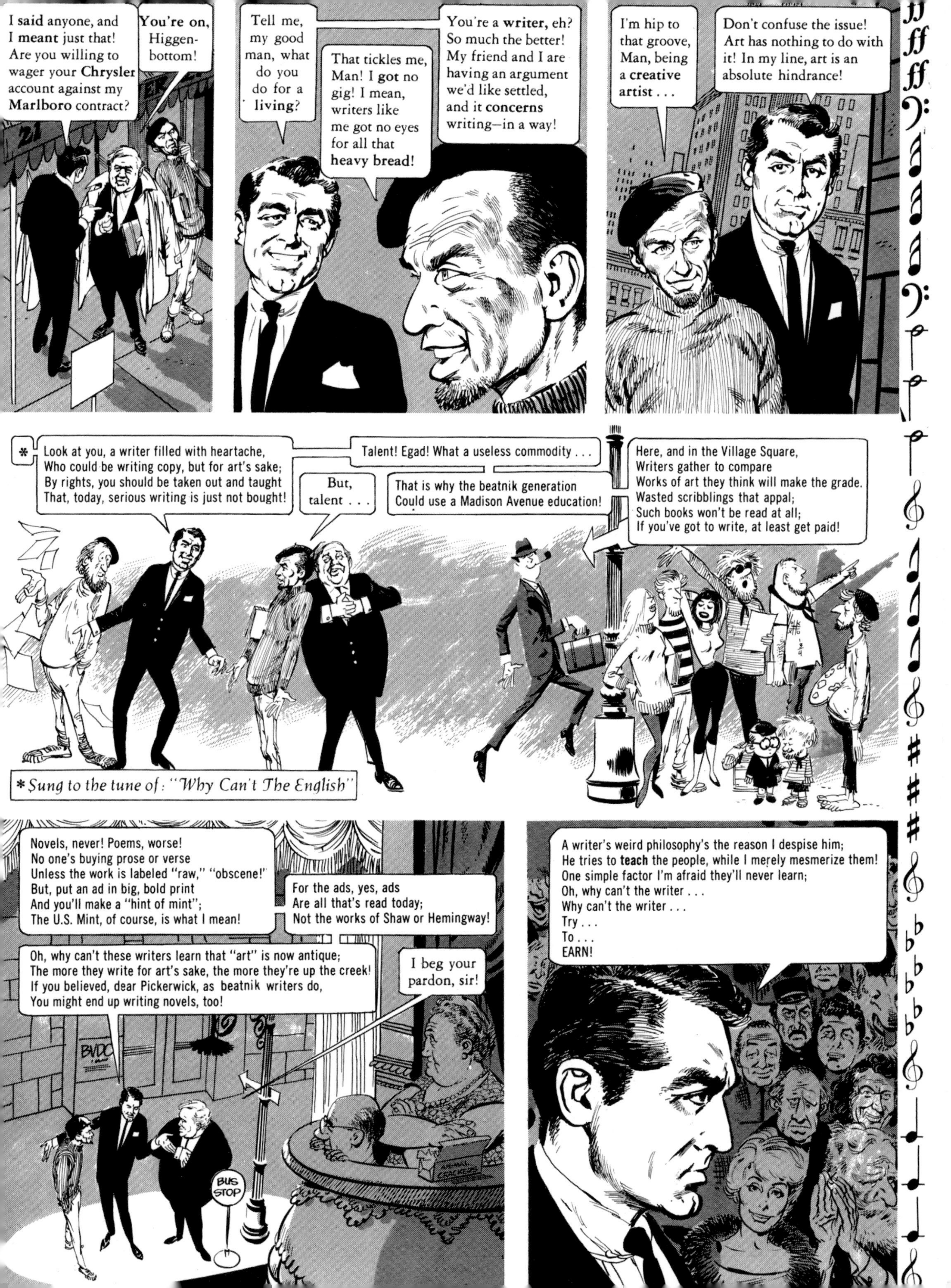
I said anyone, and I meant just that! Are you willing to wager your Chrysler account against my Marlboro contract?
You're on, Higgenbottom!
21
Tell me, my good man, what do you do for a living?
You're a writer, eh? So much the better! My friend and I are having an argument we'd like settled, and it concerns writing—in a way!
That tickles me, Man! I got no gig! I mean, writers like me got no eyes for all that heavy bread!
I'm hip to that groove, Man, being a creative artist . . .
Don't confuse the issue! Art has nothing to do with it! In my line, art is an absolute hindrance!
* Look at you, a writer filled with heartache,
Who could be writing copy, but for art's sake;
By rights, you should be taken out and taught
That, today, serious writing is just not bought!
But, talent . . .
Talent! Egad! What a useless commodity . . .
That is why the beatnik generation
Could use a Madison Avenue education!
Here, and in the Village Square,
Writers gather to compare
Works of art they think will make the grade.
Wasted scribblings that appal;
Such books won't be read at all;
If you've got to write, at least get paid!
* Sung to the tune of: "Why Can't The English"
Novels, never! Poems, worse!
No one's buying prose or verse
Unless the work is labeled "raw," "obscene!"
But, put an ad in big, bold print
And you'll make a "hint of mint";
The U.S. Mint, of course, is what I mean!
For the ads, yes, ads
Are all that's read today;
Not the works of Shaw or Hemingway!
Oh, why can't these writers learn that "art" is now antique;
The more they write for art's sake, the more they're up the creek!
If you believed, dear Pickerwick, as beatnik writers do,
You might end up writing novels, too!
I beg your pardon, sir!
BVDC
BUS STOP
ANIMAL CRACKERS
A writer's weird philosophy's the reason I despise him;
He tries to teach the people, while I merely mesmerize them!
One simple factor I'm afraid they'll never learn;
Oh, why can't the writer . . .
Why can't the writer . . .
Try . . .
To . . .
EARN!

Man, that'll **never** come on!

Why not? Listen, you'll be **well-paid** for participating in our little experiment!

Man, you just don't **dig** me! Like I don't have **eyes** for that heavy loot, Dad!

I WANT MY **MAYPO!**

Then what in the name of J. Walter Thompson **do** you want?

Well, if you gotta be put hip . . .

* All I want is a pad somewhere
Way downtown near the Village Square,
Without a phone or care . . .
Oh, wouldn't it be Kerouac!

Lots of coffee, and lots of beer,
Lots of parties that last all year,
With no landlord to fear . . .
Oh, wouldn't it be Kerouac!

Oh, so Kerouac caring nothing
How the world lives on;
I would never budge till it
Was gone, like I mean real gone!

Modern paintings
to set the mood;
They'll look normal
when we get stewed . . .

And though you'll
think me rude,
Oh, what's this thing
called "Kerouac?"

Kerouac!

Kerouac?

Kerouac!

ONE OF THESE DAYS-- I'LL CLEAN MY TOE NAILS!

YOU'RE HATEFUL!

Sung to the tune of: "Wouldn't It Be Loverly?"

Kerouac isn't a **thing!** Kerouac's A person, squares! Jack Kerouac is our **leader**—our **inspiration!** He wrote "On The Road!" Man, like I dug that book so much I wrote a **sequel** to it called "Son Of On The Road," by Irving Mallion!

Would you like it **published,** Mr. Mallion?

It would groove me the **most!** I'd give anything!

Would you give me **two months?**

Crazy, Man!

SON OF ON THE ROAD

Then it's settled! For the next two months, you belong to me. I will provide your food, your lodging, and your clothes, which I will choose! During that time, I will attempt to teach you to become an Ad-Man! At the end of the two months, if you desire to stay, I will get you a good position at BVD&O. If not, I will have your book published, and you will be free to return to your sickening existence. Are you ready to start?

Let me make **one more late scene** with the cats I dig the most, and I'll glim you in the early bright!

All right, Mallion! I'll see you at 9:00 AM **tomorrow!**

I CAN'T GET A JOB THRU THE N.Y. TIMES!

NEXT TO MY FAMILY-- I'M A PIG!

... and that's the pitch! I figure I'll play it **cool** for a double bill-payer until my **gig** comes on!

But, Glib Street, Irving! I dig that creative cats have to be bugged till they make it, but this Madison Avenue bit is, like, **too far out!**

Man! Like playing it square for two months can be a **drag!** Do you dig that it means slipping the bed before **two bells**, and scoffing a . . . *choke* . . . breakfast?

Well, like I just gotta make it, Cats! But don't worry! I may be packing my grey matter uptown, but I'm stowing my ticker here in the Village!

* For . . . I'll be an ad-man in the morning;
I'll wear a suit, and nose of brown:
Off goes my beard-o;
No more a weird-o;
'Cause I'm moving way uptown.

I've got to be there in the morning;
Can't let the boys from Westport down!
No more espresso;
My new address-o
Is somewhere with the squares uptown.

No more a beatnick . . .
I'll be a hack.
My underwear will . . .
Have buckles in the back!

Yes, I'll be an ad-man in the morning;
You needn't look at me and frown;
If it's appalling,
You I'll be calling
To take me from that place,
To snatch me from that life,
To save me from that world uptown!

* Sung to the tune of: "Get Me To The Church On Time!"

You know, Pickerwick, perhaps I was a bit too hasty in choosing a **subject** for our little experiment. I must admit that pig, Mallion, has me **worried!**

Come now, Henry! Let's not start out pessimistically. Why, I'll even **help you out**, knowing, of course, that you can't **possibly** win!

Kind of you, Pickerwick! But . . . *sniff, sniff* . . . what **is** that foul smell? Oh . . . it's **you**, Mallion! Come in. Come in! And tell me . . . why don't beatnicks believe in **bathing?** Or is your philosophy to make the rest of the world "**Pay through the nose**"?

Daddy-O! At this moment, the only smell I got eyes for is the "sweet smell of success"!

Well, if that's your goal, Mr. Mallion, the first thing you've got to learn is to be full of life . . . LIFEBOUY, I mean!

Grab him, Pickerwick!

* You've never had a clean shave or a haircut!
A bigger bum, I never hope to see!
Your taste is sad in choosing what you wear!! BUT—
With a little bit of soap;
With a little bit of soap;
You'll be looking just like him and me!

With a little bit;
With a little bit;
With a little bit of soap
you'll look like we!

Oh, I can see "your best friends haven't told you";
And I might add your breath's not "kissing sweet";
A drop of Stoppette no one's ever sold you—BUT—
With a little bit of soap;
With a little bit of soap;
You'll smell better than Palmolive-Peet!

With a little bit;
With a little bit;
With a little bit of soap
you'll smell real neat!

*Sung to the tune of: "With A Little Bit Of Luck"

You might have walked through sewers in Brooklyn . . . But with a little bit of soap you'll smell real neat!

You've got real charcoal staining your grey flannel;
I thought those shoes were for the tennis game;
If you were on TV, I'd switch the channel—BUT—
With a little bit of soap;
With a little bit of soap;
You and Cary Grant will look the same!

With a little bit;
With a little bit;
With a little bit of LIFEBOUY soap!

Look at yourself, Mallion! Tell me, do you like what you see?

Yecch! I'm disgusting!

I was hoping you'd feel that way! Now, I know we're on the right track! But, to look like an ad-man is one thing! To think like one is another! I will now teach you the most important basic principle we have here on Madison Avenue!

Repeat after me . . .

An ad that's bad will end up spoofed in MAD! *

An ad that's bad will end up spoofed in MAD!

Again!

An ad that's bad will end up spoofed in MAD!

I think he's got it!
I think he's got it!

An ad that's bad will end up spoofed in MAD!

*Sung to the tune of: "The Rain In Spain"

By George, he's got it!
By George, he's got it!

Two months, Pickerwick? Two weeks is more like it! Why, he's practically an ad-man already!

To you, perhaps, Henry! But would he pass for one of us at . . . say, the monthly account exec and copywriters' brain-storming session?

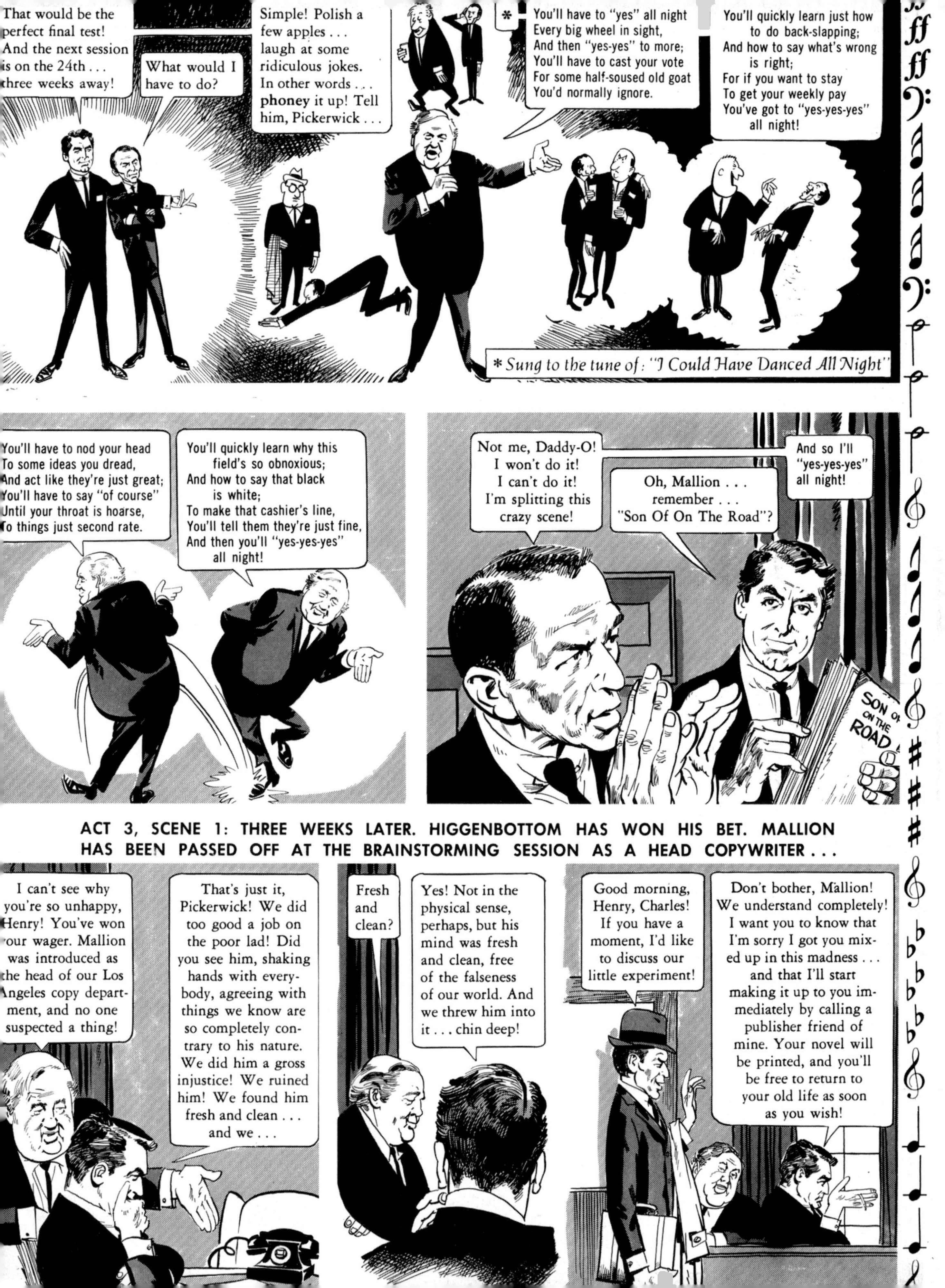

That would be the perfect final test! And the next session is on the 24th . . . three weeks away!
What would I have to do?
Simple! Polish a few apples . . . laugh at some ridiculous jokes. In other words . . . **phoney** it up! Tell him, Pickerwick . . .
*
You'll have to "yes" all night
Every big wheel in sight,
And then "yes-yes" to more;
You'll have to cast your vote
For some half-soused old goat
You'd normally ignore.
You'll quickly learn just how to do back-slapping;
And how to say what's wrong is right;
For if you want to stay
To get your weekly pay
You've got to "yes-yes-yes" all night!
* Sung to the tune of: "I Could Have Danced All Night"
You'll have to nod your head
To some ideas you dread,
And act like they're just great;
You'll have to say "of course"
Until your throat is hoarse,
To things just second rate.
You'll quickly learn why this field's so obnoxious;
And how to say that black is white;
To make that cashier's line,
You'll tell them they're just fine,
And then you'll "yes-yes-yes" all night!
Not me, Daddy-O! I won't do it! I can't do it! I'm splitting this crazy scene!
Oh, Mallion . . . remember . . . "Son Of On The Road"?
And so I'll "yes-yes-yes" all night!
SON OF ON THE ROAD
ACT 3, SCENE 1: THREE WEEKS LATER. HIGGENBOTTOM HAS WON HIS BET. MALLION HAS BEEN PASSED OFF AT THE BRAINSTORMING SESSION AS A HEAD COPYWRITER . . .
I can't see why you're so unhappy, Henry! You've won our wager. Mallion was introduced as the head of our Los Angeles copy department, and no one suspected a thing!
That's just it, Pickerwick! We did too good a job on the poor lad! Did you see him, shaking hands with everybody, agreeing with things we know are so completely contrary to his nature. We did him a gross injustice! We ruined him! We found him fresh and clean . . . and we . . .
Fresh and clean?
Yes! Not in the physical sense, perhaps, but his mind was fresh and clean, free of the falseness of our world. And we threw him into it . . . chin deep!
Good morning, Henry, Charles! If you have a moment, I'd like to discuss our little experiment!
Don't bother, Mallion! We understand completely! I want you to know that I'm sorry I got you mixed up in this madness . . . and that I'll start making it up to you immediately by calling a publisher friend of mine. Your novel will be printed, and you'll be free to return to your old life as soon as you wish!

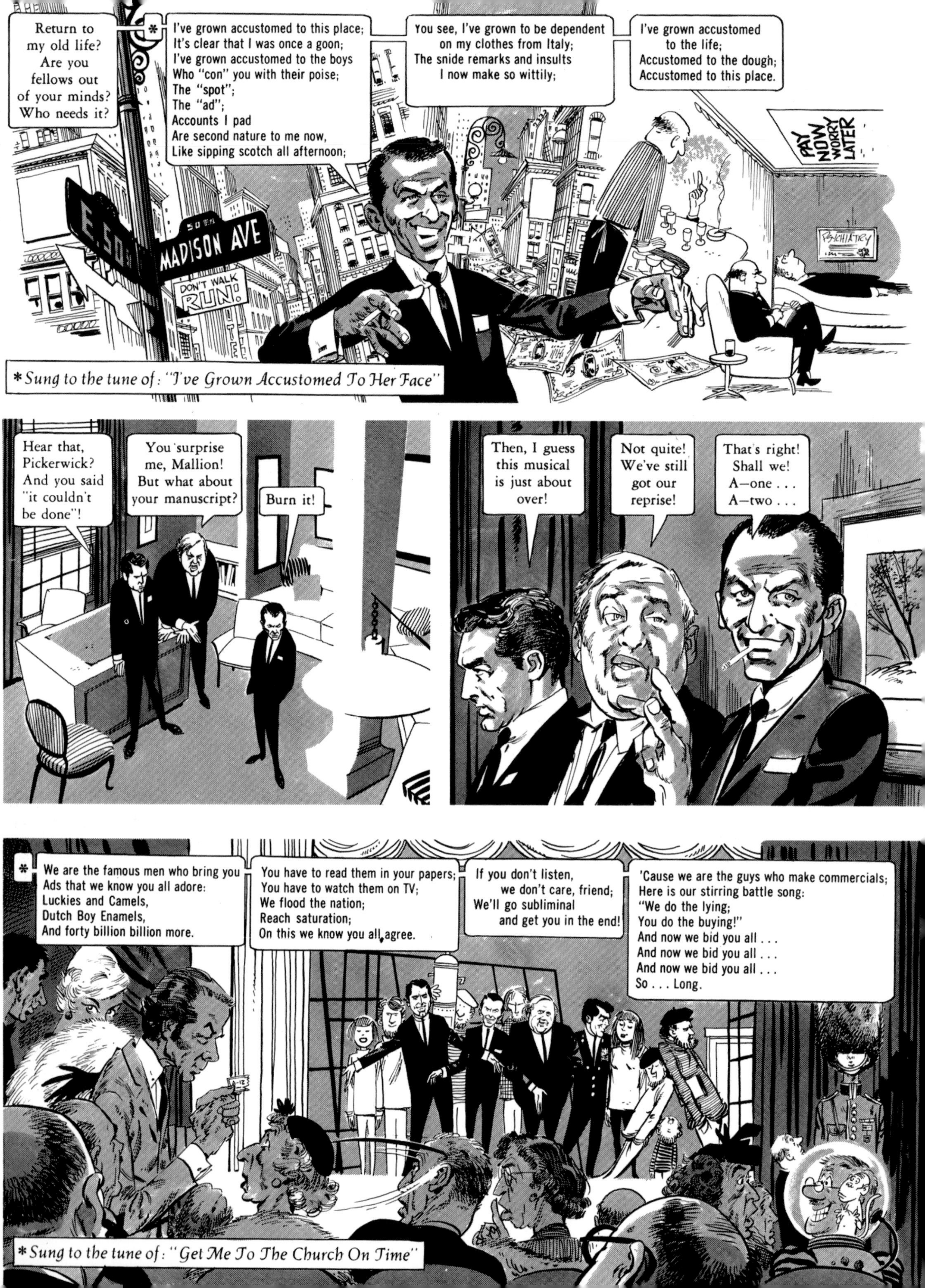
Return to my old life? Are you fellows out of your minds? Who needs it?
* I've grown accustomed to this place; It's clear that I was once a goon; I've grown accustomed to the boys Who "con" you with their poise; The "spot"; The "ad"; Accounts I pad Are second nature to me now, Like sipping scotch all afternoon;
You see, I've grown to be dependent on my clothes from Italy; The snide remarks and insults I now make so wittily;
I've grown accustomed to the life; Accustomed to the dough; Accustomed to this place.
E. 50
MADISON AVE
DON'T WALK RUN!
PAY NOW WORRY LATER
PSYCHIATRY
* Sung to the tune of: "I've Grown Accustomed To Her Face"
Hear that, Pickerwick? And you said "it couldn't be done"!
You surprise me, Mallion! But what about your manuscript?
Burn it!
Then, I guess this musical is just about over!
Not quite! We've still got our reprise!
That's right! Shall we! A—one . . . A—two . . .
* We are the famous men who bring you Ads that we know you all adore: Luckies and Camels, Dutch Boy Enamels, And forty billion billion more.
You have to read them in your papers; You have to watch them on TV; We flood the nation; Reach saturation; On this we know you all agree.
If you don't listen, we don't care, friend; We'll go subliminal and get you in the end!
'Cause we are the guys who make commercials; Here is our stirring battle song: "We do the lying; You do the buying!" And now we bid you all . . . And now we bid you all . . . And now we bid you all . . . So . . . Long.
* Sung to the tune of: "Get Me To The Church On Time"

MAD #55

June 1960
Artist: Kelly Freas
Writer: House

How many ways can he hurt himself today?

In his wonderful world called Army Basic Training, a Draftee runs an obstacle course . . . a rope breaks — and he ends up flat on his face.

The Army *tries* its best — but it *can't guarantee* that land mines won't go off prematurely, that machine gun bullets won't drop too low, that tear gas and bayonets and barbed wire and a thousand other things won't keep a Draftee from getting through the day in one piece. So a shrewd Draftee depends on Goldbrick & Goldbrick for assistance in avoiding minor injury.

Aside from GOOF-OFF* bandages, make sure you have these other great new products in your dufflebag, made by Goldbrick & Goldbrick so you can be completely confident that they'll create the effect you're looking for when you report to Sick Call!

A year's Goof-Off Aid by *Goldbrick & Goldbrick* ...about $2.

1. Cotton Balls. Perfect for stuffing into the cheeks so you'll look like you got a toothache — or a good case of the mumps. **59¢**

2. Flush Cream. Red-tinted cream gives appearance of a hot flush. Secret ingredient heats skin so it feels like you got a temperature. **59¢**

3. Throat Pills. These new pills, when dissolved on the tongue, inflame the throat. And don't ask what they do to your breath. **49¢**

4. Measle-Tape. Specially-made transparent cellophane tape has blotches and spots imprinted in large variety of alarming colors. **39¢**

*TRADE MARK   No connection with The Red Double-Cro

MAD #55
June 1960
Artist: Wallace Wood
Writer: Larry Siegel

HARD SPELL DEPT

"The MAD Horror Primer" (Issue #49) received such a GREAT response from our readers (i.e. *"A GREAT disappointment!"*—B.F., Phila., Pa.; *"It would be GREAT if you discontinued this type feature!"*—L.D., Dallas, Tex.; *"Articles like that GRATE on my nerves!"*—F.H., Fresno, Calif.) that we've decided to present another primer. This one is for the benefit of any children under seven (in other words, ALL of our readers) who may possibly be interested in working in the advertising field when they grow up.

"Take the turnpike, and you'll avoid traffic, you said. Hah!"

THE MAD MADISON AVENUE PRIMER

ARTIST: WALLACE WOOD   WRITER: LARRY SIEGEL

MY FIRST **READER**
(EDUCATION-WISE)
Rock-Bottom Slants for Little Group-Noodlers

By Batton, Barton, Durstine & Cowznofsky

Lesson 1

See the man.
He does advertising work.
He is called an "ad-man".
See his funny tight suit.
See his funny haircut.
Hear his funny stomach churn.
Churn, churn, churn.
The ad-man has a funny ulcer.
Most ad-men have funny ulcers.
But, then, some ad-men are lucky.
They do *not* have funny ulcers.
They have funny high blood pressure.

Lesson 2

See the ad-man run.
Run, ad-man, run.
The ad-man must catch the 8:02.
All ad-men must catch the 8:02.
It is a fast commuter train.
It is never more than two hours late.
And it has a club car.
"All aboard!" says the conductor.
"Chug, chug!" says the train.
"Gulp, gulp!" says the ad-man.
Wouldn't *you* like Bourbon for breakfast, too?

Rather than hit a particular campaign, this article spoofed the men (and in the '50s it was almost entirely men) who created the ads. By the time "The *MAD* Madison Avenue Primer" ran, the culture of the ad man, with his tedious daily commute, three-martini lunches, and soulless existence had entered the popular culture, thanks in part to the 1955 novel *The Man in the Gray Flannel Suit*, which soon became a movie starring Gregory Peck.

Lesson 3

See the pretty street.
It is called "Madison Avenue".
All the ad-men work here.
They write "Winston tastes good . . ." here.
Write, write, write.
They write "Mr. Clean, Mr. Clean . . ." here.
Write, write, write.
Don't you wish YOU could write like that?
You can.
You're almost *seven* now.

Lesson 4

See the nice advertising agency.
400 nice people work here.
Let us count the 400 nice people.
Count, count, count.
Hmmm! 300 nice people are missing.
The nice advertising agency must have
      lost another nice $4-million account.
Dear, dear, dear.
Where are the 300 nice people now?
At the nice Unemployment Insurance office.
Sign, sign, sign.
Isn't job security nice on Madison Avenue?

Lesson 5

See the kindly old man.
He is the President of the agency.
He has fired 132 people today.
And it isn't even lunch time yet.
Fire, fire, fire.
See the fine young man with him.
He will not be fired, today.
He is a fine ad-man.
He is a fine Vice-President of the agency.
He is a fine son of the President of the agency.

Lesson 6

See the Account Executive.
His accounts are Puffo Cigarettes,
      Bubble Soap, and Flaky Cereal.
The agency loves and trusts him.
Kiss, kiss, kiss.
Trust, trust, trust.
Next week he will resign.
He will form his own agency.
He will have three accounts in his agency.
They will be Puffo Cigarettes,
      Bubble Soap, and Flaky Cereal.
Bounce, bounce, bounce.
That's the way the ball bounces on Madison Avenue.

Written by Larry Siegel, this is one of the earliest *MAD* primers, a format the Usual Gang of Idiots
has gone on to use many times over the years.

Lesson 7

See the conference.
Ad-men have 47 conferences a day.
And even more on Sundays.
They discuss EVERYTHING at conferences.
At *this* conference, they are discussing a fire.
It has already destroyed half the agency.
It is now burning up the President's office.
Crackle, crackle, crackle.
What will the ad-men do about the fire?
Soon they will make a BIG decision.
But not at *this* conference.
Perhaps at the *next* conference.

Lesson 8

See the jolly client.
He sponsors a TV dramatic show.
He never finished the 6th Grade.
He can hardly speak English.
He can hardly write his name.
Yet, he re-writes TV scripts.
Re-write, re-write, re-write.
Why do you re-write TV scripts, jolly client?
"Because I do not like sad endings;
Because I only like happy endings."
Someday, a TV writer will shoot the jolly client.
Right in his jolly gut.
What a happy ending THAT will be!

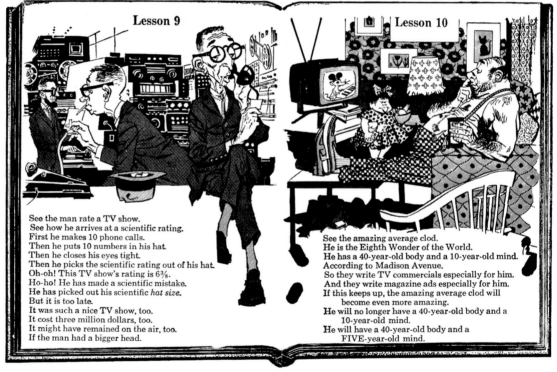

Lesson 9

See the man rate a TV show.
See how he arrives at a scientific rating.
First he makes 10 phone calls.
Then he puts 10 numbers in his hat.
Then he closes his eyes tight.
Then he picks the scientific rating out of his hat.
Oh-oh! This TV show's rating is 6⅜.
Ho-ho! He has made a scientific mistake.
He has picked out his scientific *hat size.*
But it is too late.
It was such a nice TV show, too.
It cost three million dollars, too.
It might have remained on the air, too.
If the man had a bigger head.

Lesson 10

See the amazing average clod.
He is the Eighth Wonder of the World.
He has a 40-year-old body and a 10-year-old mind.
According to Madison Avenue.
So they write TV commercials especially for him.
And they write magazine ads especially for him.
If this keeps up, the amazing average clod will
 become even more amazing.
He will no longer have a 40-year-old body and a
 10-year-old mind.
He will have a 40-year-old body and a
 FIVE-year-old mind.

MAD #55
June 1960
Photographer: Lester Krauss
Writer: Al Jaffee

PHOTO BY LESTER KRAUSS WHO'S FULLY COVERED BY INSURANCE

W̲hat? You say I'm not covered? Are you sure you're from my insurance company? The one that only insures safe drivers so that it can charge ridiculously low premiums? Are you the man from "Safe Form Insurance"? You are? Then you must be kidding about not paying for the accident I just had! You're not! Whaddayamean I should read the small print in my policy, mainly Paragraph A, Column 7, Sub-paragraph 1, Micro-line 2, where it says: "The company charges low premiums by insuring safe drivers, and anyone who has an accident is obviously not a safe driver, which cancels the policy!" Bu-but, if you don't pay I'll lose my car, my home, my family ... everything! I'll DIE!" What's that? You want to remind me that my Life Insurance policy with you says that I must die of natural causes or else it's cancelled, and dying of bankruptcy is not a natural cause! No wonder it's called **SAFE FORM MUTUAL** Insurance Company! It's safe for you ... not me! Home Office: Sneaky Wording, O.

SAFE FORM
you
can't win
INSURANCE

Based on Mental Case #34532, sickening details on request.   *In some states (where we can), we pull even niftier dodges than the one you just read.*

Beginning in the late '50s, State Farm Insurance ran a series of one-page testimonials of the downtrodden individuals who realized that they had paid too much for auto insurance premiums. Of course, that's nothing compared to finding out that even if you pay your premiums, you failed to read in the small print that you weren't covered at all.

Good things begin to happen

when you find one of 'em in your soup

(mainly, you got a chance to beat the check!)

Weekly allowance running short? Just reach for a can of Sham-bugs. It takes only a few short minutes to solve your embarrassing financial predicament.

Yes, good things begin to happen when you float a "Sham-bug" in your school lunch soup, mainly because it gives you the chance to blow your top, and stalk out without paying the check.

Good things for Daddy, too—because those high-priced fancy restaurants he dines in are particularly susceptible to this sure-fire old gag.

There are many kinds of Sham-bugs to choose from. Also steel slivers, hairs, and broken glass if you're squeamish.

Hey . . . have *you* beaten a check today?

Once a day . . . you don't pay . . . with *Sham-bugs*

A PAID TESTIMONIAL FROM FIDEL CASTRO FOR STIKKY PEANUT BUTTER

How did we get Fidel Castro to appear in our ad? Easy! WE PAID FOR IT!

A few weeks ago, we sent a whole crew of advertising people down to Cuba to visit Mr. Castro, in order to solicit a testimonial from him about Stikky. He answered by launching into a six-and-a-half hour TV speech, denouncing the evils of U.S. Imperialism, money, and Madison Avenue advertising. But as we were re-packing the suitcase of American twenty dollar bills we had planned to give him, he stopped us!

"I hate to see you Gringos make this whole trip for nothing!" he grinned, unbuckling his money-belt.

Naturally, our boys lost no time in lathering up a slice of bread with a generous portion of delicious Stikky, and Castro raised it to his mouth.

Unfortunately, he couldn't find it, and our delicious peanut butter got all over his beard, and it was one gooey mess, and he could hardly speak, and he got furious, and he started screaming and yelling and rolling on the floor, and patches of his beard stuck fast to it and were torn out of his face, and it was just awful!

So that's how we got this ad. We paid for it. *Boy*, we paid for it! *A whole advertising crew . . . shot at sunrise!*

STIKKY Gummy PEANUT BUTTER

if you like living, don't serve Stikky to bearded Cubans

MAD turned Skippy Peanut Butter's campaign, which featured all-American icons like New York Yankee Casey Stengel and *The Wizard of Oz*'s Cowardly Lion Bert Lahr, on its head when it reimagined an ad with the not-so-all-American Cuban revolutionary Fidel Castro. Although it should be noted that, like Stengel, Castro played baseball (and, like the Cowardly Lion, had a goofy beard).

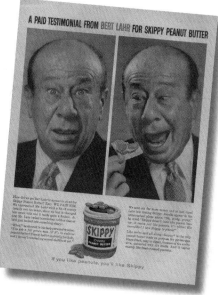

MAD #57
September 1960
Artist: Kelly Freas
Writer: Al Jaffee

INDULGE YOURSELF...
Get all the best of the coffee bean —aroma, flavor, but not caffein!
NEW AROMA-ROAST SANKA COFFEE

▼ (overleaf) *MAD #59*
December 1960
Artist: Bob Clarke
Writer: Gary Belkin

MAD #58
October 1960
Artist: Joe Orlando
Writer: Al Jaffee

INDULGE YOURSELF...

For a quick delightful "pick-me-up"

—soak in a bathtub-size coffee cup!

NEW COFFEE-FLAVORED SINKA BATH SALTS

A TURN FOR THE WORSE DEPT.

We know about "Russian Roulette" . . . the game where you have a six-shooter with one bullet and yo
keep pulling the trigger until somebody loses by getting killed. And we know about "Magazine Rou
lette" . . . the game where you have six magazines and you keep choosing one until somebody loses b
picking MAD. But the most vicious game we know is the one that millions of Americans play ever

COMMERCIA

ARTIST: BOB CLARK

. That's the game where you have six TV channels and you keep turning to each, trying to find ne entertainment. The game starts when it's time for the commercial. Mainly, when you decide to tch it off. Because the TV networks are wise to this sneaky maneuver, and they've all scheduled ir ads to come on at the same time. Here, then, is what it's like . . . when you're playing . . .

ROULETTE

RITER: GARY BELKIN

°°CHAMPS-ELYSÉES—Floyd Patterson and Ingemar Johansson are lazy.

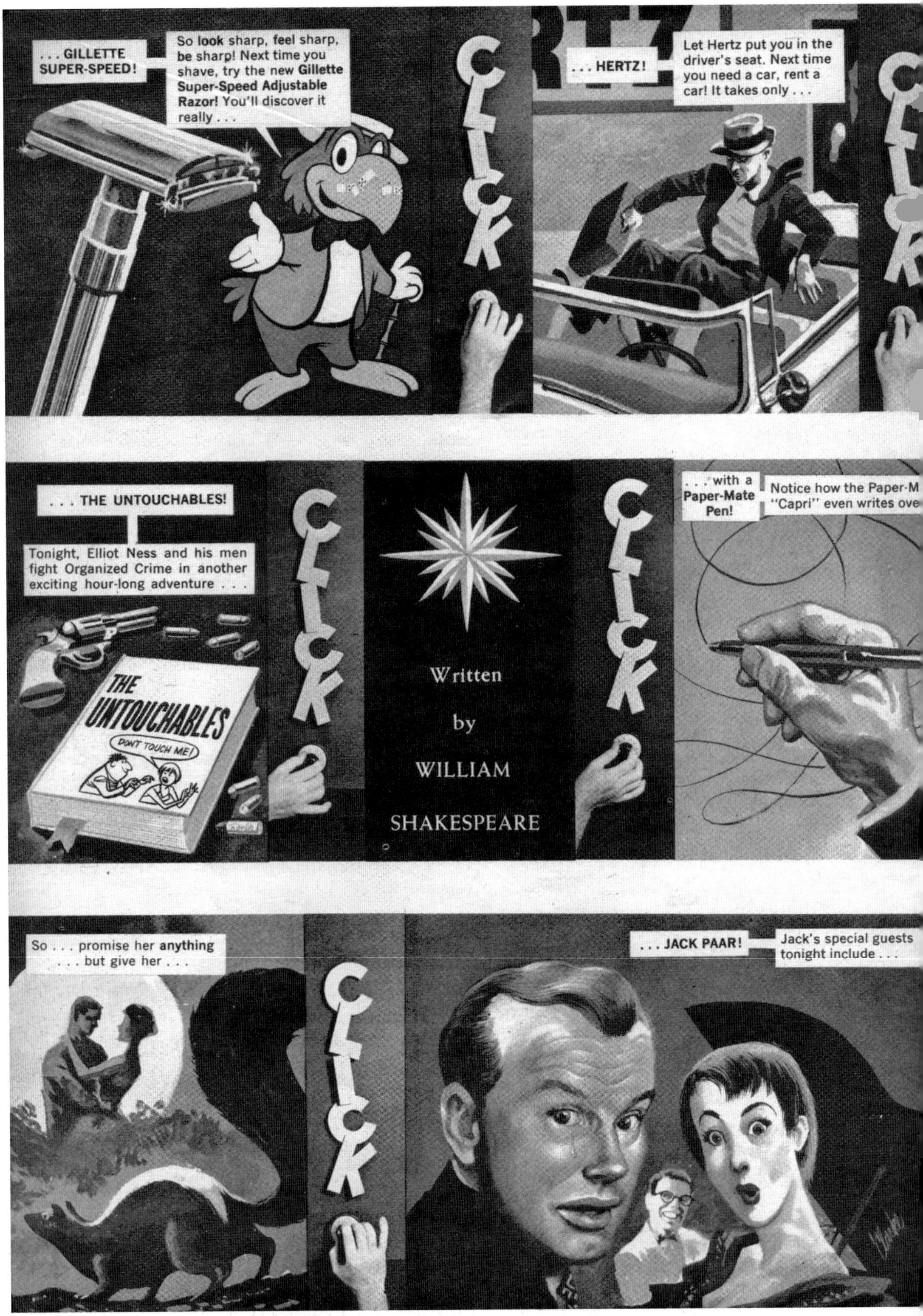
. . . GILLETTE SUPER-SPEED!
So look sharp, feel sharp, be sharp! Next time you shave, try the new Gillette Super-Speed Adjustable Razor! You'll discover it really . . .
CLICK
. . . HERTZ!
Let Hertz put you in the driver's seat. Next time you need a car, rent a car! It takes only . . .
. . . THE UNTOUCHABLES!
Tonight, Elliot Ness and his men fight Organized Crime in another exciting hour-long adventure . . .
THE UNTOUCHABLES
DON'T TOUCH ME!
CLICK
Written by WILLIAM SHAKESPEARE
CLICK
. . . with a Paper-Mate Pen!
Notice how the Paper-M "Capri" even writes ove
So . . . promise her anything . . . but give her . . .
CLICK
. . . JACK PAAR!
Jack's special guests tonight include . . .

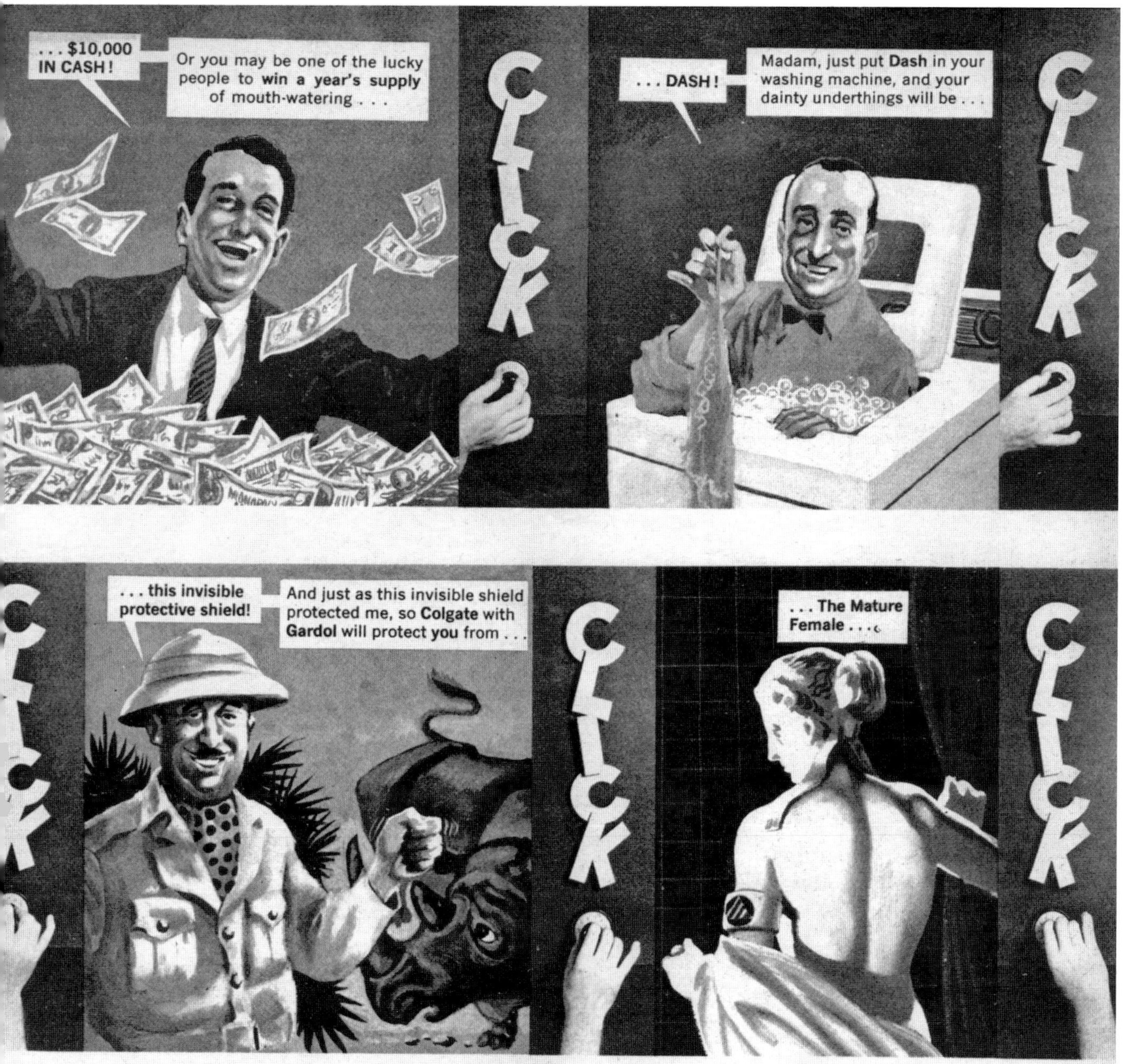

. . . $10,000 IN CASH !
Or you may be one of the lucky people to win a year's supply of mouth-watering . . .
CLICK
. . . DASH !
Madam, just put Dash in your washing machine, and your dainty underthings will be . . .
CLICK
CLICK
. . . this invisible protective shield!
And just as this invisible shield protected me, so Colgate with Gardol will protect you from . . .
CLICK
. . . The Mature Female . . .°°
CLICK

°°LA PLUME DE MA TANTE—There's a plum in my tent.

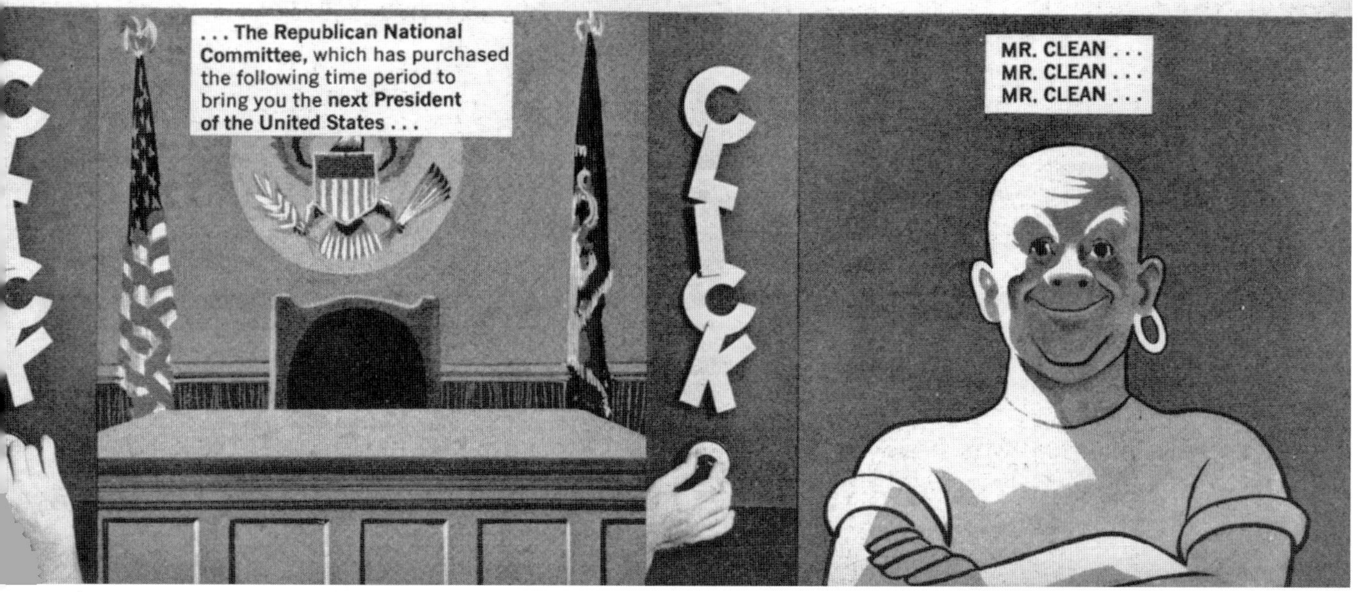

CLICK
. . . The Republican National Committee, which has purchased the following time period to bring you the next President of the United States . . .
CLICK
MR. CLEAN . . .
MR. CLEAN . . .
MR. CLEAN . . .

MAD #59
December 1960
Photographer: Lester Krauss
Writer: House

S'matter, can't you Dial?!

No, this isn't Irving! What number do you want? Well, that's your trouble, idiot! You got the wrong number! This is AT-7...not AT-6!

Why don't you learn how to Dial? People who like people Dial correctly!

Y'know, you dragged me out of a shower! Well, what's so funny about that?

Listen, do me a favor! After you learn how to Dial . . . drop dead!

When *MAD* first began using photos in the magazine, they would hire professional models for the photo shoots. Problem was, as Nick Meglin explains it, the pros were trained to look beautiful, not goofy, and it was difficult to get the proper expression out of them.

Nick and the other *MAD*men found themselves demonstrating what they wanted, invariably cracking up the model, the photographer, and themselves in the process. The editors quickly realized that it was easier to use the *MAD* staff for photo shoots—not to mention cheaper, since they didn't have to pay a modeling fee.

Different members of the Usual Gang of Idiots were used for different character types, with then-associate art director Lenny Brenner, pictured above, being called in when the shoot called for "angry."

Gee, we wonder why.

MAD #59
December 1960
Artist: Kelly Freas
Writer: House

Whenever you go — you'll look better in an Aarow shirt...

From Cuba to Argentina . . . wherever Latin American revolutionists step out of line, this new Aarow *Bye-Bye* shirt is a cool favorite. "Sanforized", it won't shrink while you're sweating out that final order. And half-sleeves allow arms to be tied behind back without wrinkling. In white and colors, $4.25. Matching blindfolds, 55¢.

AAROW

You're not kidding, Charlie Brown! Sure, you can save up to a penny a mile on gas (The Furd Foulcar averages 30 miles to the gallon!), but your doctor bills for strained muscles and slipped discs suffered getting in and out of the darn thing more than make up for it. As *Motor-Mad* Magazine put it: "The Foulcar is a great little car to own, providing you don't drive in it for longer than 12 minutes at a stretch!" We wonder why Foulcar is America's best-selling compact?

FURD DIVISION *Furd Motor Company*

WORLD'S MOST UNCOMFORTABLE SMALL CAR

FURD *Foulcar*

MAD #60
January 1961
Artist: Bob Clarke
Writer: House

There are lots of things that Doctors are not supposed to do because of *
called "Professional Ethics". However, from what we have seen, they do m
of these things anyway. But *one* thing they're not supposed to do, and real
don't, is *advertise!* Which is pretty stupid. Majnly because if you need
Doctor, how do you know which one to go to unless you hear all their claim

IF DOCTORS

ARTIST: BOB CLAR

Today as always...

IN NOSE JOBS...

**IT'S WHAT'S
UP FRONT
THAT COUNTS!**

The big difference is

TILTED-END

and only Dr. Winston does it!

The secret of Dr. Winston's famous plastic surgery is Tilted-End, an exclusive Winston development. You see, Tilted-End is what goes up front on your face when you have a Winston nose job. With Tilted-End, you not only look better but you smell better, too! Remember, Dr. Winston's idea has always been that the pleasure of smelling depends on the *shape* of the nose. (After all, isn't smelling the whole idea of having a nose?) Yes, that's one good reason why Dr. Winston is America's best-known plastic surgeon, year after year. Tilted-End up front is why you should try Dr. Herman T. Winston!

A WINSTON NOSE SMELLS GOOD

DR. WINSTON'S METHOD IS EXCLUSIVELY HIS. HE WISHES THERE WERE
OTHER DOCTORS WHO USE IT. THEN HE, TOO, COULD HAVE TILTED-END!

LIKE A CUTE LITTLE NORMAL NOSE SHOULD

HIC JACET—He may be a good jockey, but he drinks too much.

MAD ESP, PART 1

This article represents a gentler era, when doctors felt they were too respectable to advertise, and imagined a time when the medical profession would hawk its wares as if it were selling chewing gum or potato chips.

MAD #59
December 1960
Artist: Bob Clarke
Writer: Gary Belkin

rinstance, what if you need an elbow specialist, and you visit a plastic
rgeon by mistake? You end up with a shorter, cuter, turned-up elbow — only
still hurts! So, for this, and seven other reasons, MAD feels that Doc-
rs should be permitted to publicize themselves. The seven other reasons
ing the following ads . . . which are the kind of things we'd be seeing . . .

**SEMPER FIDELES—Castro is a simpering idiot.

ADVERTISED

RITER: GARY BELKIN

Memories . . . long forgotten

RECALLED UPON A COUCH

Memories . . . painted for Dr. De Beer's Collection by a patient who ran out of money

In fleeting minutes sweetly shared, you relate the story of
your life to willing, nay, anxious ears. Yes, during each
50-minute session, you talk on and on and on and on, as
only the truly neurotic can. Here is Psychology's greatest
treasure, given to you alone . . . the rapturous delight of
being able to tell people you go to a Psychiatrist. Mainly me!
Dr. Sigmund De Beers, 845 Park Ave., N.Y.C. Your analysis
may be deep — or shallow. But rest assured it will be long!
So choose your Psychiatrist with care, because you're gonna
be lying on his couch for many years to come. You may even
go the rest of your life — if you can afford it! Remember . . .

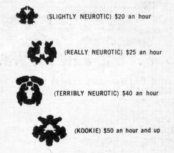

(SLIGHTLY NEUROTIC) $20 an hour

(REALLY NEUROTIC) $25 an hour

(TERRIBLY NEUROTIC) $40 an hour

(KOOKIE) $50 an hour and up

Going To A Psychiatrist Is Forever

If you've ridden the New York City subway in the last couple of decades and seen the ads for every conceivable
type of skin, dental, and hemorrhoid surgery known to man, you realize that *MAD*, unfortunately, got this one right.

KNOW THE REAL JOY OF GOOD LIVER!

"Hand me my scalpel, Shirley!"

Good operations don't just happen, you've got to make them! That goes for liver operations as well as any other kind. The same scalpels are available to all surgeons. What makes Schlitz stand out is the way he *uses* that scalpel. He gets the most out of every golden flourish. One flick of that Schlitz wrist, and your liver is as good as new. So next time you need a liver operation, go to Sam Schlitz, M.D. He may cost an extra hundred dollars but he's worth it!

SAM
Schlitz
MD
OFFICE HOURS 1-2   BILLING HOURS 2-10

move up to

THE DOC THAT MADE MILWAUKEE HOSPITAL FAMOUS

MRS. IRMA KRONKITE of Tutmere, Va., is shown in her attractive home which contains many gifts obtained with H&S Green Stamps. With her are her two allergic sons, Steve and Allen. Mr. Kronkite is in the hospital.

"I furnished my home with sickness — thanks to H&S. Green Stamps!"

says **MRS. IRMA KRONKITE**
Tutmere, Va. Housewife

— AND OVER 27,000,000 OTHER SICK, THRIFTY WOMEN AGREE...

As Mrs. Kronkite says about her own experiences with H&S (Hospitalization and Sickness) Green Stamps, "Whenever I go to Doctors and Hospitals that give Green Stamps, I know I'm dollars ahead. Because I can redeem H&S Green Stamps for lovely gifts—or more medical care!" H&S is America's oldest Hospitalization and Sickness Stamp Plan. With H&S Green Stamps you get what you want—when you're well enough to use it. As Mrs. Kronkite puts it, "H&S Green Stamps makes being sick worth it!"

SINCE 1900
H.&S.
GREEN
STAMPS

You can be dollars ahead, too! Be operated on where you get

H.&S. Green Stamps

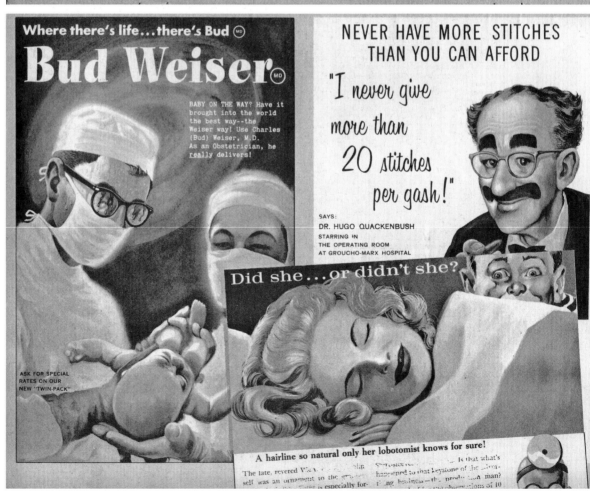

Where there's life...there's Bud ®
Bud Weiser ®

BABY ON THE WAY? Have it brought into the world the best way--the Weiser way! Use Charles (Bud) Weiser, M.D. As an Obstetrician, he really delivers!

ASK FOR SPECIAL RATES ON OUR NEW "TWIN-PACK"

NEVER HAVE MORE STITCHES THAN YOU CAN AFFORD

"I never give more than 20 stitches per gash!"

SAYS:
DR. HUGO QUACKENBUSH
STARRING IN
THE OPERATING ROOM
AT GROUCHO-MARX HOSPITAL

Did she...or didn't she?

A hairline so natural only her lobotomist knows for sure!

The late, revered V...

MAD #61
March 1961
Photographer: Lester Krauss
Writer: House

WHAT SORT OF MAN READS MAD?

SOPHISTICATED SOFT-SELL PHOTO BY LESTER KRAUSS

A young man with an open mind and a sharp sense of humor, the MAD reader has very little else to recommend him. He dresses atrociously, his tastes run to the ridiculous, and he's usually flat broke. If he does have any money, he spends it on idiotic things like the kookie car in the picture. (Incidentally, the young man beside the car isn't the MAD reader; the young man *underneath* the car is the MAD reader!) So actually, if you are an advertiser, it really wouldn't pay you to advertise in MAD. Facts: According to an obscure magazine survey, 97% of the 1,300,000 copies of MAD sold on newsstands each issue are purchased by clods. 87.3% of these clods have no visible means of support. And 79% wouldn't *believe* your advertising pitch anyway, because they've been thoroughly brainwashed by MAD articles and ad satires. So if you're looking for a magazine with a readership that seems to fall for the phony sophisticated soft sell, and has the money to do something about it, try PLAYBOY!

MAD ADVERTISING DEPARTMENT • Elevator Shaft #2 • 225 Lafayette Street, New York City , New York

This was a chance for *MAD* to spoof the "house ads" that magazines like *Playboy* ran to convince both their readers and their advertisers that the magazine appealed to a sophisticated audience. It was also a chance for *MAD* to mock its readers, something the Usual Gang of Idiots has been known to do from time to time.

That's then-associate editor Jerry De Fuccio as the *MAD*-reading man. The photograph is by Lester Krauss, who shot many of *MAD*'s early spoofs.

MAD #62
April 1961
Artist: Kelly Freas
Writer: House

Model R 270. 23" over-all diagonal. 282 sq. inch viewing area. Complete with carrying handle and folding legs.

Feast your eyes on the first
and only television set with
no picture tube at all

General Realistic

ENJOY-THE-VIEW

TELEVISION

Let your own eyes convince you that *there's a wonderful world out there!*

People have been so conditioned to watching TV these days that they no longer appreciate the real world around them. Not unless they see it on their television screen at home.

To solve this problem, General Realistic engineers have designed a whole new line of television sets — *without picture tubes!*

With any new General Realistic "Television Set-Without-A-Picture-Tube", you can once more enjoy the sights of the outside world. Merely study those sights through the vivid "Enjoy-The-View" clear-air screen.

So, get out of your living room today! Go get yourself a new General Realistic Portable "Dummy TV" set. *Put it down anywhere, and begin to observe "real life" again!*

Protest Is Our Most Important Progress

GENERAL REALISTIC

TELEVISION RELIEVER DEPARTMENT, SYRACUSE, N Y

MAD #63
June 1961
Photographer: Lester Krauss
Writer: House

Here's another example of advertisers actually wanting to be spoofed in *MAD*. Shortly after this parody ran, Jerry De Fuccio received a call from one of Scotch's competitors asking how they too could be mocked by the Usual Gang of Idiots. As De Fuccio explained to author and *MAD* writer Frank Jacobs, "I told him to just come up with an idiotic ad campaign. We'd do the rest."

After many years of looking and listening (and wincing), we've finally discovered what those one-minute television commercials are all about — They're all about one minute too short! It seems to us that the Television viewer is suffering all of the abuse and missing all of the fun . . . mainly all of the fun that goes on during . . .

THE MINUTE AFTER THAT ONE-MINUTE TV COMMERCIAL

ARTIST: BOB CLARKE
WRITER: SY REIT

TAKE TEA AND SEE

THE MAXWELL HOUSE COFFEE COMMERCIAL . . . . AND THAT MINUTE AFTER

COFFEE BEANS . . . FRESH-HOT FROM THE ROASTER!

MAXWELL HOUSE COFFEE BEANS!

THE MOST FLAVORFUL . . . THE MOST SATISFYING YET . . .

MMM! PERFECTLY ROASTED BEANS, FOR RICH, FRESH-FLAVORED COFFEE GOODNESS . . . IN EVERY CUP!

CUT!

YEEEEE EEOOW

THE GRAVY TRAIN DOG FOOD COMMERCIAL . . . . AND THAT MINUTE AFTER

GRAVY TRAIN . . . THE WORLD'S ONLY DOG FOOD THAT MAKES ITS OWN GRAVY!

SIMPLY POUR SOME INTO A BOWL, ADD WARM WATER . . . STIR FOR ONE MINUTE . . .

AND GRAVY HAPPENS! YES . . . CRUNCHY CHUNKS IN BEEFY, TASTY GRAVY! JUST LIKE THE FINEST BEEF STEW!

GRAVY TRAIN GIVES YOUR DOG A COMPLETE BALANCE OF VITAMINS, MINERALS, AND PROTEINS . . . THE BEST BALANCED DIET IN THE WHOLE DOGGONE WORLD . . . AND DOES HE LOVE IT! GRAVY TRAIN!

CUT!

MAD #63
June 1961
Artist: Bob Clarke
Writer: Sy Reit

Who says the good ol' days were always so good? At least today, annoying TV commercials typically last only 15 or 30 seconds. In 1961, they often ran a soul-stealing minute. Then again, that was probably enough time for writer Sy Reit to come up with this premise, showing what happened AFTER the cameras stopped rolling.

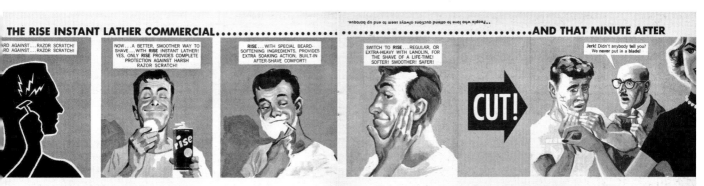

▼ (overleaf) *MAD* #64
July 1961
Artist: Bob Clarke
Writer: Sy Reit

THAT OLD AD-AGE DEPT.

After many years of jibes and insults, we've finally figured out something nice to say about Madison Avenue—namely, "It could have been worse!" What we mean is: Advertising is strictly a modern, 20th century type of plague. But supposing past centuries had been plagued with their own "Madison Avenue"? What if the Pilgrims and the Crusaders and the Cavemen had been forced to put up with advertising along with all their other troubles? Ecchh! To show how horrible this state of affairs might have been, MAD now offers a few samples of what advertisements would have been like...

if there'd been a Madisor

Camelot Stables Present...

THE ALL NEW 1361 *Horse*

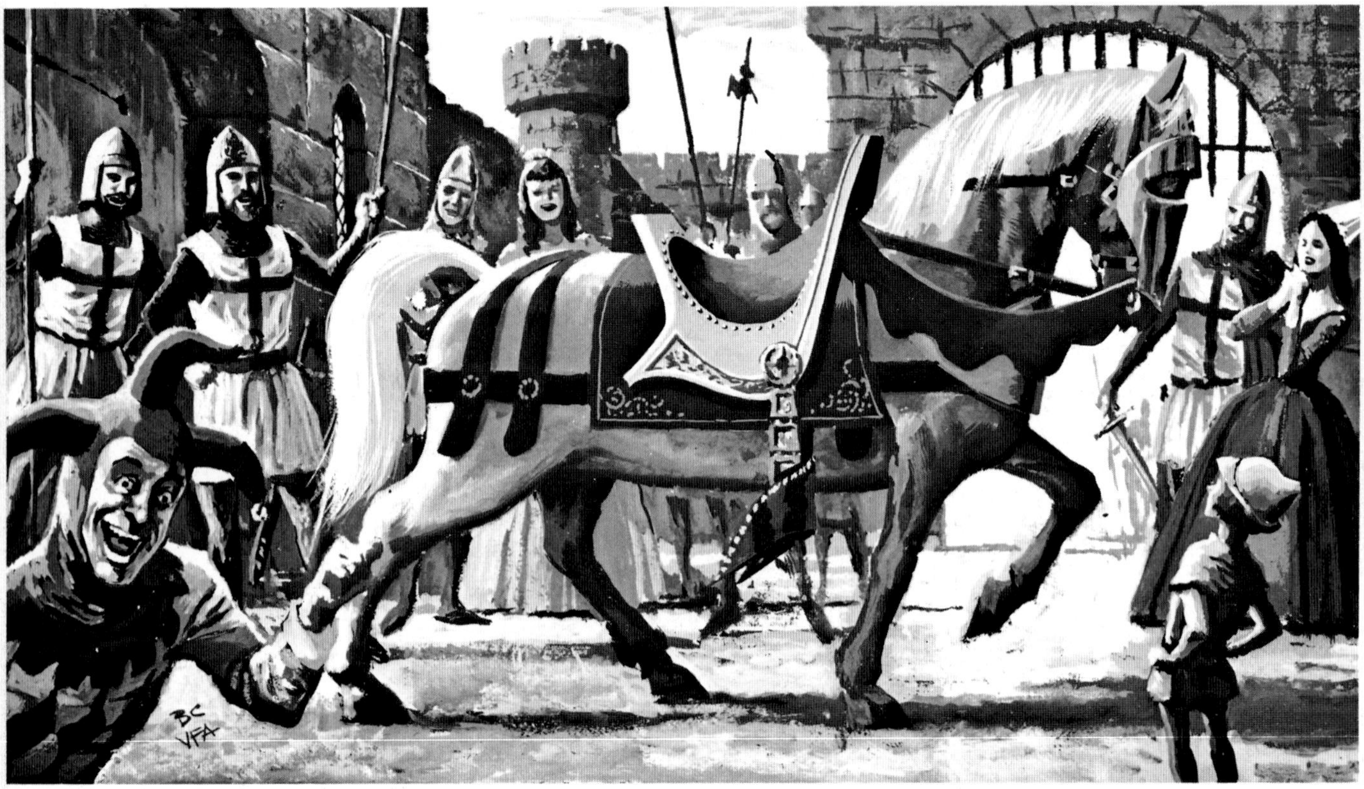

**A Situation Comedy about a *Butcher* called "What's My Loin?"

LONGER . . . LOWER . . . MORE SEATING SPACE . . . HIGHER TAIL

OPTIONAL FEATURES*:

- Puncture-Proof Hooves
- Swivel-Tilt Saddle
- Power Lance Holder
- Automatic Blinder Wipers
- Braided Tail Trim

*AT SLIGHT EXTRA COST

Here it is . . . the fastest, sleekest, most beautifully proportioned horse ever produced . . . the all-new 1361 CAMELOT! Why not drop in at your local CAMELOT stable (wear boots!) and see for yourself? Take it out for a road test! Sit on it! Start it galloping! Whip it! Listen to it whinny! Feel that exciting surge of power!

The 1361 CAMELOT HORSE is economical, too! You get 18 miles to a quart of oats! And talk about seating room . . . there's space not only for a knight in full armor, but for his fair lady as well – perched athwart the genuine leather two-toned custom saddle.

THE 1361 ***Camelot***

IS GUARANTEED ONE HORSE-POWER!

Available in your choice of colors:

WRITER: SY REIT   ARTIST: BOB CLARKE

Ave. down through History

NOW PLAYING at the COLISEUM

Rome's Off-Appian Way
"Theatre-In-The-Round"

A GREAT NEW SPECTACLE!

THUMBS DOWN

*IN GLORIOUS,
LIVID*

SLAUGHTERAMA

SEE 50 RAVENOUSLY LIVE LIONS

SEE 100 TEMPORARILY LIVE CHRISTIANS

NOT RADIATORS, IDIOT!

SEE SCARRED (AND ALSO SCARED) GLADIATORS

READ WHAT THE CRITICS SAY:

"A show that will go down in history!"
—GAUL GAZETTE

"Claws at the hearstrings!"
—PALATINE QUARTERLY

"A bloody bore!"
—THE NEW ROMER

"Of devouring interest!
Thumbs up for 'Thumbs Down'!"
—TIBERIAN TIMES

ALL SEATS RESERVED

MATINEES—280 Sesterces

EVENINGS—660 Sesterces

Announcing... An Exciting New Castle Development

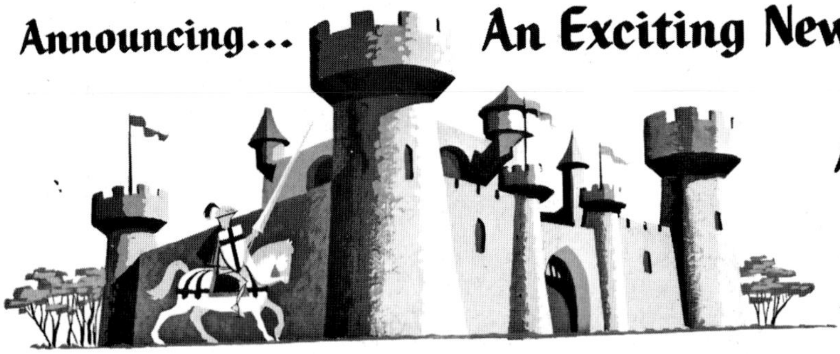

ATROCIOUS MANORS

Three Luxurious Models Available:

*48 Rooms, Two Towers

*48 Rooms, Three Towers

*49 Rooms, Four Towers

plus Knotty Pine Family Torture Chamber

16,990 PIECES OF GOLD and up

no down payment for veteran knights

Only 20 minutes from your front door to the field of honor
Only 20 minutes from your front door to your own room

DIRECTIONS: Take horse path to Lancelot Brook, make rt. turn at Oak Tree into Sherwood Forest, remove arrows from your wife and lackey, chalk robbery up to Real Estate Loss, continue on dirt road which leads to development, pay ten pence toll, go left to moat, and you are there.

FEATURING:

*all rooms off the drawbridge
*guest dungeon
*oversized 2-horse stable
*sunken living room (in the moat)
*70x100 acre plots

**A Play about Horses called "Life With Fodder."

Praying You'll Get There Is Halfe Ye Funne!

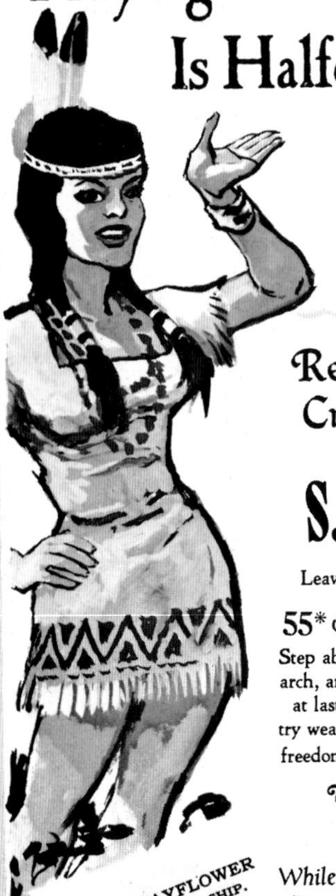
THE S.S. MAYFLOWER IS YE ONE-CLASS SHIP. ALL QUARTERS ARE THE SAME—CRAMPED! ACT NOW, A FEW CHOICE SLEEPING PLANKS ARE STILL AVAILABLE!

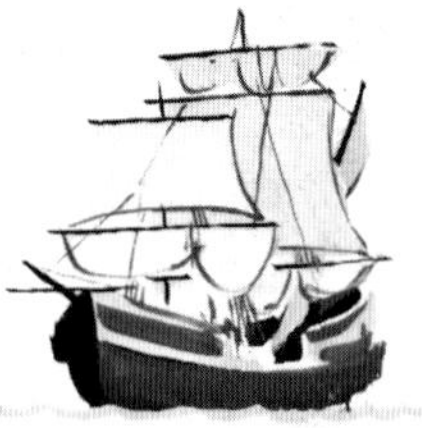

Reserve Now for the Cruise of a Lifetime on the

S.S. Mayflower

Leaving England on September 16, 1620

55* GLORIOUS DAYS AT SEA 55*

Step aboard this modern 100-foot ocean monarch, and say goodbye to all your cares! Now, at last, you can enjoy freedom from ye wintry weather, freedom from ye London fog, and freedom from ye RELIGIOUS PERSECUTION!

Visit The New World

With its breathtaking scenery and bloodthirsty natives

While In Port, The Ship Is Your Hotel**

*Give or take a few weeks

**On account of there's no place else that's safe

For Information, Apply To:

Pilgrim Tours, Ltd.

Fleet Street, London

Revere

Messenger Service

"For People Who Care To Send The Very Best!"

Reliable! Dependable! *Known Throughout the Colonies!*

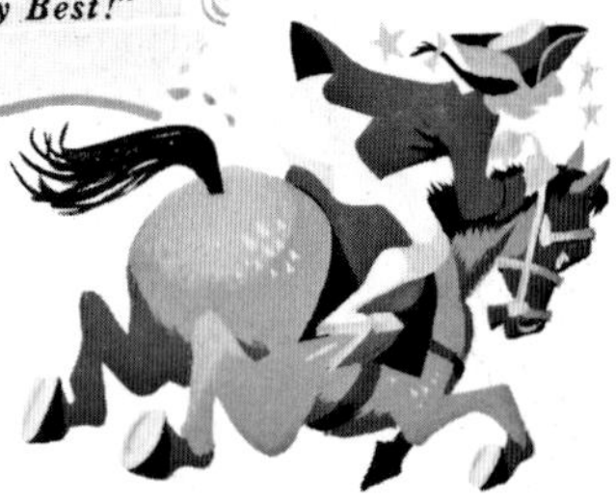

THE BEST WAY TO –

- *Send Messages*
- *Deliver Packages*
- *Warn Minute Men*

REVERE

Messenger Service

ON CALL ANY HOUR—DAY OR NIGHT
OUR MOTTO:
"Let Paul Do It!"

A Complete Art Service for all your needs!

Michelangelo

ASSOCIATES, INC.

An "easy-to-work-with" creative art studio that offers top talent backed by years of "know-how." Let us help you with your art problem. No ceiling too large or too small!

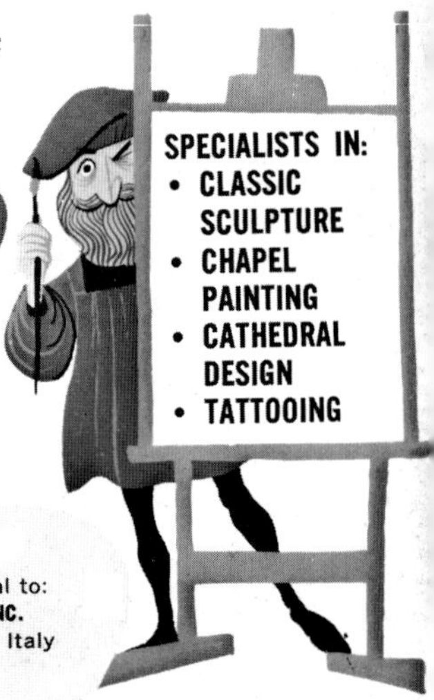
SPECIALISTS IN:
• CLASSIC SCULPTURE
• CHAPEL PAINTING
• CATHEDRAL DESIGN
• TATTOOING

Send 25 Lira for Sample Mural to:
MICHELANGELO ASSOCIATES, INC.
522 Medici Road, Florence 24, Italy

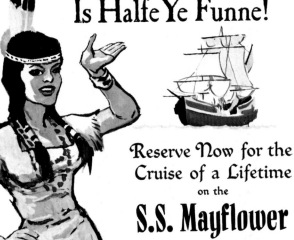

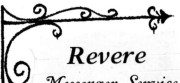

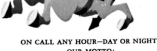

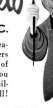

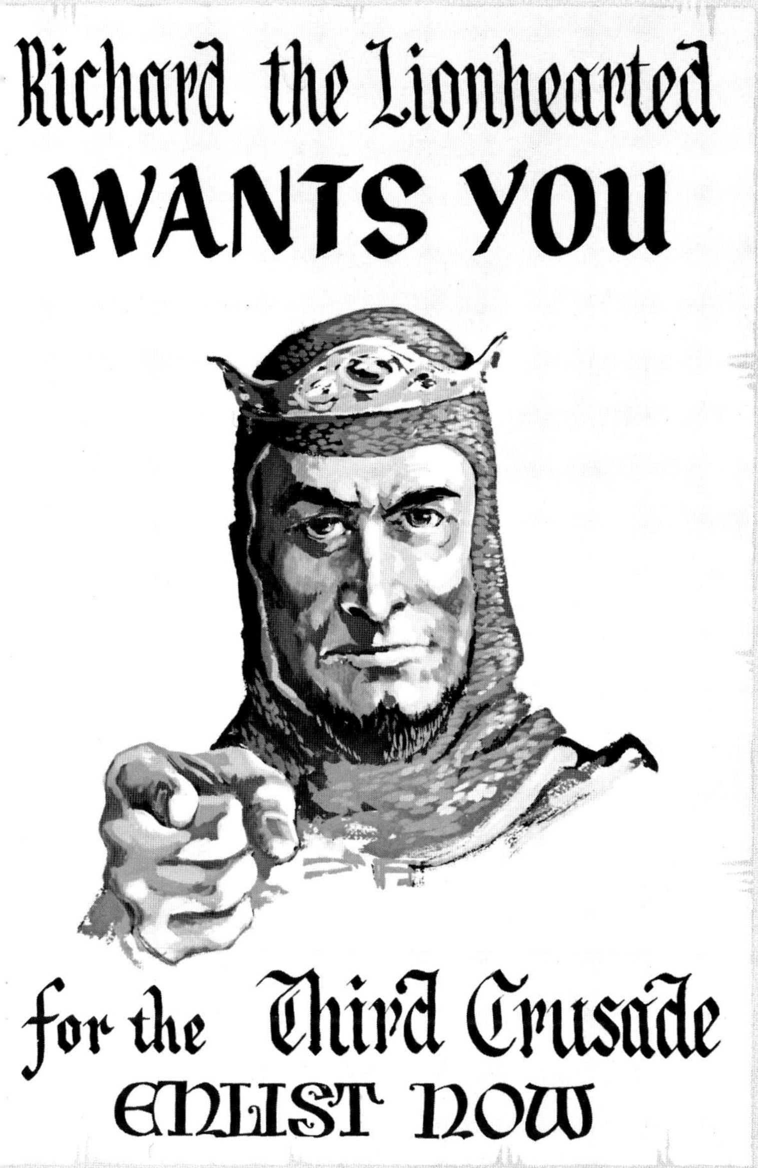
Richard the Lionhearted
WANTS YOU
for the Third Crusade
ENLIST NOW

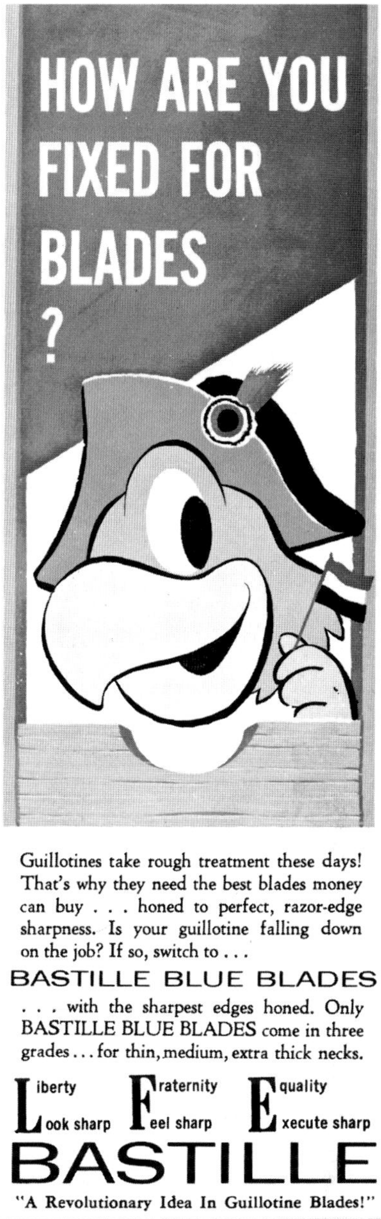
HOW ARE YOU FIXED FOR BLADES ?
Guillotines take rough treatment these days! That's why they need the best blades money can buy . . . honed to perfect, razor-edge sharpness. Is your guillotine falling down on the job? If so, switch to . . .
BASTILLE BLUE BLADES
. . . with the sharpest edges honed. Only BASTILLE BLUE BLADES come in three grades . . . for thin, medium, extra thick necks.
Liberty Fraternity Equality
Look sharp Feel sharp Execute sharp
BASTILLE
"A Revolutionary Idea In Guillotine Blades!"

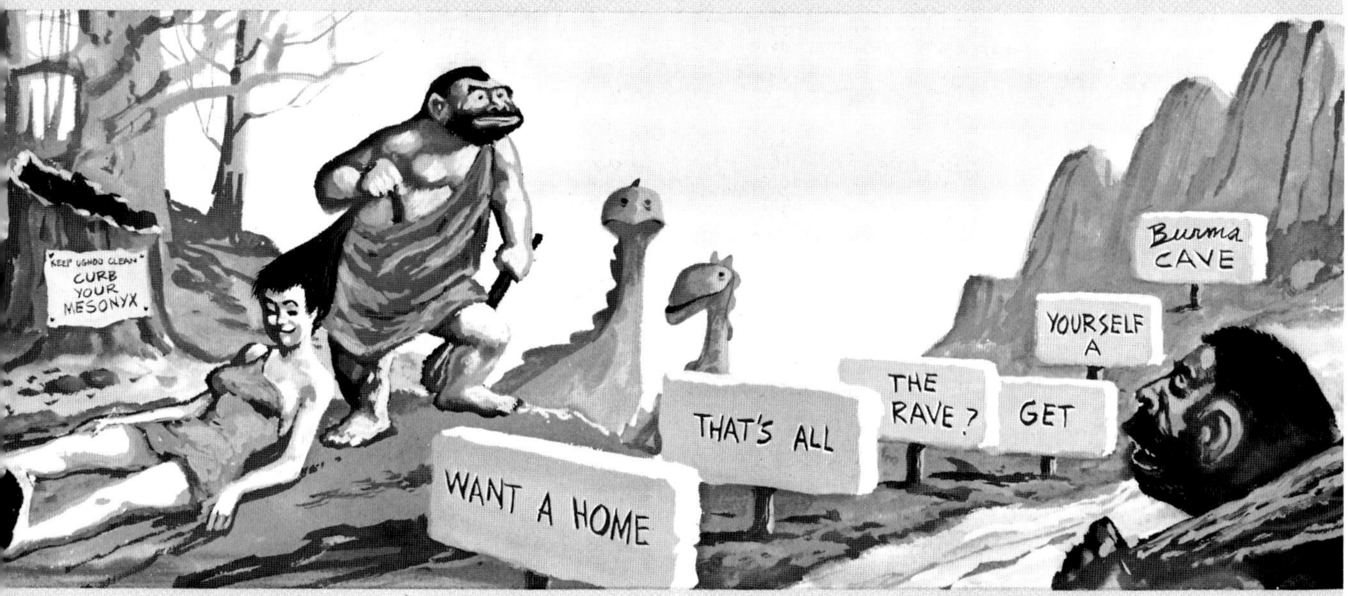
KEEP UGHOO CLEAN
CURB YOUR MESONYX
WANT A HOME
THAT'S ALL
THE RAVE ?
GET
YOURSELF A
Burma CAVE

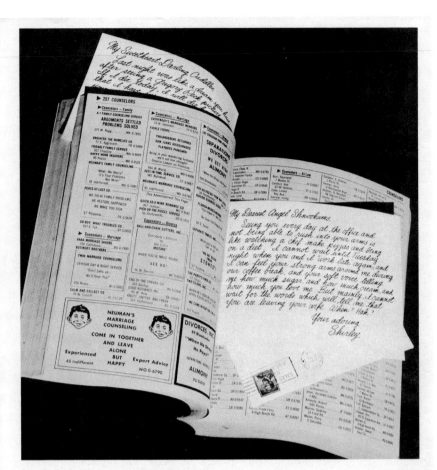

How to find things you never expected

Look something up in the Yellow Pages — and discover things your husband figured would be safely hidden from you — like some torrid love letters from his secretary.

Get the facts — read them letters carefully. Find out what's been going on behind your back. Then use the Yellow Pages to locate the exact service you need.

Select to suit your needs. After you decide what steps to take, you're ready to contact folks who can help you— like a Marriage Counselor, or a competent Divorce Lawyer.

Yellowed Pages

THE WORST PLACE
TO HIDE ANYTHING

MAD #66
October 1961
Artist: Bob Clarke
Writer: Al Jaffee

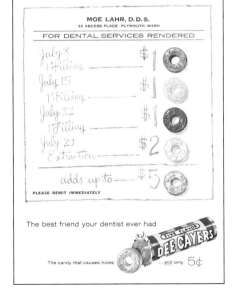

MAD #66
October 1961
Artist: Kelley Freas
Writer: House

The trouble with owning a Cadillac is: you gotta leave it in the parking lot. Now, wherever you go, you can let the whole world know you own that fabulous status-symbol—by wearing Cadillac Jewelry.

Car-Shaped Cadillac Jewelry Box in your Model by Ideal Toy Co.

CADILLAC JEWELRY DIVISION, GENERAL MOTORS CORPO

MAD ESP, PART 2

As we all know, *MAD* has had a huge influence on rap culture, and here's another example.

Okay, it hasn't, but when this ad spoof ran in 1961, who knew that one day hood ornaments would indeed become especially popular as jewelry among status-conscious hip-hoppers? (We'll know *MAD*'s really got some pull when 50 Cent records the single "Straight Outta Potrzebie Axolotl!")

MAD #65
September 1961
Artist: Kelly Freas
Writer: House

MAD*vertising* **67**

BUY THE WAY DEPT.

ARTIST: BOB CLARKE

With Russia waging an all-out "anti-America" campaign to win new countries to their side, we figure it's time for action! Mainly, what better way to sell America around the world than to let Madison Avenue handle the problem. Then they could treat "democracy and freedom" as they would the commercial products they push. F'rinstance, here are a few sample ads to show you . . .

HOW MADISON AVENUE COULD SELL AMERICA TO T

KNOW THE REAL JOY OF FREE LIVING!

"How come we ain't seen you at The Clan lately, Jack?"

That's American democracy for you! The only nation in the world where a President from Harvard and a Singer from Hoboken can sit down together, side-by-side, and talk about old times over a cold glass of beer. In no other nation on earth are people from different levels treated as equals. Try refreshing democracy yourself!

MOVE UP TO EQUALITY

move up to

America

THE NATION THAT MADE A CLASS-FREE SOCIETY FAMOUS

Everybody knows...

It's who's in front that coun

IF IT HASN'T GOT IT HERE

NUCLEAR WEAPONS
AMERICA
RUSSIA

IT HASN'T GO

King Size H-Bombs or Regular Size A-Bon

America's got it — Atomic Stock-Pile — the effective deterrent specially processed to keep you-know-who from getting any ideas!

You get something special when you team up with America. Democracy and dom to begin with . . . plus America's up-to-date Atomic Stock-Pile to back
After all, if you haven't got deterrent strength . . . you'll miss the whole of being an independent nation. Mainly, *you-know-who* may decide to includ in its satellite program. America has that strength with Atomic Stock-Pile powerful energy specially designed and specially processed to insure freedom where in the world. Try America!

AMERICA'S ARMED GOOD
LIKE A FREE NATION SHOULD

MAD ESP, PART 3

This idea seems pretty silly and far-fetched, huh? Some forty years later it became a reality, as the U.S. State Department launched a TV network, magazine, and radio station in the Middle East with the sole purpose of persuading Arab youth that the U.S. isn't a bunch of shallow, morally bankrupt infidels (which may explain why they refuse to add *Fear Factor* to the lineup).

UNITED NATIONS
To the countries of
the World
An examination of
*America, shows it to be
free of any colonies!
Dag Hammarskjold*
Secretary-General

"Look, World—no colonies!"

Yes, America is the only leading world power which does not
have any colonies. So if you
are thinking about keeping
your newly-won independence
clean and shiny, try an alliance with America. Mainly,
we could keep you from getting your teeth knocked out.

COMMENDED BY THE U.N. ASSEMBLY

Guaranteed by Good Government

MAD #65
September 1961
Artist: Bob Clarke
Writer: Paul Laikin

Revolutionary 3-way plan for relief of

COLD WAR MISERIES AND POPULATION CONGESTION

POVERTY AREA — DROUGHT AREA — FAMINE AREA — DISEASE AREA — OVERPOPULATION AREA — UNDERDEVELOPED AREA — NO EDUCATION AREA — NO PARKING AREA

HELPS DRAIN ALL 8 PRESSURE AREAS
(critical *causes* of *Communist infection*)

ASSISTANCE Decongestion Money, working
through the International Monetary Fund,
brings dramatic relief from Cold War miseries, starvation allergies, and overpopulation
congestion with its painful pressures.

ASSISTANCE, amazing diplomatic achievement, contains (1) The scientific decongestant most prescribed by leading economists.
In minutes, it reaches into affected areas —
quickly shrinks swollen recessions — promotes
recovery — restores free enterprise. (2) An
exclusive Anti-Communism ingredient to
block Dictatorship often associated with internal strife. (3) Prosperity to help build
a country's resistance to Communist infection. **NOTE:** Today's U.S. ASSISTANCE is
being widely imitated by you-know-who. But
the fact remains . . . the exclusive American
ASSISTANCE formula cannot be duplicated!

This Exclusive ASSISTANCE
THOUSAND $ LOANS
MILLION $ LOANS   Loan
BILLION $ LOANS   Formula
Cannot Be Duplicated!

ASSISTANCE is the exclusive 3-
way discovery which makes it possible to unite certain economically-proven ingredients into one
fast-acting recovery system. Accept
no substitutes!

ASSISTANCE
DECONGESTANT MONEY
LOANS FOR RELIEF OF
POPULATION CONGESTION
AND COLD WAR MISERIES

There's Nothing like **ASSISTANCE** *Decongestion Money*

MAD #67
December 1961
Writer: House

MAD #67
December 1961:
Writer: House

There's always need for Fool-Aid. The hideous grin on the pitcher tells you it's indispensable. Warm weather brings out hordes of enterprising kids who set up soft drink stands in every neighborhood. The only trouble is: you can't be sure what the little monsters use to make the stuff. So be prepared! Always carry Fool-Aid — the instant antidote for poisons taken internally.

MAD #67
December 1961
Artist: Kelly Freas
Writer: Al Jaffee

MAD #67
December 1961
Photographer: Lester Krauss
Writer: Al Jaffee

Three (*MAD*)men and a lady: editor Al Feldstein (Nausea), Jerry De Fuccio (Ulcers), art director John Putnam (Hysteria), and a friend of *MAD* in this spoof of Bayer Aspirin.

MAD #69
March 1962
Photographer: Lester Krauss
Writer: House

LIBERTY MUTILATE
The company that stages auto accidents

PHOTO BY LESTER KRAUSS

Hoo Boy! This is gonna be a gory one!

THIS ACCIDENT NEVER HAPPENED! It was staged by us to catch your beady little eyes . . . so we can sell you some insurance. The way we figure, everybody has a little bit of sadism and a little bit of masochism in them. First we grab the sadist in you with a gory accident scene, and then we appeal to the masochist in you by insidiously implying that this mess could easily have happened to you. Then, when you're good and scared, we make our pitch. You'd be amazed at how much insurance we've sold lately using this great ad campaign. Incidentally, here's how Liberty Mutilate stages an auto accident: ■ First, we visit a "Used Car" lot and pick up a beat-up old second-hand car — cheap. ■ Then we drive it out to a likely spot, and smash it into a tree, or a wall, or another beat-up old second-hand car. ■ Next, we add a few finishing touches with sledge hammers and crow bars. ■ Then, we hire some actors, bandage them up, squirt ketchup all over them, and pose them around the phony wreck. And finally, to cover us, because "location shots" often run into legal difficulties, we insure the entire crew with some reliable company — like "All-State".

LIBERTY MUTILATE INSURANCE COMPANY • HOME OFFICE: BOSTON, MASOCHISTIC

Liberty Mutual's slogan in 1961 was "the company that stands by you," but given their propensity for running ads with gruesome auto accidents in them, you probably didn't want them to stand too close.

MAD #70
April 1962
Photographer: Lester Krauss
Writer: House

I dreamed my husband caught me posing in my *maidinfirm bra*,

PURPLE RAGE . . . that's what he was in . . . especially since I'd told him it was for "Pepsi-Cola"! But what's a professional model supposed to tell her guy . . . when lingerie ads are getting sexier and sexier, and they're just about the only jobs available these days? Hah?

MODEL-FORM BOOKS, INC.—PUBLISHERS OF "HOW TO TELL YOUR GUY YOU'RE POSING FOR A LINGERIE AD"

What happened to the coverage? . . . that big umbrella which The Travailers Insurance Company uses as a symbol of adequate insurance protection? In the picture above, we see a couple that had the foresight to buy adequate insurance protection many years ago. They felt secure under that big umbrella (the dotted lines). But when they retired, were they surprised! The big umbrella turned out to be very small. *That's because no one has yet figured out how to SANFORIZE insurance umbrellas against the ravages of inflation.*

PHOTO BY LESTER KRAUSS

THE TRAVAILERS Insurance Companies HEARTACHE 1 CONNECTICUT

To create this spoof of the Travelers Insurance Companies, Nick Meglin (with plunger), John Putnam, and a model posed outside the famously slovenly Putnam's Greenwich Village apartment, surrounded by a pile of junk that was Putnam's actual stuff.

MAD #71
June 1962
Photographer: Lester Krauss
Writer: Al Jaffee

▼ (overleaf) *MAD* #70
April 1962
Artist: Wallace Wood
Writer: Gary Belkin

*If Celeste HOLM had a brother, FOSTER . . .

Various industries, in an effort to invest themselves with dignity and importance, have taken to collecting their historical artifacts for exhibition in museums. The Automobile Industry has "The Henry Ford Museum," the Glass Industry has the "Corning Museum of Glass" and the Baseball Industry has the Cooperstown "Hall of Fame." So, we here at MAD figure it won't be long before the Advertising Industry opens . . .

THE NEW, IMPROVED, HOSPITAL TESTED AND APPROVED

MVSEVM OF MADISON AVENVE

Hi, there! I'm Helen Hubbard, your guide! I'll be showing you average people around our Museum. And folks, this museum looks good —like an Ad Museum should! So why not do as thousands of others have done? Follow me on our money-back guaranteed tour! You'll be awfully glad you did!

GEE, DAD...IT'S A WVRLITZER
DOES SHE—OR DOESN'T SHE?
EVEN YOVR BEST FRIENDS WON'T TELL YOV
TELL YOVR FRIENDS ABOVT IT
WOVLD YOV BELIEVE IT, I HAVE A COLD
I WAS A 97-POVND WEAKLING!
QVICK HENRY, THE FLIT ☆ TAKE TEA AND SEE
IF YOV CAN WALK, YOV CAN DANCE
A DIAMOND IS FOREVER ☆ TIME TO RETIRE
T WILDROOT CREAM OIL CHARLIE ☆ IT'S TOASTED
'S LOVELY, SHE'S ENGAGED, SHE VSES POND'S
IT LOATS ☆ THEY SAID IT COVLDN'T BE DONE
IT'S WHAT'S VP FRONT THAT COVNTS ☆ 99$\frac{44}{100}$% PVRE
PROGRESS IS OVR MOST IMPORTANT PRODVCT

ARTIST: WALLACE WOOD   WRITER: GARY BELKIN

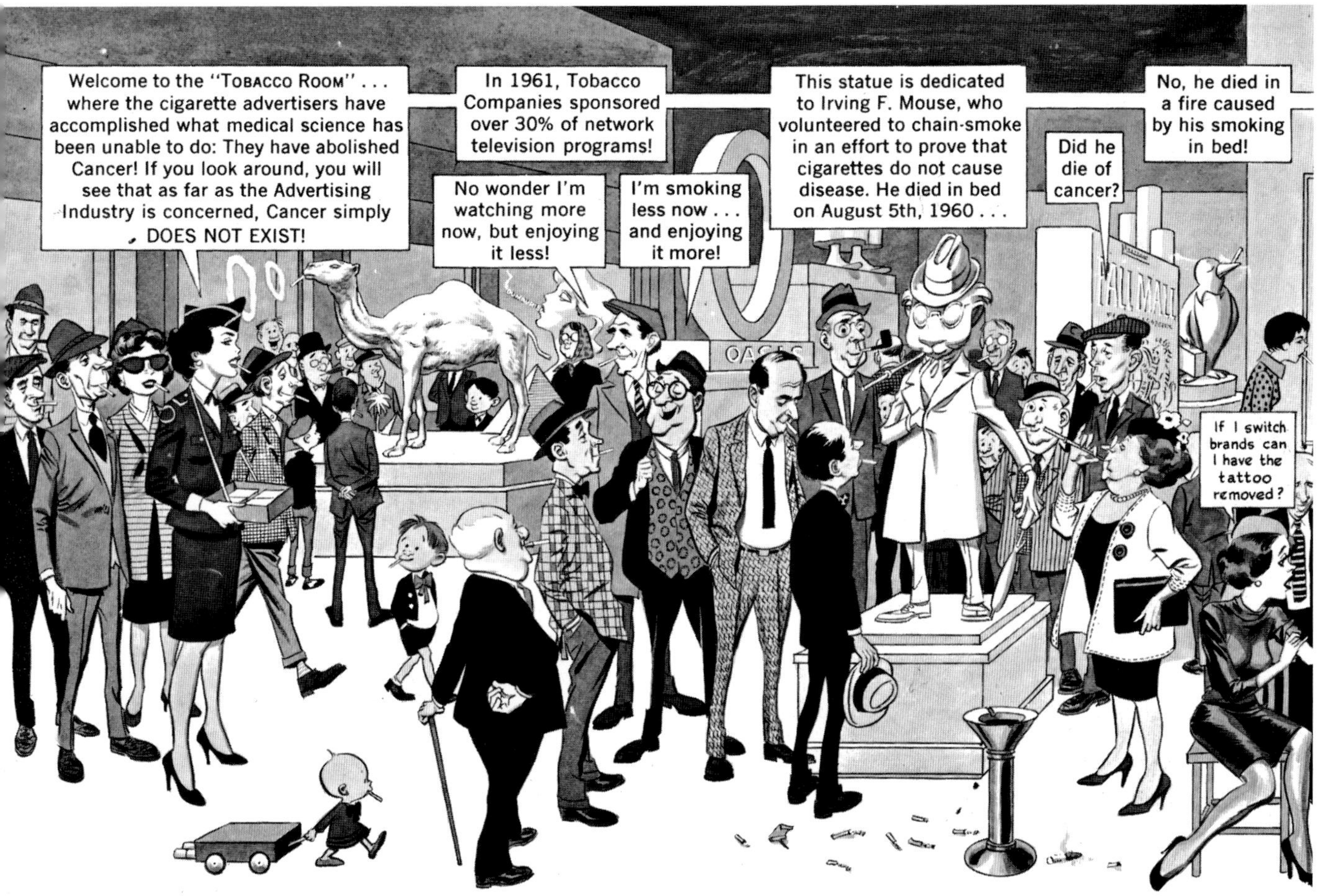

Welcome to the "TOBACCO ROOM" . . . where the cigarette advertisers have accomplished what medical science has been unable to do: They have abolished Cancer! If you look around, you will see that as far as the Advertising Industry is concerned, Cancer simply DOES NOT EXIST!
In 1961, Tobacco Companies sponsored over 30% of network television programs!
No wonder I'm watching more now, but enjoying it less!
I'm smoking less now . . . and enjoying it more!
This statue is dedicated to Irving F. Mouse, who volunteered to chain-smoke in an effort to prove that cigarettes do not cause disease. He died in bed on August 5th, 1960 . . .
Did he die of cancer?
No, he died in a fire caused by his smoking in bed!
If I switch brands can I have the tattoo removed?
OASIS
PALL MALL

*If Lynn BARI had a brother, HUCKLE . . .

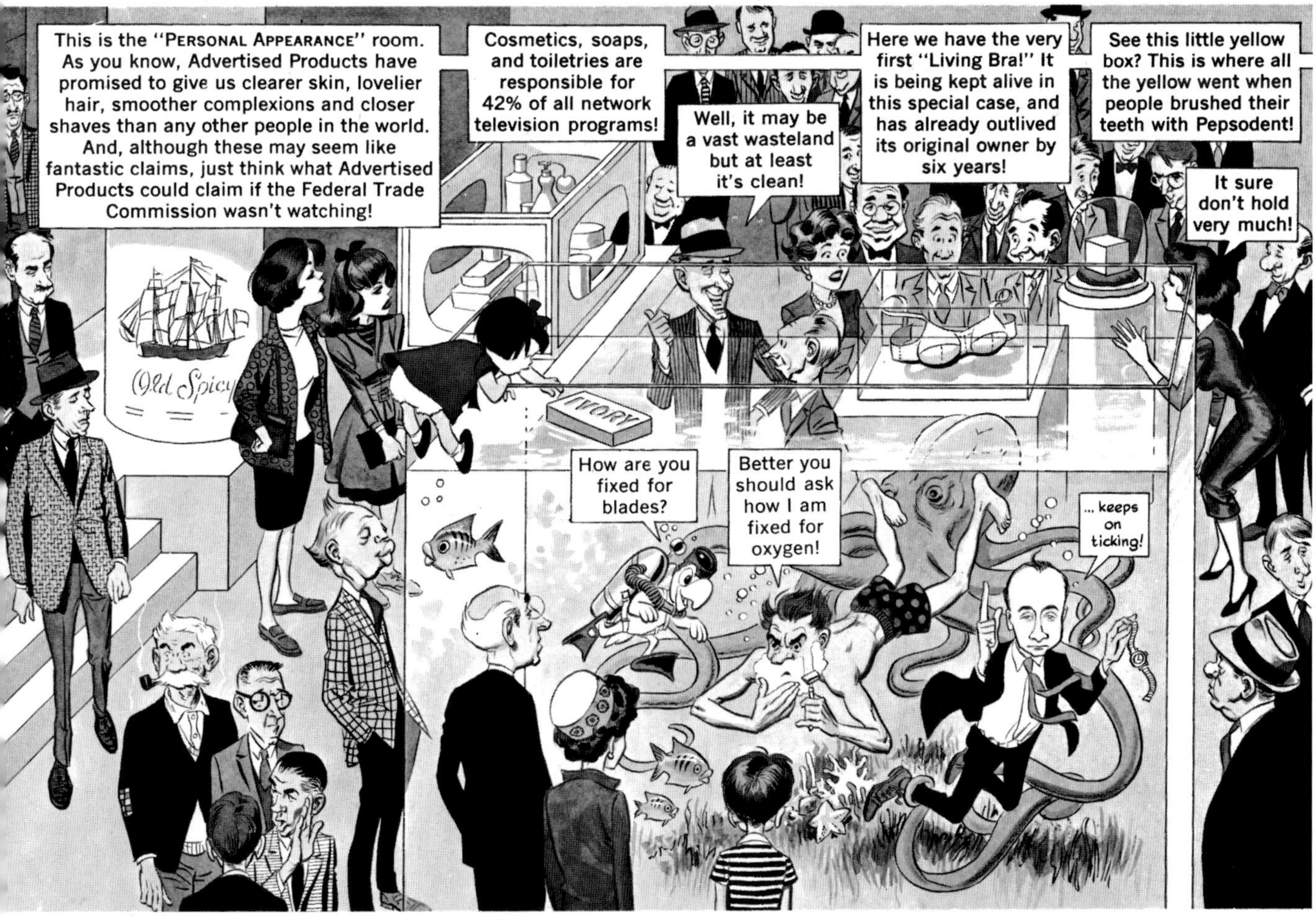

This is the "PERSONAL APPEARANCE" room. As you know, Advertised Products have promised to give us clearer skin, lovelier hair, smoother complexions and closer shaves than any other people in the world. And, although these may seem like fantastic claims, just think what Advertised Products could claim if the Federal Trade Commission wasn't watching!
Cosmetics, soaps, and toiletries are responsible for 42% of all network television programs!
Well, it may be a vast wasteland but at least it's clean!
Here we have the very first "Living Bra!" It is being kept alive in this special case, and has already outlived its original owner by six years!
See this little yellow box? This is where all the yellow went when people brushed their teeth with Pepsodent!
It sure don't hold very much!
Old Spice
IVORY
How are you fixed for blades?
Better you should ask how I am fixed for oxygen!
... keeps on ticking!

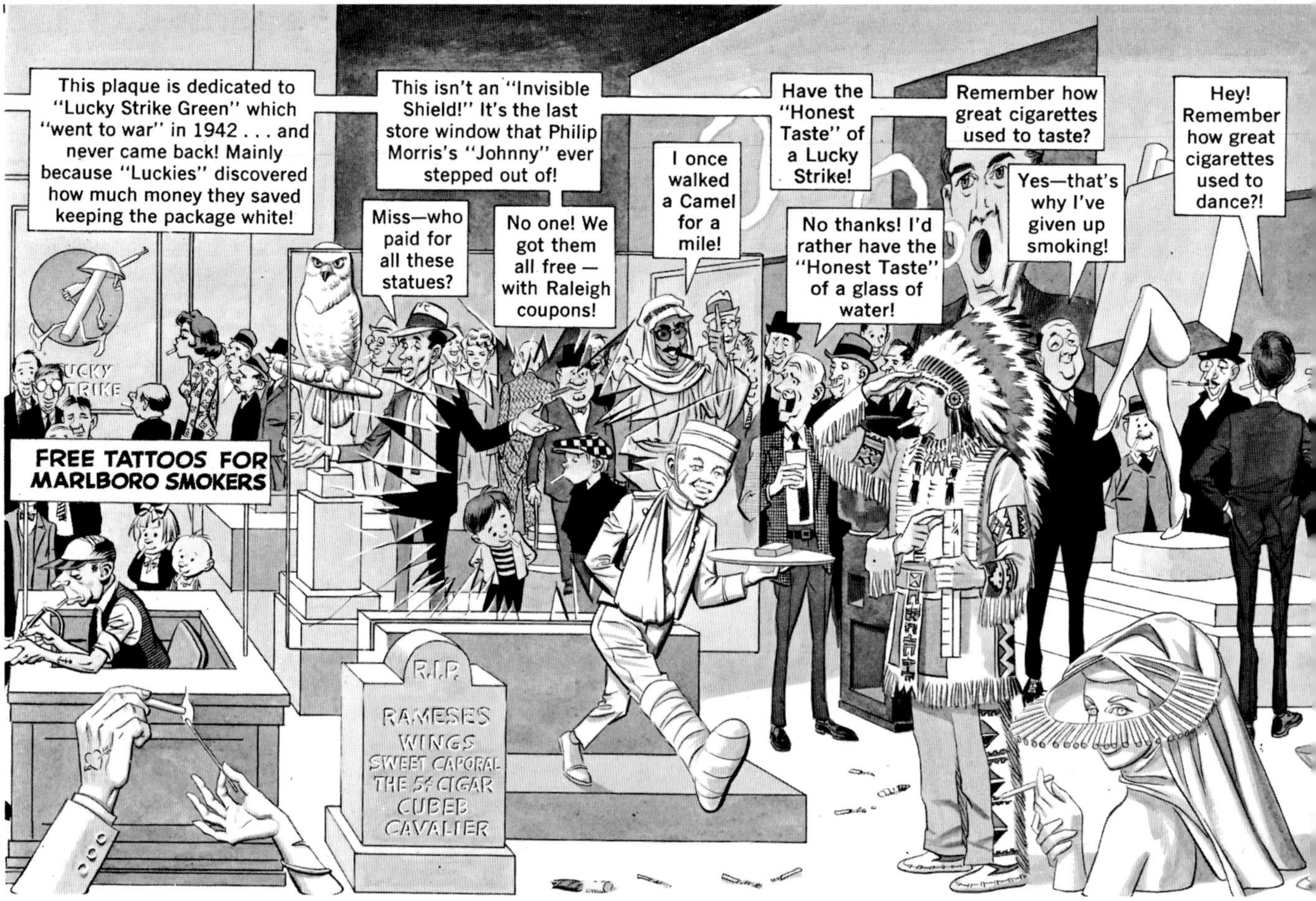

This plaque is dedicated to "Lucky Strike Green" which "went to war" in 1942 . . . and never came back! Mainly because "Luckies" discovered how much money they saved keeping the package white!
This isn't an "Invisible Shield!" It's the last store window that Philip Morris's "Johnny" ever stepped out of!
Have the "Honest Taste" of a Lucky Strike!
Remember how great cigarettes used to taste?
Hey! Remember how great cigarettes used to dance?!
Miss—who paid for all these statues?
No one! We got them all free—with Raleigh coupons!
I once walked a Camel for a mile!
No thanks! I'd rather have the "Honest Taste" of a glass of water!
Yes—that's why I've given up smoking!
LUCKY STRIKE
FREE TATTOOS FOR MARLBORO SMOKERS
R.I.P. RAMESES WINGS SWEET CAPORAL THE 5¢ CIGAR CUBEB CAVALIER

*If Frank GORSHIN had a brother, ATLANTIC . . .

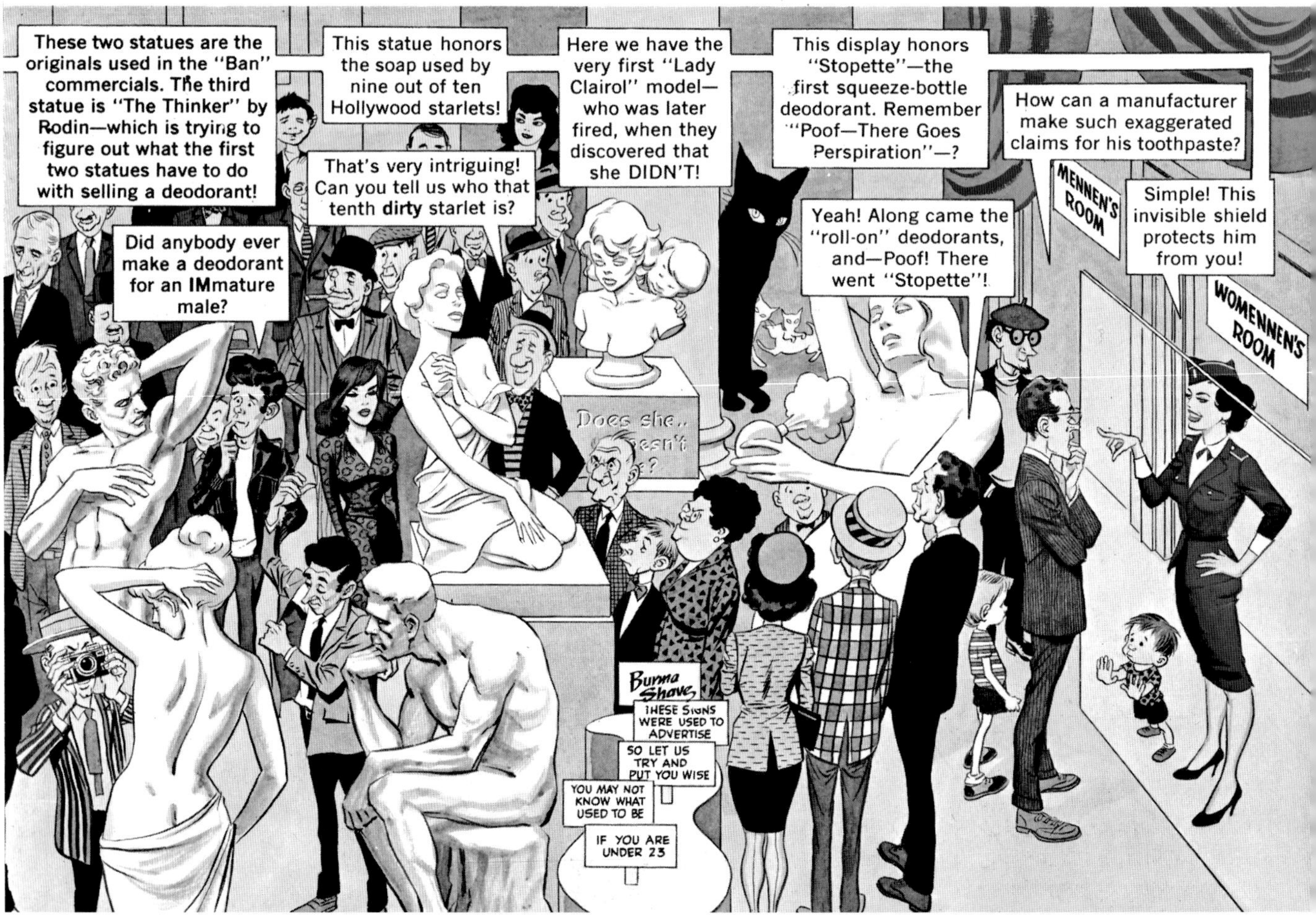

These two statues are the originals used in the "Ban" commercials. The third statue is "The Thinker" by Rodin—which is trying to figure out what the first two statues have to do with selling a deodorant!
This statue honors the soap used by nine out of ten Hollywood starlets!
Here we have the very first "Lady Clairol" model—who was later fired, when they discovered that she DIDN'T!
This display honors "Stopette"—the first squeeze-bottle deodorant. Remember "Poof—There Goes Perspiration"—?
How can a manufacturer make such exaggerated claims for his toothpaste?
That's very intriguing! Can you tell us who that tenth dirty starlet is?
Did anybody ever make a deodorant for an IMmature male?
Yeah! Along came the "roll-on" deodorants, and—Poof! There went "Stopette"!
Simple! This invisible shield protects him from you!
MENNEN'S ROOM
WOMENNEN'S ROOM
Does she..
Burma Shave
THESE SIGNS WERE USED TO ADVERTISE
SO LET US TRY AND PUT YOU WISE
YOU MAY NOT KNOW WHAT USED TO BE
IF YOU ARE UNDER 23

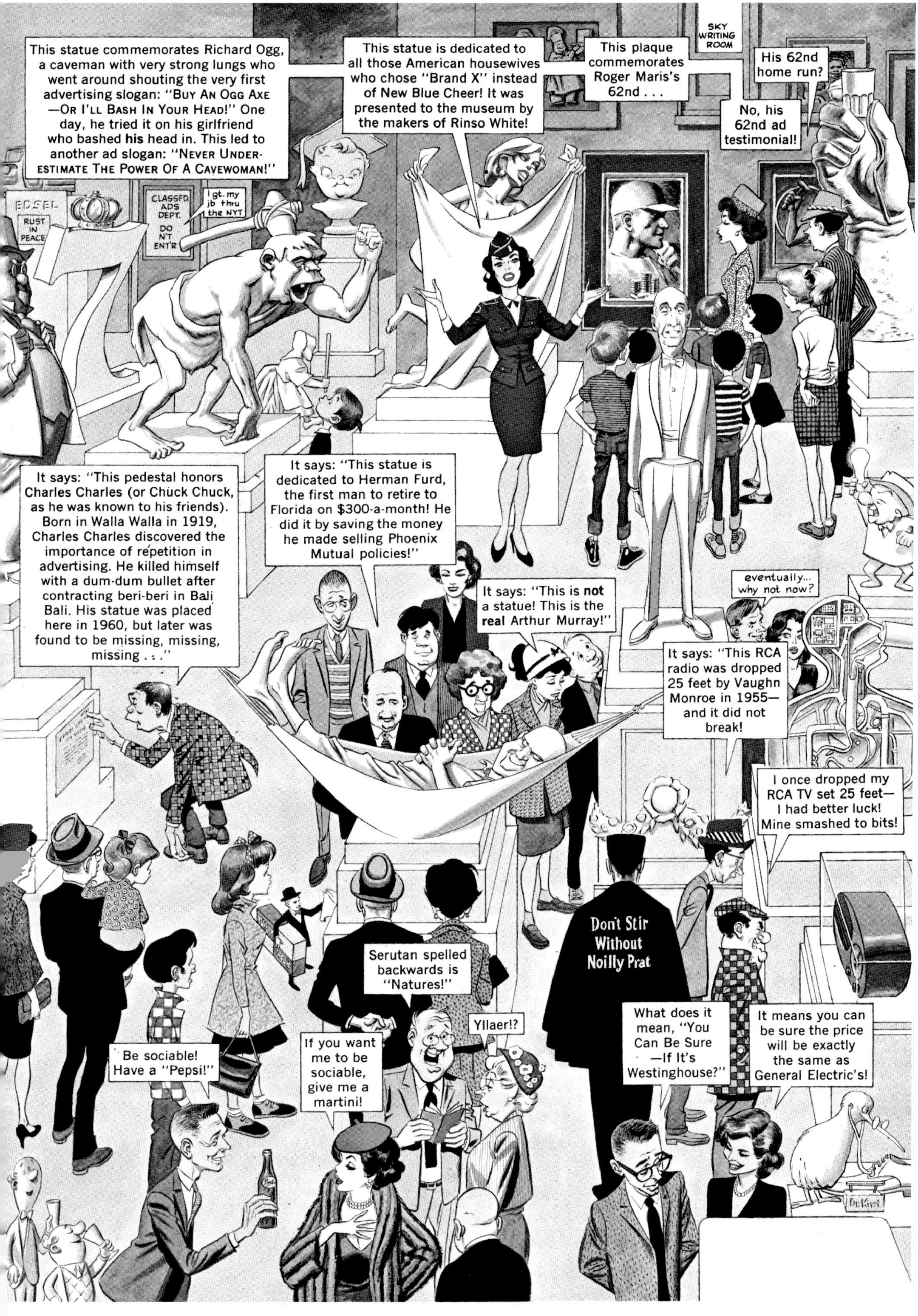
This statue commemorates Richard Ogg, a caveman with very strong lungs who went around shouting the very first advertising slogan: "BUY AN OGG AXE —OR I'LL BASH IN YOUR HEAD!" One day, he tried it on his girlfriend who bashed **his** head in. This led to another ad slogan: "NEVER UNDERESTIMATE THE POWER OF A CAVEWOMAN!"
This statue is dedicated to all those American housewives who chose "Brand X" instead of New Blue Cheer! It was presented to the museum by the makers of Rinso White!
SKY WRITING ROOM
This plaque commemorates Roger Maris's 62nd . . .
His 62nd home run?
No, his 62nd ad testimonial!
EDSEL
RUST IN PEACE
CLASSFD. ADS DEPT. DO N'T ENT'R
I gt. my jb thru the NYT
It says: "This pedestal honors Charles Charles (or Chuck Chuck, as he was known to his friends). Born in Walla Walla in 1919, Charles Charles discovered the importance of repetition in advertising. He killed himself with a dum-dum bullet after contracting beri-beri in Bali Bali. His statue was placed here in 1960, but later was found to be missing, missing, missing . . ."
It says: "This statue is dedicated to Herman Furd, the first man to retire to Florida on $300-a-month! He did it by saving the money he made selling Phoenix Mutual policies!"
It says: "This is **not** a statue! This is the **real** Arthur Murray!"
eventually... why not now?
It says: "This RCA radio was dropped 25 feet by Vaughn Monroe in 1955—and it did not break!
I once dropped my RCA TV set 25 feet—I had better luck! Mine smashed to bits!
Don't Stir Without Noilly Prat
Serutan spelled backwards is "Natures!"
Yllaer!?
Be sociable! Have a "Pepsi!"
If you want me to be sociable, give me a martini!
What does it mean, "You Can Be Sure —If It's Westinghouse?"
It means you can be sure the price will be exactly the same as General Electric's!
Dr. Kiwi

MAD #71
June 1962
Artist: George
Woodbridge
Writer: Walter Farley

ARTIFICIAL DISSEMINATION DEPT.

Every once in a while, we get to wondering just what kind of thinking goes into the creation of some of the absurd product-names that are advertised today. Namely, what these names they've come up with have to do with the purpose of the product beats us! So we've dreamed up our own MAD version of 5 Madison Avenue "Brain-Storming Sessions" which resulted in—

THE BIRTH OF A

MADISON AVENUE B

THE HOUSEHOLD CLEANSER

Gentlemen, our client has come up with a **new household product** designed to clean out sinks, tile, porcelain, and mainly the consumer's pocketbook! We've got to think of a **catchy name** for it! Something **new** and **different!**

How about "Mr. Whiz"?

I've got it! "Mr. Quick"!

I like "Mr. Spotless"!

"Mr. Sheen"!

"Mr. Gallagher"!

Hold it! **Hold it!** This is getting us nowhere! What **we** need is a **fresh point of view!** Smedley—ask that **window washer** to come inside . . .

THE UNDERARM DEODORANT

Men—we've got to create a brilliant name for our client's new **spray deodorant** . . . so I've decided to try something **different** this time. Namely, we're going to stay in this sealed room, **inhaling its fragrance,** in hopes that it will **inspire** us . . .

Okay Charlie . . . open up that valve . . .

"We knew GEORGE RAFT when he was just a Floater.

Sounds like a great idea, T.B.!

Here it comes! No, shout out your immediate impressions—

Coff-Coff . . . What do you think of "Misty"?

Gasp . . . "Heaven Scent"?

Choke! How about "Cloud"?

Keep trying— *Cough-Cough!!* We'll get it!

RAND NAME

TIST: GEORGE WOODBRIDGE   WRITER: WALTER FARLEY

"We knew HOWARD FAST when things were Slow."

THE HAND SOAP

THE BOURBON WHISKEY

THE NATIONAL MAGAZINE

"Palm-Onion"?

"Palm-Cherry"?

Sir—not to change the subject, but I have looked around and—

Perkins! I get the distinct impression that you're not **with** us completely in this brainstorming session! Just what's **bothering** You?

Sir . . . I get the distinct impression that we better **forget** this brainstorming session before it's **too late!** Mainly because that **volcano** there is about to **erupt all over** this clean, clear, sweet-smelling tropical island, covering us all with . . .

By George, you've **got** it, Perkins!

**We knew BARBARA NICHOLS before she made any Cents.

"Sheven Roses"?

"Shixteen Roses"??

Arnold! What's going **on** here! You're supposed to be **working** . . . not getting stoned with those drunken employees of yours! **Get out of here! All of you! GET OUT** . . .

See! Wha'd **I tell** you! My wife don' approve of drinkin'! She's nuthin' but an ol' . . . an ol'—

Thash it, A.A. . . . **Thash it!**

"Everywoman's mily Argument"!!

"The Reader's Gobbledegook"!!

"U.S. News and Halavah"!!!

What kind of a magazine would make a great Madison Avenue talent like **him** go off the deep end . . .?

Look! He's waving a piece of **paper** . . .

It says, "This new magazine will be devoted to **Humor & Satire!** It's main stock-in-trade will be to make fun of—" **Oh, no! Get this!!** "—**MADISON AVENUE ADS!"**

No wonder That's enough to drive **any** advertising man . . .

GWOODBRIDGE

MAD has always been a paragon of good taste, never going for the cheap laugh by running scatological humor. (Okay, so advertisers aren't the only people who lie to you.)

MAD #72
July 1962
Artist: Kelly Freas
Writer: House

6:01 pm
add warm water...
and stir a minute

6:02 pm
things happen fast —
now Doggy is dying
to go for a walk

World's only dog food that regulates your doggy
(right in the bow-wow-el!)

Ex-Lax's
DOGGY TRAIN
DOG FOOD
NEW! ADD WATER
MAKE WAY FOR DOGGY

No more interruptions: New Doggy Train fixes it so you can watch your favorite TV show in peace.

No more emergencies: New Doggy Train eliminates any sudden barking or scratching during the night!

Just add water...and your dog is ready to go for a walk in one minute—at your convenience, not his!

NEW DOGGY TRAIN *shows him who's boss!*

INSTANT PHOTOGRAPHY BY LESTER KRAUSS

Why we always look angry in these ad? I tell you why! We work hard — 12, maybe 14 hour a day — grow finest coffee tree — pick ripest bean — lift heavy sack — carry to boat — sweat and strain — and for what? So big company can grind it into lousy instant coffee because American housewife too lazy to brew real coffee, and American husband too spineless to object! **SUCKA INSTANT COFFEE...** for "sucka" husband.

INSTANT
Sucka coffee
98% WORK-FREE

GASEROUS FOODS PRODUCTS

MAD #74
October 1962
Photographer: Lester Krauss
Writer: House

6:01 pm
add warm water...
and stir a minute

6:02 pm
gravy happens —
crunchy chunks
in beef-tasty gravy

World's only dog food that makes its own gravy
(right in the bowl!)

Gaines
GRAVY TRAIN

Nothing to add for flavor: New Gravy Train has everything your dog loves: crunchy chunks, real beef flavor, and rich home-style gravy.

Nothing to add for nourishment: New Gravy Train gives your dog a complete balance of vitamins, minerals and 10 different proteins.

Nothing to add but warm water...for the best balanced banquet in the whole doggone world!

NEW GRAVY TRAIN *looks like, tastes like beef stew!*

MAD #75
December 1962
Photographer: Lester Krauss
Writer: House

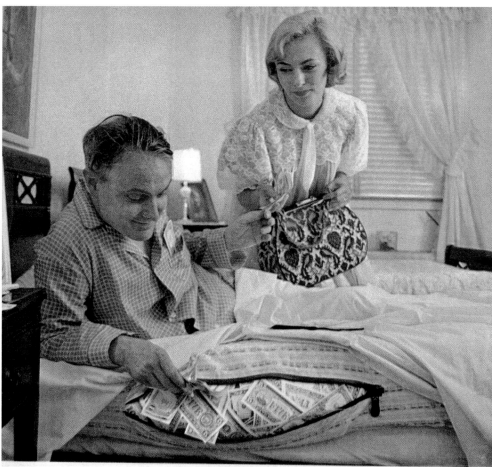

PHOTO BY LESTER KRAUSS WHO KEEPS HIS MONEY IN HIS SHOES

Bootyrest...for the Money that Can Buy Happiness

Good night, sweet principal!

Here's a thought to sleep on: Why toss when the economy turns? Now you can provide yourself with a soft cushion for those hard times that may lie ahead.

When you sleep on a Bootyrest "Night Depository," you rest insured. Because your security rests with you. Just open the convenient side zipper, stuff in your hard-earned cash, and sleep tight. Enjoy peace-of-mind over mattress.

Then, if the stock market collapses or business sags, you won't lie awake nights. You'll doze off peacefully — counting that extra support you've got in your Bootyrest.

It's much better than counting sheep!

Buy a Bootyrest "Night Depository" and start hoarding today. It's the mattress with the money-back guarantee!

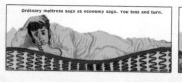

Ordinary mattress sags as economy sags. You toss and turn.

Bootyrest has support of firm cash. You sleep like a log.

**BOOTYREST
by ZIPPIN$**
THE MATTRESS WITH
THE SAVING GRACE

The Temptation of Beautyrest Another story about the kind of comfort that's kind to your back. The highway man came riding, riding up to the motel door. And when his traffic-tired eyes spotted the "Beautyrest" sign, he knew that he and his Bess had found the Oasis. Can't you almost hear him saying to her: "Let the unpacking wait, old girl. Drop everything. It's revival time for the road-weary. Your Beautyrest awaits."

Single-bed comfort in a double bed! Because each spring is separate, the heaviest husband cannot disturb his wife's rest. The best costs the least! All tests by the United States Testing Co. prove Beautyrest lasts 3 times longer than ordinary mattresses. So Beautyrest, firm or extra firm, at $79.50, is least expensive to own. Another reason why more people, including smart motel hosts, insist on Beautyrest. **Beautyrest by Simmons**

Sometimes you need a little help from Mom, so Nick Meglin's mother, Elizabeth, a professional seamstress, was enlisted to create a fake mattress that could be unzipped and stuffed with cash for this takeoff on Beautyrest Mattresses.

That's John Putnam lying atop the pile of cash.

DAS SPIEL VON DER AUTOMOBILE OR, HOW TO LOOK FUNNY WHILE DRIVING

DER VATER: ACH DU LIEBER! I GET BETTER THAN 35 MPW MIT MEIN VOLKSWAGEN! (DER MPW STANDS FOR "MILES PER WIND".) ALL I GOTTA DO IS GIVE BY DER KEY A COUPLE TURNS, UND I CAN GO 35 MILES BEFORE IT RUNS DOWN UND I GET SHTUCK IN DER TRAFFIC UND MAYBE GET SQUASHED BY A CADILLAC. BUT MIT DER PARTS GIVES NO TROUBLE. ALL OVER DER COUNTRY IS DEALERS MIT A SUPPLY OF ELVES!

Die Mutter: Vun thing I like is der Volkswagen ain't got der shtoopid hole by der roof so der crazy kids ain't flying those balloons oudtside und lifting up der car from der road. DAS KINDER: Ve don't like it! Better ve should have gotten a Renault! **DER DEALER:** UND REMEMBER, MIT DER VOLKSWAGEN, YOU DON'T HAVE TO COMING OUDT A NEW MODEL, BUT KEEP UP MIT DER JONESES! BECAUSE EVERY YEAR IS VE KEEP ALVAYS DER SAME OLD DOODLE-BUG STYLE!

Der Car Kraut: **VOLKS W agen**

Deutschland, Deutschland über alles, über alles in Detroit!

MAD #52
January 1960
Artist: Kelly Freas
Writer: House

MAD #75
December 1962
Artist: Bob Clarke
Writer: Al Jaffee

Pesky Import

Fooled yuh, hah? No, this is not a car, it's a beetle—a German beetle—a Volksbuggen!

Unknown before World War II, today it is multiplying fast and spreading all over the world. Some people think it's cute. They even keep it as a pet and brag about it to everyone they meet. Other people simply can't stand it. They call it a pest, and are always afraid of running into one and squashing it.

Then there are the commercial bug-breeders! They really hate it! They were scared that this tough little foreigner might hurt their larger, less-maneuverable American bugs. So they created our own home-grown variety of small bugs—with fancy names like Valiant, Corvair, Falcon, etc.

But, as of today, the intrepid Volksbuggen seems to be holding his own. And where the mighty battle of the bugs will end—who knows? One thing is certain, the Volksbuggen won't be easy to dislodge now that he is firmly entrenched.

 Unless, maybe, a new Japanese beetle comes along!

Perhaps no campaign better represents the creative revolution that shook up Madison Avenue in the '60s than the Volkswagen Beetle ads created by the New York firm of Doyle Dane Bernbach. During that period, advertisements became dynamic and clever, and, as author Warren Berger puts it in his book, *Advertising Today*, "Now, suddenly, there were ads with an unspoken message and complex personality; ads that were capable of engaging you in a dialogue, and that challenged you to keep up with their level of wit and intelligence."

Amazingly, *MAD*, a magazine that prides itself on possessing neither wit nor intelligence, managed to keep up just fine.

After you let your fingers do the walking!

Yep, after you shop the Yellow Pages way, you'll have to soak your fingers in Epsom salts! Why? Because fingers just aren't made for all that walking! We'll show you what we mean. Let's say you're out of Epsom salts. Okay, you'll shop by phone for some. Simply look up "Epsom Salts" in the handy Yellow Pages. There it is—No, that's an "Epsom Salts Manufacturer"! Now what? Try "Drug Stores"—they should carry it! Let's see: "Drug Importers," "Drug Manufacturers," "Drug Store Fixtures"—Ahh, here it is: "Druggists, Retail—See 'Pharmacists'"! More walking! Okay – "Pharmacists"—Hmmm—"Pharmaceutical Machinery," "Pharmaceutical Research Laboratories," "Pharmaceutical Manufacturers" – Ahh! At last! "Pharmacists"! Ho-Boy! Did you ever see so many "Pharmacists"? Okay, let's find one nearby. Start walking down the list. By now, your poor sore fingers are really killing you! See what we mean? You better let your feet do the walking next time. They're made for it!

Yellow Pages

A penny can make your conscience feel better

Here's a helpful hint for making things right with the little woman next time you're out late, boozing it up with the boys:

As soon as you step up to the bar, ask the bartender for an empty glass and set it down beside you.

Now you can get down to business.

Order your first drink, and drop a penny into the glass.

And every time you order another drink, drop another penny into the glass.

When you've spent all your money, and you're thoroughly soused, and you're ready to stagger home, you'll find you've put aside enough pennies to buy your wife a thoughtful peace offering—something to shut her up when you fall in the front door. A corsage will do it. Try Three, maybe Four Roses!

Association Of American Florists

"After 33 years, our Mayjag is a-workin' still"

"Yep, we got our Mayjag 33 years ago!" writes (or rather — dictates) Mrs. Alma Funk of Ozark, Arkansas. "Cousin Luke, who went to the big city an' made good, sent it to us! The only thing he fergot was — we don't have no 'lectricity up here in the hills!

"Which is why our Mayjag is a workin' still now! She jus' sat in the barn fer 29 years until Paw got the idea to use it fer makin' moonshine whiskey!

"Today, our Mayjag makes twice as much moonshine whiskey as that fool refrigerator Cousin Luke sent us, which we also rigged up to be a workin' still.

"Now if only Cousin Luke'd send us one of them dryin' contraptions! What a still that would make!!!"

MAYJAG
the dispensable automatics

MAD #79
June 1963
Photographer: Lester Krauss
Writer: Sergio Aragonés

MAD #79
June 1963
Photographer: Lester Krauss
Writer: House

MAD #80
July 1963
Photographer: Lester Krauss
Writer: House

Yeehaw! It was a family affair for John Putnam (back row, far right), as he was joined for this Maytag parody by his wife and kids. Artist George Woodbridge (no relation, as far as we know) also appeared.

MAD #80
July 1963
Photographer: Lester Krauss
Writer: House

Is it true... blondes have more fun?

Just being a blonde is no guarantee, honey! Take our word for it! Because even if you do suffer thru 3 or 4 hours . . . stripping your hair of its old color with cream developer and protinator (which burns like hell), then washing the gook out, then towel-drying it, **then coloring your hair** with chemicals and peroxide, then rinsing, setting, combing it out, and starting all over again in a week — when the roots begin to show . . . Well, men will *still* get nauseous when they see you — if you happen to be ugly in the first place!

Even hairdressers will tell you an ugly blonde's best friend is **Lady Clinic** Plastic Surgeons

SEND FOR THIS FOLDER TODAY!

In this spoof, longtime contributor Frank Jacobs plays the "lady." Reacting in disgust is Nick Meglin, who probably holds the record for appearing in more *MAD* photos than any other *MAD*man.

Nick's record is due to either A) his uncanny gift for brilliant comedic expressions and model-like good looks; or B) longevity, as Nick has been a member of *MAD*'s editorial staff for over forty years.

Looking at the photo, we can safely say it's B.

(By the way, the chances of ever getting Frank to agree to pose in drag again are thankfully slim.)

MAD #82
October 1963
Photographer: Lester Krauss
Writer: House

You think you're alone on the highway. Now to test that premium gas you've been paying so much for. You push the pedal to the floor—and then you hear the siren. "Where's the *Fire, Chief?*" sneers the Trooper. And as he writes your ticket, you realize that having "the nearest thing to perfect gasoline" is pretty ridiculous when speed limits won't let you use it!

Trust your car
will be stopped
by the man who
wears the star

When Texaco used the slogan "You can trust your car to the man who wears the star," they were thinking of the smiling attendant who checked your oil and washed your windows, not the frowning cop (played by Nick Meglin) who wrote up some poor schlub (Al Feldstein) for driving too fast.

As Meglin remembers it, they had to shoot quickly on Long Island's Southern State Parkway since, as usual, no one had bothered to get permits and they were "concerned that a REAL state trooper would come by."

A large gathering of friends of *MAD* and the *MAD*men themselves, many of whom longtime readers will recognize, like writer Dick DeBartolo, *Spy vs. Spy* creator Antonio Prohias, Lenny Brenner, artist-writer Sergio Aragonés, Jerry De Fuccio, William M. Gaines, and way, way in the back, *MAD*'s longtime publicist, Sid Asher (the one holding up the watch).

367 angry workers yell, "Next year—watch out!"

That's right! Next year, old man Buluva better not try giving each of us another watch for a Christmas bonus! Nosirree! That's out! O-U-T!

Besides, how many watches can one person use? We been getting these crummy watches as bonuses every Christmas for the last seventeen years!

And what's the big deal, anyway? We can always pick one up for eight or ten bucks, using our 40% employee's discount, if we wanted to pay for one — which would be pretty ridiculous, considering how

easy it is to swipe one off the conveyer belt and slip it into a pocket for free!!

So listen good, all you crumbs up in them executive offices: Next year, the "Christmas Bonus Watch" is out! O-U-T! We want cold cash — or we go out! O-U-T! On strike, that is! Just try it and see!

We're sick of bonus watches from **BULUVA**

"Never again!"—says our Union President

This ad presented as a public warning by the Amalgamated Watchmakers of America-Buluva Local

MAD #82
October 1963
Artist: John Putnam
Writer: House

MAD #83
December 1963
Photographer: Lester Krauss
Writer: House

Does this ad look blurred to you?

It should look blurred to you. Mainly because it really is blurred. We photographed it out of focus on purpose, and we're printing it exactly like this in millions of magazines all over the country.

Why are we doing this? So you'll strain your eyes to read it, that's why!

We're also running ads with blurred pictures—so you'll strain your eyes on them, too!

We figure if you strain your eyes bad enough on all our ads, you'll end up needing glasses. Pretty sneaky, eh?

Well, it was the best way we could think of to get you into our offices and shops so we could take you for plenty by overcharging for lenses and frames and eye-drops and like that. We, being all the greedy Optometrists & Oculists in the Better Vision Business Assoc.

A trade group called The Better Vision Institute ran ads (including one in Braille) that, out of a deep and profound concern for the American consumer's ocular health, encouraged people to have their eyes checked every year. Although it might—just *might*—be possible that the BVI's concern was also inspired, as this piece suggests, by its deep and profound concern for selling more eyeglasses.

MAD #84
January 1964
Photographer: Lester Krauss
Writer: House

Ex-Life Insurance Policy Owner Elmer Greedy at a PONY Track

"Life insurance? I'd rather play the horses!"

"Because a PONY man showed me that betting to win makes a lot more sense."

Rocky Gumbah talks it over with Elmer Greedy

"'When you buy life insurance,' PONY man Rocky Gumbah told me, 'You're betting to lose! Mainly, the Company that issues you that Insurance Policy is making book you stay alive—while you're betting you kick off. Now what kind of a gamble is that? If you win, you lose! When the pay-off comes, you ain't around to collect!'

"'Hey, I never thought of it that way, Rocky,' I said. 'But what do I do with all the insurance policies that I've been paying premiums on?'

"'Cash 'em in!' he said. 'Take the loot and come down to a PONY track with me. I'll show you some gambling that makes sense. When you bet on a horse and win, you do the collecting, not some crumby beneficiary!'"

PONY MEN TALK HORSE SENSE

They'll be glad to discuss gambling with you, and show you what kind of idiot you are for buying life insurance. For more information about PONY *gambling, mail coupon at right.*

PARIMUTUELS OF NEW YORK

PONY
Dept. M 35
Dream Street at Easy Street
Pie-In-The-Sky, New York
Please send me your free booklet, "The ABC of Playing the Horses at PONY Tracks in N. Y. State"
NAME
ADDRESS
CITY ZONE
STATE
CASH-ON-HAND AND IN BANKS
CASH VALUE OF INSURANCE

Shot at the now-defunct Roosevelt Raceway on Long Island, this spoof, featuring Nick Meglin and Al Feldstein, parodied the insurance company MONY (Mutual of New York).

I'm the guy who puts eight great tomatoes in that little bitty can!!

All day long – squashing, squooshing, slamming, splattering . . . Yeccch, what a mess! Thank goodness it's my last week at this gooky job! Next week my company starts using a new-type can, and I'll be able to stuff those eight great tomatoes in that little bitty can without ending up looking like I've been attacked with a "meat cleaver. Mainly because our new "little bitty can" expands into a "biggy wiggy can" like an accordion.

Concertina

EXPANDING CAN

MAD #84
January 1964
Photographer: Lester Krauss
Writer: House

Model Lenny Brenner says this mess was created by putting a small can inside a larger one, in effect creating an unwieldy hydraulic system that would splatter tomatoes everywhere when he slammed on the contraption with his mallet. Then-editor Al Feldstein recalls that after each shot the editors would have to clean and reset the studio. Fortunately, they eventually got this photo . . . after about twelve takes.

By the way, this is Lenny on a good day.

MAD #87
June 1964
Artist: Bob Clarke
Writer: Al Jaffee

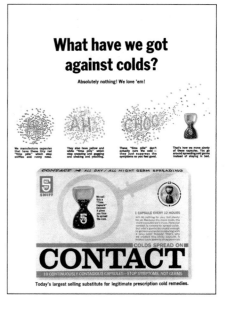

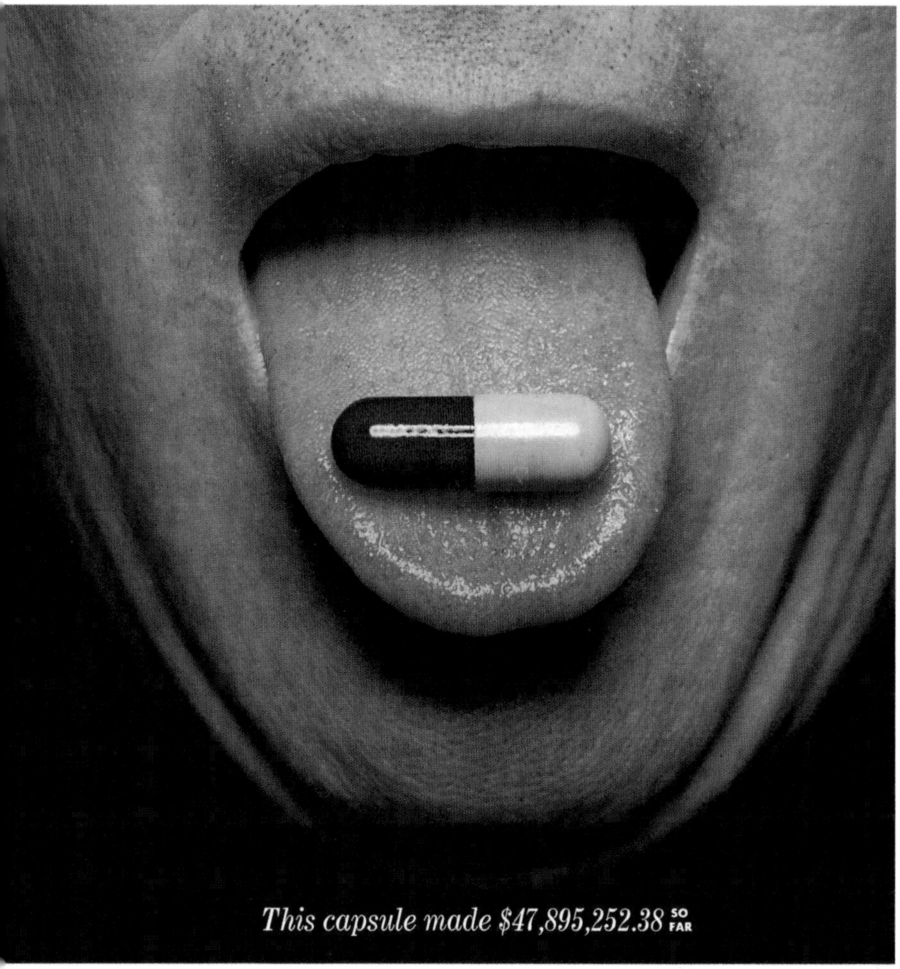

What have we got against colds?
Absolutely nothing! We love 'em!
We manufacture capsules that have these tiny red "time pills" which stop sniffles and runny nose.
They also have yellow and white "time pills" which stop sneezing and gagging and choking and yeeching.
These "time pills" don't actually cure the cold — they just suppress the symptoms so you feel good.
That's how we move plenty of these capsules. You go around spreading cold germs instead of staying in bed.
CONTACT ALL DAY / ALL NIGHT GERM SPREADING
SNIFF
We call this a "Time Capsule" because it gives you time to spread the cold.
12
1 CAPSULE EVERY 12 HOURS
COLDS SPREAD ON
CONTACT
10 CONTINUOUSLY CONTAGIOUS CAPSULES—STOP SYMPTOMS, NOT GERMS
Today's largest selling substitute for legitimate prescription cold remedies.

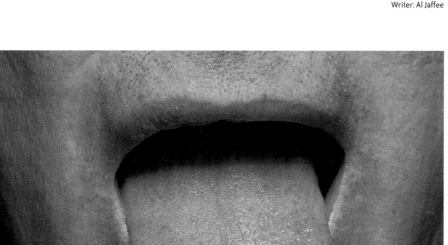

This capsule made $47,895,252.38 SO FAR

PHOTOGRAPHY BY LESTER "PLACEBO" KRAUSS

Millions of dollars in research went into the creation of this drug. But it was peanuts compared to the really expensive part—Advertising it! Those brochures in 33 glorious colors, including silver and gold, that we send every doctor cost us $7.83 each. You can see what this can run into when you consider the AMA has over 200,000 members and each one gets a brochure with a load of free samples.

But it was all worth it. Believe it or not, 33 days after the drug appeared on the market, the original investment of $3,517,103 was completely recouped and we began to spoon in the pure gravy. And what is even more remarkable is that this fantastic record was compiled by a relatively unknown and untested drug. It sure shows you the effectiveness of our promotion, the faith doctors have in us, and the power of a well-placed article in Reader's Digest. Let's hope that there are no unpleasant "side-effects" to mar this heart-warming beginning.

We are proud of this dedicated and humanitarian role that we, the members of the Drug Manufacturers Association, play in every American citizen's life. Sure there are grumblers, malcontents and Congressional investigators who try to impugn our motives. They claim that we're not so much interested in saving lives as we are in making money. They claim that the wonderful capsule shown here could be sold for 1.3¢ instead of 89¢ and still allow a reasonable profit. So what! If the American public wants to pay 89¢ instead of 1.3¢ for a capsule, that's their privilege as a Free People, and no Un-American agitators should try to stop them. We don't want no "Commie-type Socialized Drug-Selling" here!

All right, all you 100%-Americans out there! Let's hear it for the 100%-American Drug Manufacturers Association!

This advertisement is sponsored by that dedicated bunch of swell guys, all members of the Drug Manufacturers Association, whose aim it is to keep coming up with newer drugs at higher prices.

MAD #85
March 1964
Photographer: Lester Krauss
Writer: House

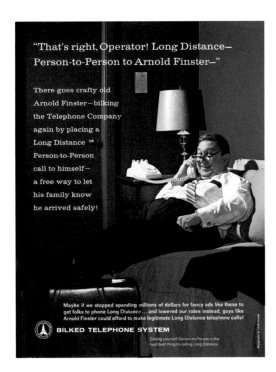

MAD's own cheapskate, William M. Gaines, played cheapskate Arnold Finster in this Bell Telephone parody.

MAD #89
September 1964
Photographer: Lester Krauss
Writer: House

MAD #90
October 1964
Artist: Frank Frazetta
Writer: House

In an era when young men were causing outrage among the establishment by wearing their hair longer than a crew cut, *MAD* asked, "Who better to represent the ultimate fantasy of the bouncy-haired Breck Girl than Beatle Ringo Starr?" in this painting by renowned fantasy artist Frank Frazetta.

I JUST PUT A GAS STATION ATTENDANT IN MY TANK!

"URP!"

MAINLY BECAUSE I GOT SICK AND TIRED OF BEING EXPLOITED!

1 First there was that idiotic Tiger on all them boxes of Sugar Frosted Flakes—used by

2 Then came them ads for those Tiger paw tires on Pontiac's GTO Tiger to sell you

3 Then there's that ridiculous broad lying all over the Tiger skin on TV for

4 And finally there's this stupid idea of putting a Tiger in your car's tank by using

Kellogg's   **U.S.Royals**   **'TOP BRASS'**   **HUMBLE (Esso)**

WELL, THAT'S THE LAST STRAW! HONESTLY, I'M JUST FED UP WITH MADISON AVENUE'S PREOCCUPATION WITH TIGERS! NOW, MAYBE THEY'LL THINK TWICE BEFORE THEY COME OUT WITH ANOTHER ADVERTISING CAMPAIGN FEATURING ME!

MAD #92
January 1965
Artist: Bob Clarke
Writer: House

Artist Bob Jones was one of many *MAD* artists who also worked in advertising. In fact, he created the original illustration for the Exxon tiger that is spoofed in the ad you see here. Only, in the *MAD* parody the tiger was illustrated by a different Bob—Bob Clarke, who was *also* one of many *MAD* artists who came to the magazine with a background in advertising.

Got that?

By the way, you may be wondering why the editors didn't just ask Jones to draw the character he had created. According to Nick Meglin, they had two fears: 1) Jones might lose his Exxon account if the company found out their own illustrator was spoofing their character; and 2) *MAD* might get sued if they used the actual Exxon artist for their spoof.

Let's **Kill off**
RIDICULOUS AD CAMPAIGNS
Before Our Minds Go SNAP! CRACKLE & OOM-PAH-POP!

If you advertisers have to blow your own horns, why tie your products to unrelated activities? Mainly, what's eating a Breakfast Cereal got to do with playing a musical instrument. Boy...we just can't swallow that!

"Nuts to you each morning"

All right, the fact is, even though he had a reputation around the *MAD* offices for his supposed temper, everyone knew that deep down Lenny "The Beard" Brenner was a lovable bear of a man, which made his cherubic face perfect for this Kellogg's spoof.

MAD #96
July 1965
Photographer: Irving Schild
Writer: House

MAD #97
September 1965
Photographer: Irving Schild
Writer: House

Photography by Irving "Sudsy" Schild

MAD's
Great Moments In Advertising

THE DAY THEY SHOT THE "TEN-FOOT-TALL WASHING MACHINE" COMMERCIAL IN AN 8-FOOT HIGH BASEMENT

No apartment floors were harmed in the making of this photo. That's an actual washing machine, but it's being rammed through a stage that photographer Irving Schild built in his 50th Street studio.

On the couch being caught in a make-out session are Susan Feldstein, daughter of then-editor Al Feldstein, and *MAD*'s office boy, Richard Grillo.

MAD #99
December 1965
Photographer: Irving Schild
Writer: House

MAD's Great Moments In Advertising

THE DAY THEY FORGOT TO PUT THE TOP DOWN FOR THE HERTZ COMMERCIAL

Photography by Irving "Avis" Schild

"Let Hertz put you in the driver's seat" was the slogan of the car rental company's TV campaign, which featured drivers literally dropping down from the sky into a moving convertible.

Amazingly, photographer Irving Schild convinced a Manhattan Hertz location to let him shoot their storefront for a *MAD* back cover making fun of their ads. Even more amazingly, the rental agency also let him cut a hole in the roof of one of their cars. And most amazingly, Irving didn't pay a dime for the damage he caused, although he did have to pay a $50 modeling fee since the car was going to appear in a national magazine.

By the way, the woman with the shocked look was an actual Hertz employee. Perhaps she was gasping at the enormous stupidity of her bosses.

MAD #98
October 1965
Photographer: Irving Schild
Writer: House

MAD's
Great Moments In Advertising

THE DAY THAT "AJAX" GOT THE HOUSEWIFE
OUT OF THE KITCHEN A LITTLE TOO FAST!

After dealing with the complicated set of the "Dash" parody, the set for this spoof of Ajax detergent was much easier for Irving Schild to build: a simple living room with rug, sofa, television set . . . oh, and a double wall that appeared to be exploding as a woman was shot through it.

To create the illusion of flight, Schild suspended the model on a 2 x 6 ft. board, which was hidden beneath the folds of her skirt. The illusion of motion was created by an off-set assistant throwing wood chips into the frame.

The man on the couch is Sergio Aragonés. Among his many claims to fame, Aragonés was responsible for bringing Irving into the *MAD* fold. Aragonés introduced Schild to Al Feldstein after Sergio and Irving got to know each other at a coffee shop around the corner from both Irving's studio and the *MAD* offices. (In fact, Irving jokes that the reason he became a *MAD* mainstay was because, with his studio nearby, Feldstein didn't have too walk too far.)

MAD's
Great Moments In Advertising

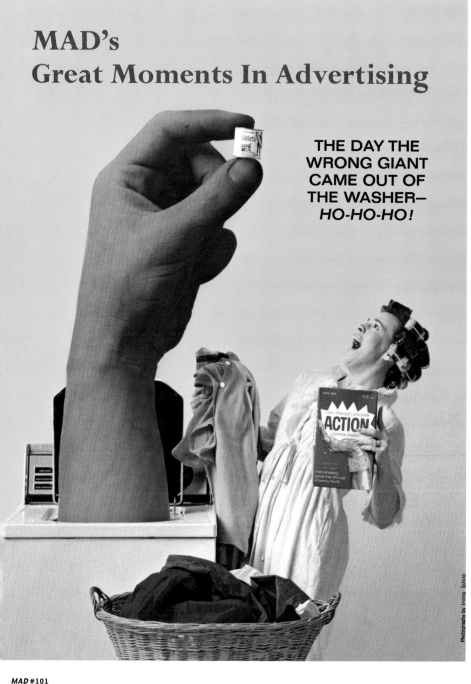

THE DAY THE WRONG GIANT CAME OUT OF THE WASHER— HO-HO-HO!

Photography by Irving Schild

MAD #101
March 1966
Photographer: Irving Schild
Writer: House

Today, in an era when computers make almost any type of trick photography possible, creating a photo-realistic Jolly Green Giant hand to pop out of the washer (spoofing Action detergent's claim that it could make your clothes look hand-washed) would be no problem. In 1966, it was a lot trickier.

Like many of photographer Irving Schild's assignments, this one began with a drawing from Al Feldstein. "He'd always give me a sketch and say, 'Can you do this?'" And I'd always say, 'No problem.'"

Which was a lie, since Irving usually had no idea how he would pull it off.

"Every assignment was a new problem, a new experience, a new way to do something," Schild says. After he received the assignment, Irving would go back to his studio and get to work. A week might go by before Feldstein would call for an update, and Irving, still trying to iron out the kinks, would stall his editor, saying confidently, "I'm working on it."

In the case of this spoof, Irving had to solve several problems on, er, *hand*: First, he had to figure out the correct proportion for a giant's hand that would be large enough for the shot, but also have the proper amount of space between the thumb and forefinger to perfectly accommodate the can. Irving decided to shoot a black-and-white photo of an empty hand, and, using his photo enlarger, projected several versions of the hand on the wall until he calculated the exact size he needed.

Then he took the negative to a lab that specialized in large-sized photos, blew up the shot, mounted it to a board, and sprayed it with a transparent green dye, giving it the proper Jolly Green Giant look.

When Schild set up the final shot, he had to make sure that the lighting on the model was exactly the same as the lighting he had used on the hand, otherwise they wouldn't match. The whole process took about a week. Today, using a computer, Schild estimates creating this shot would take "about ten minutes."

MAD #112
July 1967
Photographer: Irving Schild
Writer: House

Put your hand over the bald half and see how much younger he looks.

Sure, dark hair makes you look young, and gray hair makes you look old. But NO hair makes you look even older!

So why fool around with dyes and chemicals and other junk, trying to darken what little gray hair you've got, when you may be taking a chance on losing it all?

GREAT GRAY For Men

Be satisfied with your gray hair. And take good care of it.

Remember, a man with gray hair looks distinguished. A heck of a lot more distinguished than if he suddenly goes bald.

Photography by Irving Schild

WHAT WOULD BE A PERFECT SLOGAN FOR THE ADVERTISING INDUSTRY?

A▶ FOLD THIS SECTION OVER LEFT

HERE WE GO WITH ANOTHER RIDICULOUS
MAD FOLD-IN

Madison Avenue advertising agencies are forever creating slogans for others, but they've never created a slogan for themselves. Fold page in as shown at right, and you'll see what MAD thinks would make a perfect slogan for "Madison Avenue."

FOLD PAGE OVER LIKE THIS

◀B FOLD BACK SO "A" MEETS "B"

FINSTER, FENSTER AND BLECH ADVERTISING AGENCY

SLOGAN IDEAS

BECAUSE MOST CONSUMERS ARE TOTALLY UNAWARE OF THE AD INDUSTRY'S REAL CONTRIBUTION, THE BUSINESS NEEDS A SLOGAN TO EXPLAIN IT ALL

MAD #112
July 1967
Artist and Writer: Al Jaffee

The *MAD* Fold-In has been a staple since artist-writer Al Jaffee created it in 1964. The monthly feature, which runs on Cover III (the inside back cover), was originally created to spoof other magazines' fold-out sections, such as *Playboy*'s centerfold. And it has always served as a place where Jaffee, working with the magazine's editors, can take shots at . . . well, just about anything, from politics to the latest trend to suggesting the proper way to respond to Madison Avenue's come-ons.

WHAT WOULD BE A PERFECT SLOGAN FOR THE ADVERTISING INDUSTRY?

FOLD PAGE OVER LIKE THIS

A▶ ◀B FOLD BACK SO "A" MEETS "B"

BEWARE OF THE BULL

Yep. That just about sums it all up.

Higher taxes? Special surtaxes? Increase the National Debt? It seems to us at MAD that there ought to be other ways for the Government to raise the money to finance our "Great Society" (not to mention unpopular wars!). For example, why not turn to the place where fantastic sums of money are spent for advertising testimonials. Mainly, Madison Avenue! We're sure the boys at the Ad Agencies would pour plenty into the Government coffers to have

CONCEIVED BY:
MAX BRANDEL

PRESIDENT JOHNSON ON MADISON AVENUE

FORGET YOUR TROUBLES!

Take **Miltown** (meprobamate)

"Whenever I'm tense—with problems like Vietnam and Bobby Kennedy—I simply reach for my "Miltown"! In a few minutes, I'm perfectly relaxed! All my troubles are

GOT A HEADACHE?

Bayer works wonders

"And believe me, I got plenty headaches! This "Great Society" program I'm pushing can really

BAYER ASPIRIN

WHICH HAND HAS THE M&M'S?

M&M Candies melt in your mouth—not in your hand!

"When you like chocolate candies like I do, but you have a tendency to get a little hot under the collar once in a while, you want a chocolate candy that

"When you're out of Schlitz, you're out of beer."

"Yep, when the gang gathers down at the Ranch and the Schlitz starts flowing, you can bet we run out fast. And when that happens, I always say, "When you're out of Schlitz, you're out

Schlitz

THE DODGE REBELLION WANTS YOU!

I know I'm not as pretty as that little blonde who used to be in these ads, but the folks over at Chrysler thought I could command a lot more authority. So they asked me to do the pointing and order you to join the Dodge Rebellion

DODGE

"MY GROUP HAD 38% FEWER CAVITIES!"

CREST TOOTHPASTE WITH FLUORISTAN

With **Crest** Crest with fluoristan

"When the 'Crest' folks asked me to take part in a toothpaste test, I agreed. My group brushed regularly with 'Crest', and Dean Rusk's group used another toothpaste without Fluoristan. After six months, both

---

MAD #114

October 1967

Conceived by: Max Brandel

No. 2 says he tries harder!

Than who?

When you've been a "No. 1" for as long as I have, you know a little bit about what it takes to stay "No. 1" ... like experience, and know-how. That's why, when I need a car—which isn't often, since the Government supplies me with all I need—I rent a car from the "No. 1" Rent-A-Car Company—Hertz! Now Hubert . . . he uses Avis, which just goes to show you how much a "No. 2" knows about things. I

Hertz RENT-A-CAR

Is this the day you finally do something about your weight?

I'll never forget the shock of looking down one day, while delivering a State Of The Union Message to Congress, and noticing that paunch I'd developed. I knew right there and then that I would have to do something about it. And the best way I knew was to go on a Metrecal diet. Unfortunately, I never bothered—what with State Dinners and such. But if you have a weight problem, that's my advice. Don't do as I do—do as I say.

Take **METRECAL**

As Long As You're Up, Get Me A Grants!

"Yes, sir—whenever I'm down—and your President is down pretty often these days—the best "pick-me-up" I know is a double shot

GRANTS SCOTCH WHISKEY

ITCHY SCALP? TIME FOR *Head & Shoulders*

It Works! This Dandruff Shampoo Doesn't Kid Around!

"Take my word for it. You won't see me scratching my head any more, except maybe at a meeting of the Presidential Advisory Committee, because I discovered "Head & Shoulders". It's the...

TOILET TISSUE TOO ROUGH?

There's A Definite Difference In Delsey!

"You can rest assured that the folks who spend the night at the White House are never troubled by rough toilet tissues. That's because all 28 baths are stocked with "Delsey"—the tissue with a definite difference. So be my guest! Go out and

Delsey

BUY A "BRAND NAME"

...OR I'LL TAN YOUR HIDE!

Aviz can't afford dirty plugs!

But we can afford sneaky plugs—like these ads! Ever notice how we cry the blues and tell how hard we try and make like the underdog?

We got a clever reason for doing this!

It's an old American tradition to root for the underdog. We figure you'll feel sorry for us, and give us your rent a car business.

That way, we might get to be No. 1! Then we can afford to be independent and rent unwashed cars with cigarette butts in the ash trays, and worn wipers, and dry batteries...and if you complain, we can afford to say, "Nuts to you, Buddy!"

Right now...it hertz to be No. 2!

MAD #85
March 1964
Photographer: Lester Krauss
Writer: House

▶ **MAD #110**
April 1967
Produced by: Max Brandel

When this spoof ran in 1964, Avis was the number two car rental agency behind Hertz, and tried to capitalize on its underdog status by claiming that it "tried harder," and—unlike Avis's larger rival—went the extra distance in customer care by doing the little things, like making sure the cars were clean and the ashtrays empty.

Perhaps sensing that Avis was onto something, *MAD* tried its own version of the "try harder" campaign on the cover of issue #115, but, as usual, didn't get it quite right.

MAD #115
December 1967
Artist: Bob Clarke
Writer: House

ADS WE'D LIKE TO SEE

...and Pillsbury says it best. Pillsbury

Old Grand-Dad
Head of the Bourbon Family

Come to the U.N.
A trip to United Nations Headquarters can be educational and inspirational. What's more, it's fun.

Let Hertz put you in the driver's seat

(Isn't that where you belong?) HERTZ RENT A CAR

KEEP AMERICA BEAUTIFUL

The further she is...the closer you should look!*

MAD #117
March 1968
Photographer: Irving Schild
Writer: House

Remember what we said on page 87 about never getting Frank Jacobs to dress in drag again? We were wrong. But man, we wish we weren't.

The 60-second disappointment

It happens too often with a Parloraid Color Pack Camera! That's why we can't take a chance. We photograph these ads with a Nikon loaded with Ektachrome!

MAD #127
June 1969
Photographer: Irving Schild
Writer: House

Clockwise, from top middle, the MADmen featured are Lenny Brenner, Nick Meglin, Antonio Prohias, John Putnam, Al Feldstein, and Jerry De Fuccio. The female models, as well as the gentleman at the upper left, are unidentified.

MAD #129
September 1969
Artist: Jack Rickard
Writer: Dick DeBartolo

A  AD WE'D LIKE TO SEE

The Ultra-White Toothpaste Commercial

New Ultra-White Toothpaste...

...has the taste you can really feel!

New Ultra-White gives your mouth...

...SEX...

...APPE...E...E...E...

...E...E...EEEEEAL!

ARTIST: JACK RICKARD   WRITER: DICK DE BARTOLO

MAD #148
January 1972
Photographer: Irving Schild
Writer: Al Jaffee

MAD #178
October 1975
Photographer: Irving Schild
Writer: Dick DeBartolo

It was a challenge to execute the above spoof of a TV campaign for Caesar's salad dressing that began as a sketch by writer-artist Al Jaffee. After all, it's one thing to show a group of Romans lounging around a courtyard in a drawing, but it's a whole other thing to make it come alive in a photo.

Photographer Irving Schild relied on a front-projection system he had built at his studio, which allowed him to create realistic backgrounds that would have otherwise required a cost-prohibitive location shoot. (Bill Gaines may have been famous for flying his staff around the world on the *MAD* trips, but chances are he wouldn't have sprung for twenty folks to head to Rome for a day to get this photo.)

Irving then brought in the props and togas, and, once again, relied on friends and the *MAD* staff to serve as his models. Jaffee's the one with the beard sitting on the floor.

One of the problems that arose during the two-hour shoot was of Schild's own making. "Somehow through the middle of shooting it looked like there were less people than I started with," Schild says. And he was right. Choosing to create a true bacchanalian atmosphere, Irving had decided to serve actual red wine.

"They got so drunk, they fell off the back of the set," laughs Schild. "I found them after the shoot."

MAD #212
January 1980
Photographer: Irving Schild
Writer: House

Hey, Dad! You know all those Long Distance calls I made to you and Mom last month...?

Reach out. Reach out and put the touch on someone.

Wherever you are, you're never too far away to spend a half hour or so on the phone with your folks back home. And don't worry about the cost. Just reach out. Reach out and put the touch on someone—mainly, them—with another phone call.

 Bilk System

A MAD LOOK AT... HALF TRUTHS IN T V ADS

ARTIST: AL JAFFEE   WRITER: PAUL PETER PORGES

MAD #207
June 1979
Artist: Al Jaffee
Writer: Paul Peter Porges

▼ (overleaf) **MAD #218**
October 1980
Artist: Jack Davis
Writer: Tom Koch

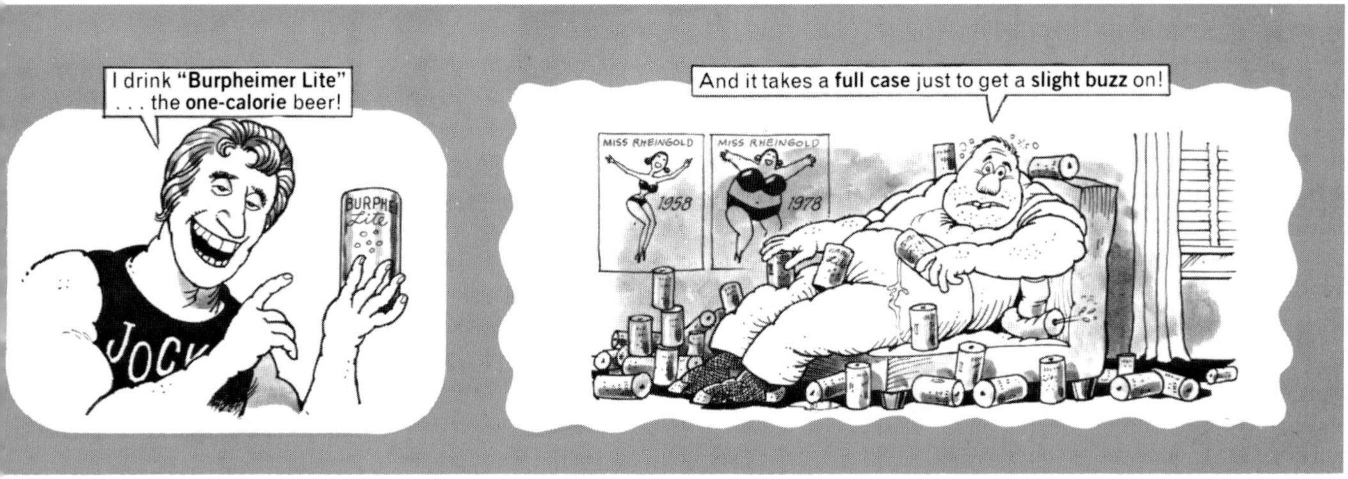

I drink "Burpheimer Lite" . . . the one-calorie beer!
JOCK
BURPHE Lite
And it takes a full case just to get a slight buzz on!
MISS RHEINGOLD 1958
MISS RHEINGOLD 1978

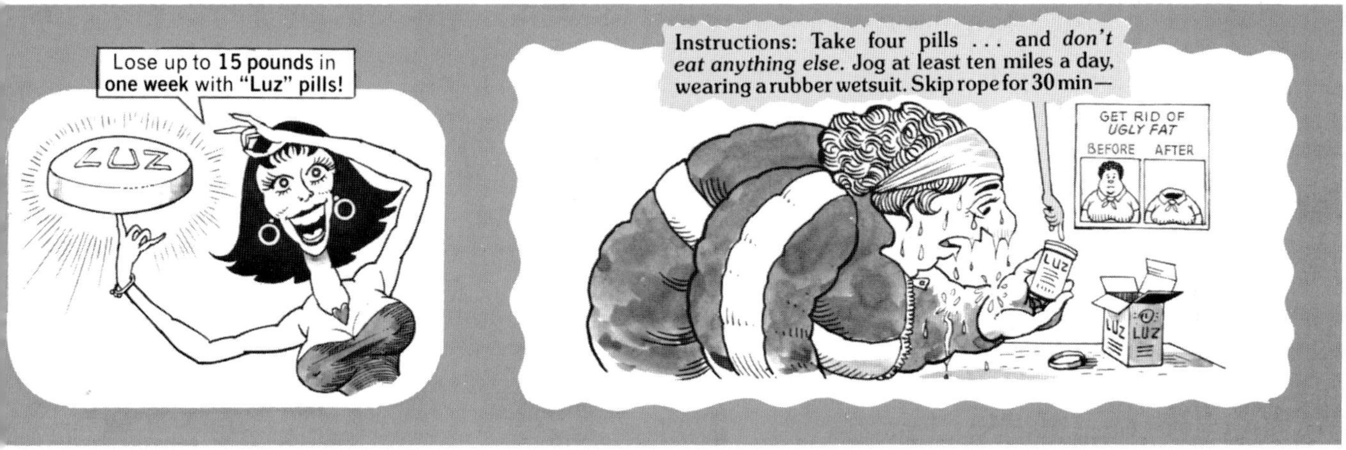

Lose up to 15 pounds in one week with "Luz" pills!
LUZ
Instructions: Take four pills . . . and don't eat anything else. Jog at least ten miles a day, wearing a rubber wetsuit. Skip rope for 30 min—
GET RID OF UGLY FAT
BEFORE AFTER
LUZ

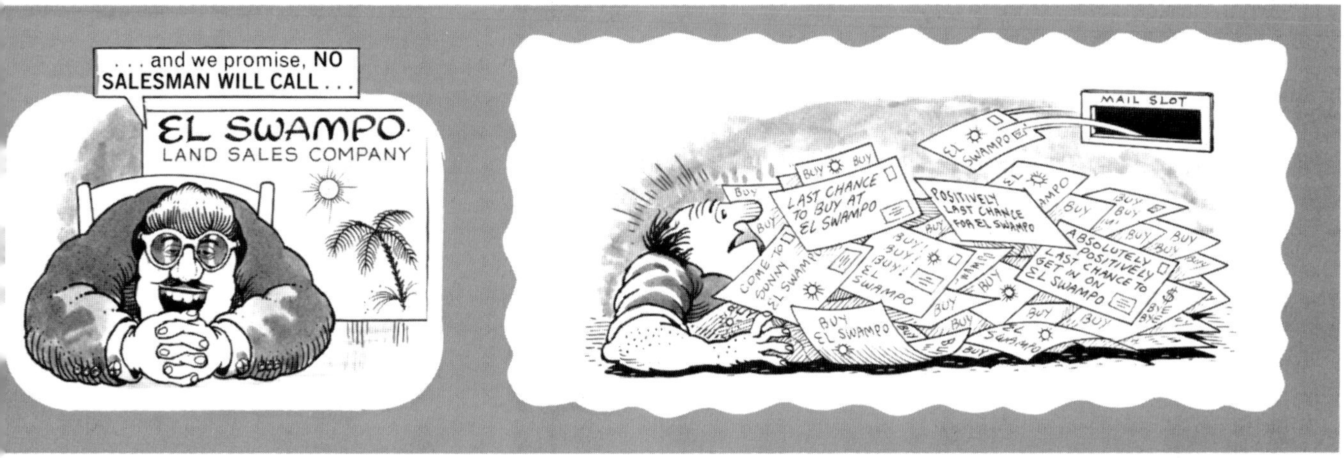

. . . and we promise, NO SALESMAN WILL CALL . . .
EL SWAMPO LAND SALES COMPANY
MAIL SLOT
LAST CHANCE TO BUY AT EL SWAMPO
POSITIVELY LAST CHANCE FOR EL SWAMPO
ABSOLUTELY POSITIVELY LAST CHANCE TO GET IN ON EL SWAMPO
COME TO SUNNY EL SWAMPO
BUY EL SWAMPO

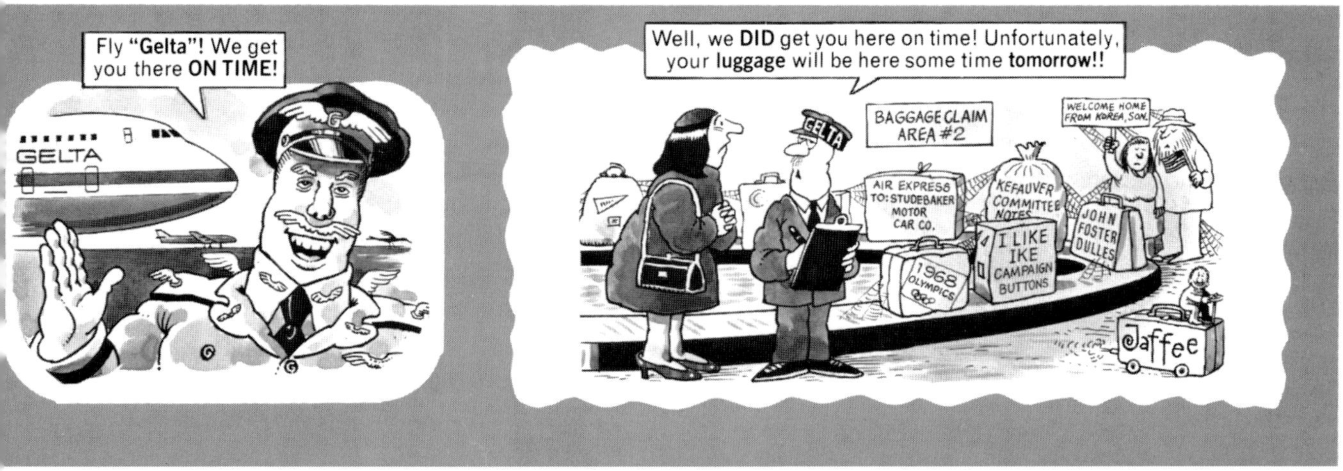

Fly "Gelta"! We get you there ON TIME!
GELTA
Well, we DID get you here on time! Unfortunately, your luggage will be here some time tomorrow!!
GELTA
BAGGAGE CLAIM AREA #2
WELCOME HOME FROM KOREA, SON.
AIR EXPRESS TO: STUDEBAKER MOTOR CAR CO.
KEFAUVER COMMITTEE NOTES
JOHN FOSTER DULLES
I LIKE IKE CAMPAIGN BUTTONS
1968 OLYMPICS
Jaffee

AD INSULT TO INJURY DEPT.

Advertising has become so unbelievable that we no longer expect products to cost as little or perform as well as we're promised they will. In fact, the approach taken by advertisers has lost all touch with reality. Se we browse through magazines or stare glassy-eyed at TV let the sponsors' incredible claims flow right past

ADVERTISING MA

ARTIST: JACK DA

ADVERTISING MAKES YOU WONDER...

. . . whether anyone in real life would actually walk into a crowded drug store and loudly start discussing his hemorrhoids with the pharmacist.

ADVERTISING MAKES YOU WONDER...

. . . what the banning of cigarette commercials on radio and TV has proved, except that the tobacco companies can save advertising money and still sell their products!

ADVERTISING MAKES YOU WONDER...

. . . why stores only offer real bargains at their "Going Out of Business" sales when they wouldn't have had to go out of business if they'd lowered their prices earlier!

ADVERTISING MAKES YOU WONDER...

. . . why a politician would spend $10,000 on a full-page newspaper announcement to tell you he's a poor man in need of your contribution!

thout even bothering to resent the fact that we're being fed a steady diet of baloney. MAD urges its readers become more alert amid the snow jobs that are piling up drifts all around them. Start analyzing those ads you now ignore, and see how few you can force yourself to swallow once you actually pay attention to them! Because

KES YOU WONDER...

WRITER: TOM KOCH

ADVERTISING MAKES YOU WONDER...

BADRICH TIRES

"We're The Other One!"

... why a company that doesn't own a blimp should necessarily make better—or worse—tires than a company that does own a blimp!

ADVERTISING MAKES YOU WONDER...

... what's so great about being able to call anywhere in the country after 11 P.M. for 85¢, unless you have lots of faraway friends you love to wake up in the middle of the night!

ADVERTISING MAKES YOU WONDER...

... how companies invariably know that their offers are being made "... for a limited time only!" but they never seem to be able to tell you what that time limit will be!

ADVERTISING MAKES YOU WONDER...

... why your choice of deli products should be influenced by what an inarticulate three-year-old on TV tells you he prefers to eat!

ADVERTISING MAKES YOU WONDER...

. . . how breweries can claim their "New Light Beer" is a "major scientific discovery" when simply adding water doesn't seem like much of a discovery at all!

ADVERTISING MAKES YOU WONDER...

. . . whether any marriage was ever actually saved because the wife found a product that reduced static electricity in her husband's newly-laundered socks!

ADVERTISING MAKES YOU WONDER...

. . . how you get on mailing lists to receive sales letters that speak of "busy executives like yourself" when you're not even out of high school yet!

ADVERTISING MAKES YOU WONDER...

. . . why radio stations buy commercials on TV stations merely to announce that you'll encounter fewer commercials on radio stations than you will on TV stations!

ADVERTISING MAKES YOU WONDER...

. . . what oddball type of car can use those tires you see offered for "only $19" when the size that fits your compact always seems to cost $49.50!

ADVERTISING MAKES YOU WONDER...

. . . how a coffee company that just raised its price by a dollar a pound has the gall to send you coupons good for 50¢ off on every pound you buy at the new price!

ADVERTISING MAKES YOU WONDER...

. . . how companies that make up a patented name for their own particular variety of plastic think that's going to prevent you from noticing that the stuff is still plastic!

ADVERTISING MAKES YOU WONDER...

. . . why a gorgeous model, who has the world at her feet, would ever have to worry about choosing the right brand of "kitty litter"!

ADVERTISING MAKES YOU WONDER...

. . . exactly how the "cheapest motel in town" cuts corners on room maintenance so it can afford all those big expensive billboards out on the highway!

ADVERTISING MAKES YOU WONDER...

. . . why the auto makers, who have always known how to make gasoline engines that go 25 miles to the gallon, never showed any interest in doing so until recently!

ADVERTISING MAKES YOU WONDER...

. . . where Supermarkets, claiming to sell at rock bottom prices, get all that extra money to run contests that give away free Hawaiian vacations!

ADVERTISING MAKES YOU WONDER...

. . . why 75 million American men placidly ate mashed potatoes all those years if every one of them would have really preferred stove-top stuffing with his chicken!

MAD #222
April 1981
Artist: Jack Rickard
Writer: Tom Koch

<u>AD NAUSEA DEPT.</u>

No matter how many new laws the Government passes, and no matter how many new Agencies they set up to protect us gullible consumers from Madison Avenue . . .

WE'LL ALWAYS BE SUCKERS FOR CLEVER ADVERTISING...

ARTIST: JACK RICKARD   WRITER: TOM KOCH

WE'LL ALWAYS BE SUCKERS FOR CLEVER ADVERTISING

BASE PRICE	$3,899
NEEDED OPTIONS	960
NEEDLESS OPTIONS	370
RIDICULOUS OPTIONS	855
TOTAL	$6,084

. . . because invitations to "buy one, get the second one free" sound so appealing, we quickly forget we can't even use one!

. . . because we're already inside the dealer's showroom with our tongue hanging out before we realize that $3,899 cars really cost over $6,000 by the time wheels, windows and other "optional equipment" are added in

WE'LL ALWAYS BE SUCKERS FOR CLEVER ADVERTISING

. . . because we don't find out until too late that it costs less to keep the junk we buy from mail order houses than it does to pay the postage to return it.

. . . because we're lured to muffler shops that offer "30-Minute Service," even though we know it takes longer than that just to get a mechanic's attention.

WE'LL ALWAYS BE SUCKERS FOR CLEVER ADVERTISING

LIMITED EDITION! "BUGS OF AMERICA" SOUVENIR PLATES

. . . because few realize that "a collector's item much in demand" will stop being in demand as soon as every collector orders his from the same ad we're reading.

Regularly $495.00. SALE PRICED — $199.95!

. . . because draping a beautiful model across cheap furniture makes any sofa look much better in the ad than it's ever going to look in our living room.

WE'LL ALWAYS BE SUCKERS FOR CLEVER ADVERTISING

. . . because we invariably buy pills promising "temporary relief from minor pain" after we see how they provide the actor in the commercial with permanent relief from major pain.

. . . because supermarkets promoting those sweepstake games act as if the prize money is coming out of their profits . . . and not your pockets.

WE'LL ALWAYS BE SUCKERS FOR CLEVER ADVERTISING

. . . because we never add up all those items that cost "only pennies a day" to see how their total cost can amount to thousands of dollars a year.

. . . because liquor companies always mention their product's mellow aging and smooth taste, but never warn us of the rotting liver and wild convulsions we can get from drinking it.

WE'LL ALWAYS BE SUCKERS FOR CLEVER ADVERTISING

. . . because a chance to get ten free albums for joining a record club blinds us to the fact that there's no way we can drop out once we've joined.

. . . because hardly anybody remembers that the sales items "drastically reduced" from $89.00 to $69.00 are the same ones that were drastically increased from $49.00 last year.

WE'LL ALWAYS BE SUCKERS FOR CLEVER ADVERTISING

. . . because we stupidly assume that anything sold by Farrah Fawcett-Majors has to be great.

. . . because they deviously bunch items of different prices together, hoping we'll think the one we want is cheap.

. . . because a TV announcer with a British accent has a way of making even worthless trash sound like high-quality merchandise.

WE'LL ALWAYS BE SUCKERS FOR CLEVER ADVERTISING

. . . because banks don't remind us that we could also have doubled our money in the past ten years investing in light bulbs, blue jeans, shoes or kitty litter.

. . . because it impresses us to read how "Mrs. J. M. of California" has praised a product, even though we have no idea who she is, or if she even exists.

WE'LL ALWAYS BE SUCKERS FOR CLEVER ADVERTISING

... because we mistakenly assume that the models pictured demonstrating "body-building equipment" were as scrawny as we are until they started using the stuff.

... because every parent wants to believe that a $500 set of encyclopedias is all that's needed to transform his stupid kid into a Rhodes Scholar.

WE'LL ALWAYS BE SUCKERS FOR CLEVER ADVERTISING

... because we desperately want to believe that "low-tar" cigarettes are a heaven-sent discovery that'll let us keep smoking and still keep alive.

... because it boggles the mind to imagine a wonderful person like Pat Boone lying when he tells us that hot dogs are nutritious, even when they're not particularly.

WE'LL ALWAYS BE SUCKERS FOR CLEVER ADVERTISING

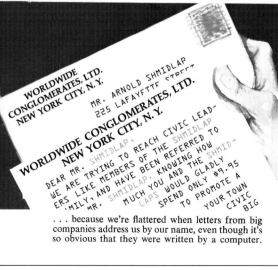

... because we're flattered when letters from big companies address us by our name, even though it's so obvious that they were written by a computer.

... because we lack the foresight to realize that 'easy monthly car payments' won't seem so easy when the car falls apart, and we're still paying for it.

▼ (overleaf) **MAD #242**
October 1983
Artist: Jack Davis
Writer: Tom Koch

AD NAUSEA DEPT.

MAD has often denounced advertising as a deliberate insult to our intelligence. We've never quite believed that future happiness depended upon using a razor that cuts whiskers off below the skin line, or that friends would turn on us if the fish we were cooking smelled like fish cooking. So the ads that preached

AN ADVERTISER WOU

ARTIST: JACK DAV

An Advertiser Would Have Us Believe...

...that guests will soon be rushing into our homes, flinging open our kitchen cabinets and subjecting us to humiliation if our glassware has a few water spots.

An Advertiser Would Have Us Believe...

...that if we lose our possessions in a hostile country, our chances of survival will depend upon what brand of travelers' checks we were carrying.

An Advertiser Would Have Us Believe...

...that a slick, big city announcer becomes more trustworthy when he puts on a grocer's apron, and speaks with a New England twang.

An Advertiser Would Have Us Believe...

...that no matter how totally our home is destroyed, the phone will still work to call our Insurance Agent...but only if we've had the good sense to pick the right Agent.

ese doctrines struck us as dumb. But from the Adan's point of view, our limited vision is not his ult. If only we'd see life as he wants us to see it, then every TV commercial would make sense. It's just a matter of dropping our sales resistance (and our sanity) to accept the following points that...

D HAVE US BELIEVE...

ITER: TOM KOCH

n Advertiser Would Have Us Believe...

...that the Post Office Department's fast service "Express Mail" is a bargain at $9.35, even though it's the very same hing that used to be called "Special Delivery" and cost 30¢.

An Advertiser Would Have Us Believe...

...that veterinarians actually recommend a cat food that is composed of 10% fish heads, 10% chicken guts and 80% water.

n Advertiser Would Have Us Believe...

...that we would expect to pay "$200... $300...even $400" for the polyester suit that's now being offered to us for $79.95.

An Advertiser Would Have Us Believe...

...that it will sell no wine before its time, so we should be happy and grateful that it just became time to sell all ten million bottles they've got stored in their warehouses.

An Advertiser Would Have Us Believe...

...that acquiring a 36-inch bust, a 22-inch waist, wavy blonde hair and perfect bone structure all depends upon choosing the right low-calorie diet cola.

An Advertiser Would Have Us Believe...

...that we can get a neighbor to spend his who weekend doing free labor for us if we'll just r ward him with his favorite beer when he's finishe

An Advertiser Would Have Us Believe...

...that the preservation of our American Way depends upon re-electing some idiot to Congress who hasn't done anything for us in twelve years.

An Advertiser Would Have Us Believe...

...that our kids will beg to spend the whole eveni brushing their teeth if only we'll buy them the goo tasting toothpaste with the red stripe down each glo

An Advertiser Would Have Us Believe...

...that its stockbrokers apparently work for the sheer fun of it, since they could all easily become rich and retire just by following their own investment advice.

An Advertiser Would Have Us Believe...

...that anxiety neurosis can be cured withou expensive psychiatry, merely by switching to it brand of decaffeinated coffee for a few weeks

An Advertiser Would Have Us Believe...

...that the Army is very finicky about the enlistees it accepts because of all the high-skill job training and free travel it gives to the lucky ones who get in.

An Advertiser Would Have Us Believe...

...that its brand of 87-octane gasoline will make our car run like new even though every other brand of 87-octane gasoline makes it sputter and wheeze.

An Advertiser Would Have Us Believe...

...that we can easily combat 10% inflation by putting our money in a savings bank that pays us 5¾% interest and gives us a free toaster.

An Advertiser Would Have Us Believe...

...that serious Mother-Daughter talks consist of spreading the word that liberated women no longer must accept static electricity in their laundry as a burden of life.

An Advertiser Would Have Us Believe...

...that the exorbitant amount of money we're paying for gasoline is being used to finance the search for new oil that will someday enable the company to lower its prices.

An Advertiser Would Have Us Believe...

...that no one taking a "Comparison Taste Test" among cola drinks ever concluded that they all seem pretty much alike after all.

Back in 1968 (MAD #116), we published some "Ads We Never Got To See" ... a collection of ill-fated advertising campaigns that sounded good when they were first created, but upon reflection certainly didn't say what the advertisers intended to say. Well, it's taken sixteen years for the laughter to die down. And now that everyone's had a chance catch his breath, we're ready to go again with

MORE ADS WE NEVER GOT TO SEE

ARTIST: HARRY NORTH   WRITER: DICK DE BARTOLO

MAD #248
July 1984
Artist: Harry North
Writer: Dick DeBartolo

PREPARATION H

For temporary hemorrhoid relief, it leaves all the others behind!

Brillo

SOAP PADS

We're always working to improve them and we've just started to scratch the surface!

Let our cheerful drivers take you for a ride!

The Yellow Cab Co.

SUNSWEET Prunes

IN THE MORNING WILL GET YOU GOING ALL DAY!

Every year advertisers spend millions of dollars on campaigns that have no cultural value other than persuading us to buy various products. How then, you ask, can companies improve their ads and give **them more culture? Well, one way would be to let the world's great painters and sculptors provide the artwork. What, you ask, would be the result? Look no further, because Mad now reveals what we'd see**

IF ADVERTISERS MADE USE OF OLD MASTERS

WRITER: FRANK JACOBS

reach out and touch someone

Let your fingers get you talking! From Adam to Zachariah, you're only digits away from communication! It's the next best thing to hand-to-hand contact!

AT&T our creation is divine

When you take on the world, you're not alone.

Reach in and pull out your American Express Credit Card— it's welcomed from Waterloo to Corsica! Don't leave your homeland without it!

First the SCOPE... ...then the KISS!

The *modern* way to handle the *classic* problem of romance after pizza with everything!

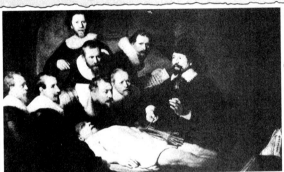

when E.F. Hutton talks, people listen.

MAD #256
July 1985
Writer: Frank Jacobs

"I Want My Alka-Seltzer!"

When you've eaten like a pig and feel nauseous. When you're belching in public and embarrassing your friends. When you're bloated and yecchy and kind of feel like throwing up—

TAKE

Alka-Seltzer

FOR ACID INDIGESTION, HEARTBURN, SOUR STOMACH AND OTHER DISGUSTING THINGS.

ARE YOU SEEING RIGHT?

Or is everything fuzzy and blurred and giving you head-aches and making you think you're swacked when you haven't had a drink since last Thursday? Maybe you should have your eyes examined. Could be you really don't have cataracts or glaucoma or some incurable eye disease. Maybe you're just nearsighted or astigmatic or wobble your head a lot when you look at things. So see your eye profes-sional today. You'll be glad you did. So will we.

SEEING

how many lenses and other optical stuff we can peddle from ads like this

IS OUR BUSINESS

BAUSCH & LOMB

THE BEST TEST OF A SEALY POSTUREPEDIC IS YOU.

WHAT AM I THINKING? I'M THINKING HOW SQUEEZABLY SOFT CHARMIN IS. AND THAT I USED UP THE LAST ROLL YESTERDAY.

CHARMIN Toilet Tissues

YOU KNOW WHEN YOU NEED RIGHT GUARD.

Your nose tells you. So do your friends, who stay up-wind when you're around. Not to mention the people who get off the elevator when you get on. So pick up the stick or the spray, and for the sake of everyone around you—USE IT.

By the early '80s, *MAD* was doing fewer and fewer ad parodies on its back cover, opting instead to have artist Don Martin draw a color cartoon for almost every issue.

When Martin left *MAD* in a dispute over artists' rights in 1987, the editors saw a chance to liven up a page that had grown stale and somewhat toothless. They decided to use Cover IV (back cover) to return to *MAD*'s roots by doing more pointed material, an editorial direction that would include plenty of ad spoofs.

Charlie Kadau and Joe Raiola, who had recently joined the magazine as associate editors, were among the first to reinvigorate the back cover, parodying their experiences with record clubs (the precursor to today's CD clubs) like Columbia House that always seem like a good a deal when one signs up, but quickly lead to a severe case of buyer's remorse.

Or, as Charlie puts it, "Once you get the 15 records for a penny, your first thought is, 'How do I get out of this?'"

MAD #262
April 1986
Photographer: Irving Schild
Writers: Charlie Kadau and Joe Raiola

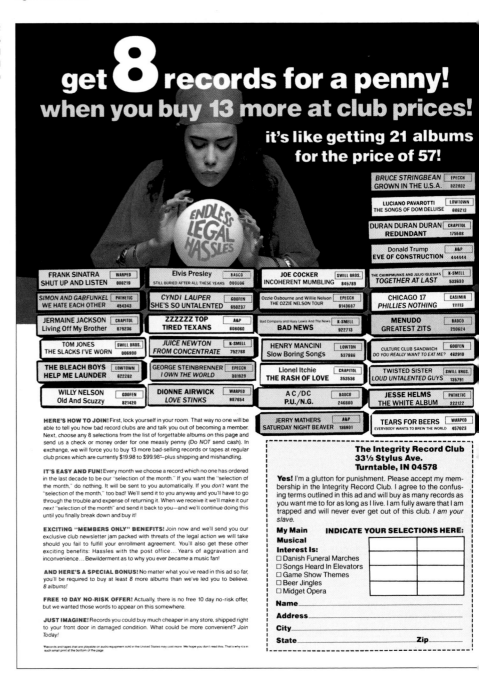

MAD #263
June 1986
Artists: Harvey Kurtzman
and Will Elder
Writer: J. Prete

Are you one of those people Madison Avenue ad-men dream about? Drool over?   Here's your chance to find out just how easy a mark you are by taking…

MAD'S ADVERTISING GULLIBILITY TEST

ARTIST: AL JAFFEE   WRITER: MIKE SNIDER

1) Do you believe that people in the real world would carry on a 30-second conversation about hemorrhoids in a crowded drug store?
☐ YES ☐ NO

2) Do you believe that those "respected wine authorities" would continue to be respected if they really did recommend a $2.98 California wine to their friends?   ☐ YES ☐ NO

3) Would you truly be surprised to find some soap suds in your kid's clothes right after you washed them?   ☐ YES ☐ NO

4) Would you buy anything just because it ha the words "DIET" or "LITE" on it?   ☐ YES

5) Do you really believe that it's the designer label on the backs of jeans that are attracting all the attention?   ☐ YES ☐ NO

6) Do you wholeheartedly believe that anything labeled "100% natural" must be good for you?   ☐ YES ☐ NO

7) Do you believe that the only thing stopping a beautiful woman from finding an absolute nerd "irresistible" are "fresher breath and whiter teeth"?   ☐ YES ☐ NO

8) Do you take Bob Hope's advice on motor o even though he hasn't driven or cared for a c in over 40 years?   ☐ YES

9) Do you actually think the military offers the best career training for future civilian life?
☐ YES ☐ NO

10) Do you think nothing terrible can happen to you just because you remembered to leave home with your American Express Card?
☐ YES ☐ NO

11) Do you believe "squeezability" is the definitive test for determining the quality of toilet tissue?   ☐ YES ☐ NO

SCORING

Tally up all your "YES" answers.

0–2 LOW GULLIBILITY Go forth and watch comme without fear!

3–5 AVERAGE GULLIBILITY Try and "keep your gua little better. No more $50 jeans!

6–9 HIGH GULLIBILITY *Never* shop alone; get the a *three* friends before you buy *anything*!

10–11 FIRST-CLASS SUCKER But all is not lost—if y NOW and sign up for our at-home Anti-Gullibilit spondence Course. ONLY $695.99. Mastercard a accepted.

MAD #271
June 1987
Artist: Al Jaffee
Writer: Mike Snider

MAD #271
June 1987
Artists: Harvey Kurtzman
and Will Elder
Writer: J. Prete

A TV COMMERCIAL WE'D LIKE TO SEE

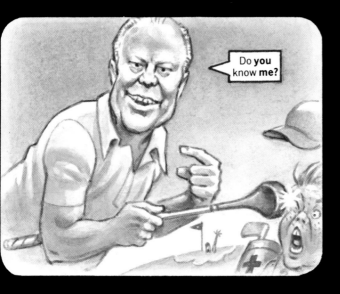

ARTISTS: HARVEY KURTZMAN AND WILL ELDER   WRITER: JOHN PRETE

MAD #274
October 1987
Artist: Bob Clarke
Writer: Frank Jacobs

REQUIEM MASS-COT DEPT.

If you live to 80, you're doing fine. If you live to 90, you've really beaten the odds. However, there are some among us who believe they'll live forever. We're referring to Mr. Clean, Cap'n Crunch and the rest of that copyrighted gang. Well, we've got some news for them! Eventually *everyone* dies, them included! So, to show them what's in store, we've prepared these...

OBITUARIES
For Merchandising Characters

FRED WHIPPLE DIES AT 54

Fred Whipple died today of suffocation after being squeezed to death under a truckload of toilet tissues. He was 54.

Whipple began his career at the Charmin Company as a sheet counter, and later became chief roll inspector and scent supervisor.

"We shall miss him greatly," said a Charmin spokesman. "After all, we have lost our Number Two man."

In accordance with Whipple's last request, his body will be wrapped in 5,000 squeezably soft sheets and placed on permanent display at a local supermarket.

Mr. Clean Dies at 33; Victim of Pollution

Mr. Clean died today after losing a fight with lung cancer. He was 33.

He was a battler to the last," said his son-in-law, Brawny, "but the filthy air and polluted environment were too much for him."

During his final months, the once-muscular Mr. Clean wasted away to a shadow of his robust size. Despite his terminal illness, he poured himself into his work, continuing to attack his sworn enemies, grease, dirt and soot.

"We tried to keep him alive with ammonia transfusions," said a hospital spokesman, "but by then it was hopeless. Still, he fought to the last drop before throwing in the sponge."

In his will, Mr. Clean left his entire estate to the EPA, except for his earring, which he bequeathed to Miss Clairol.

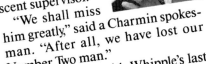

Campbell Kids Die

Boris and Doris Campbell, famed for decades as the Campbell Soup Kids, died today within hours of each other.

Doctors at the scene believe both succumbed to the Smurf Disease, otherwise known as "acute cuteness."

ARTIST: BOB CLARKE
WRITER: FRANK JACOBS

Cap'n Crunch Dies After Gallant Fight

Cap'n Crunch, beloved hero to young people the nation over, died last night after struggling valiantly against the Soggies.

Famed for his crisp, dry manner and tough grain, Crunch wilted under the Soggies' attack, which only last week claimed the lives of Snap, Crackle and Pop.

According to eyewitnesses, the Cap'n fought bitterly, refusing to surrender. Wet and weakened, he shouted, "Better croaked than soaked!" Shortly thereafter he was drenched and overwhelmed.

A colorful character, Cap'n Crunch was considered eccentric by those who knew him. "He was a real flake," said his close friend, Tony the Tiger.

REEN GIANT, 42, 'S OF OVERDOSE

he Green Giant collapsed and d yesterday from a chlorophyll rdose. He was 42.

he body was found ly this morning occupying parts of seven unties in northern alifornia and southn Oregon. The imact measured 8.5 on ne Richter scale and was felt as far away as Ohio.

Observers at the scene believe that more than 4,000 victims are trapped beneath the Green Giant's body. Health officials say that unless the immense rotting hulk is removed soon, a massive epidemic could result. He is survived by a nephew, the Little Green Sprout.

Charlie the Tuna Dies; Starkist Reject Was 92

Charlie the Tuna, 92, believed to have been the oldest fish in existence, died today of natural causes.

Charlie was orphaned at an early age when his parents gave their lives to Starkist. As an adult, he vowed to carry on the family tradition, but was constantly rejected as "undesirable."

Ever optimistic and hopeful, Charlie never lost his will to die. Yet despite numerous self-improvement courses and body-building exercises, he never managed to improve his image.

In his will, he asked to be broiled under a medium flame with a dash of lemon. So far, no one has claimed the body, which is still floating on the ocean surface off Newfoundland.

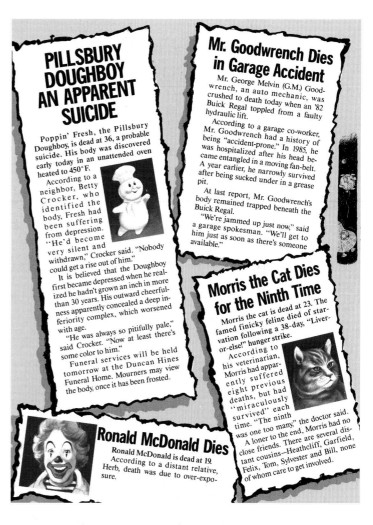

PILLSBURY DOUGHBOY AN APPARENT SUICIDE

Poppin' Fresh, the Pillsbury Doughboy, is dead at 36, a probable suicide. His body was discovered early today in an unattended oven heated to 450°F.

According to a neighbor, Betty Crocker, who identified the body, Fresh had been suffering from depression. "He'd become very silent and withdrawn," Crocker said. "Nobody could get a rise out of him."

It is believed that the Doughboy first became depressed when he realized he hadn't grown an inch in more than 30 years. His outward cheerfulness apparently concealed a deep inferiority complex, which worsened with age.

"He was always so pitifully pale," said Crocker. "Now at least there's some color to him."

Funeral services will be held tomorrow at the Duncan Hines Funeral Home. Mourners may view the body, once it has been frosted.

Mr. Goodwrench Dies in Garage Accident

Mr. George Melvin (G.M.) Goodwrench, an auto mechanic, was crushed to death today when an '82 Buick Regal toppled from a faulty hydraulic lift.

According to a garage co-worker, Mr. Goodwrench had a history of being "accident-prone." In 1985, he was hospitalized after his head became entangled in a moving fan-belt. A year earlier, he narrowly survived after being sucked under in a grease pit.

At last report, Mr. Goodwrench's body remained trapped beneath the Buick Regal.

"We're jammed up just now," said a garage spokesman. "We'll get to him just as soon as there's someone available."

Morris the Cat Dies for the Ninth Time

Morris the cat is dead at 23. The famed finicky feline died of starvation following a 38-day, "Liver-or-else!" hunger strike.

According to his veterinarian, Morris had apparently suffered eight previous deaths, but had "miraculously survived" each time. "The ninth was one too many," the doctor said.

A loner to the end, Morris had no close friends. There are several distant cousins—Heathcliff, Garfield, Felix, Tom, Sylvester and Bill, none of whom care to get involved.

Ronald McDonald Dies

Ronald McDonald is dead at 19. According to a distant relative, Herb, death was due to over-exposure.

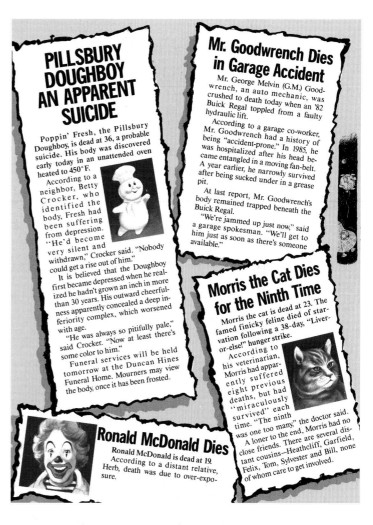

MAD #275
December 1987
Artist: Bob Clarke
Writer: Lou Silverstone

Big Books For Small Minds™

AN INCREDIBLE OFFER FROM THE

FAT-BOOK-OF-THE-MONTH CLUB

...Because Sometimes Quantity <u>Is</u> Better Than Quality! We have them all! Just take a look at our **FAT** collection of extremely **FAT** books and join today!

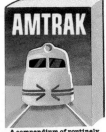

AMTRAK

A compendium of routinely ignored safety regulations
Publisher's price $768.50

NANCY WHO ?

Everything President Reagan claims he forgot
Pub. price $116.95

THE CONGRESSIONAL PAYROLL

A complete guide to your Congressmen's relatives
Pub. price $720.95

Steven King

18 novels written last April
Pub. price $250.00

AMERICAN TRAITORS

Secrets divulged by the marines in Russia, Vol. 9
Pub. price $544.97

HAND GUNS

People killed by the weapons they bought for protection
Pub. price $199.29

FRANCE

A history of appeasements of and surrenders to terrorists and dictators
Pub. price $275.00

THE PUBLISHERS CLEARINGHOUSE SWEEPSTAKES

A complete listing of all those who have never won
Pub. price $171.50

Saturday Night Live

Sketches that have no ending
Pub. price $199.50

THROWING PUNCHES, SNEERING AND SPITTING

A pictorial history of Sean Penn
Pub. price $599.49

Joan Rivers

Ways the faltering star can improve her act
Pub. price $1.95

Facts About Membership. After years of running this ad, we've discovered that no one who orders books from us ever reads this paragraph. In fact, we've also discovered that the people who order books from us *can't* read! They hope that by ordering a few impressive looking fat books to leave on their coffee table or bookshelf, they'll be able to hide the shameful secret of their illiteracy from their friends and neighbors! That's okay with us, because since they can't read, we can charge them any amount we feel like! If you *can* read this, then you know what a rip-off book clubs are and can share in our mocking of those less fortunate than yourself!

VERY THIN BOOKS

The complete catalogue
Pub. price $519.87

GOD

The first zillion years
Pub. price $620.86

ABOUT SMOKING AND CANCER

Facts distorted by the RJ Reynolds Company
Pub. price $222.50

1001 GRIPES!

Consumer complaints against book clubs
Pub. price $400.00

Billy Idol ON EGO

Pub. price $394.59

TAMMY BAKKER'S The ART of MASCARA

Pub. price $169.79

GARY HART'S LITTLE BLACK BOOK

Pub. price $537.50

LETTERS TO Dear Abby from "CONFUSED"

Pub. price $116.95

Choose any 4 books and save up to $2,731.17.

You simply agree to send us a blank check every month for the next two years!

The Fat-Book-of-the-Month Club, Inc.
461 Voluminous Rd., Manypages, PA 17011

Please enroll me as a member of the Fat-Book-of-the-Month Club. I understand that the books I order will not necessarily be the books you send. That's fine with me. The fact that I have enclosed a blank check made payable to you is proof that I am just the kind of gullible customer you're trying to attract. I agree to say good things about your club even if it turns out to be the worst thing in my life.

Indicate by number the 4 books you want.

Name_____
Address_____
City_____
State_____ Zip_____

ARTIST: BOB CLARKE   WRITER: LOU SILVERSTONE

A TV COMMERCIAL WE'D LIKE TO SEE

ARTIST: ANGELO TORRES   WRITER: BILLY DOHERTY

MAD #277
March 1988
Artist: Angelo Torres
Writer: Billy Doherty

Why are we giving away the Bulgin' Belly Burner™ for only $10?
(Because we tried to give it away for $20 and that didn't work!)

Bulgin' Belly Burner™

AS SEEN ON TV*

Don't waste your hard-earned cash on inferior imitations when you can get the inferior original for the same price!

*On Nationwide Consumer Fraud Reports

Intensive back-stretch sends blood rushing to lower abdomen and thighs!

Reverse leg-lifts leave hands free to take important nutritional supplements!

Power sit-ups work your arteries to their bursting point!

To see how desperate overweight people are, our Special Consumer Alert Movement (**SCAM**) is offering this truly amazing device.

NOT AVAILABLE IN ANY STORE
The amazing Bulgin' Belly Burner will not be sold in any store! It's only offered by mail, where you can't get your hands on one until you have already paid for it!
Use it to flatten your tummy, firm your buttocks, mow your lawn, grate your cheese, slice your eggs—just about anything you can think of!
Forget about expensive gyms, difficult rowing machines and all the ridiculous claims in this ad. Just 10 minutes with the Bulgin' Belly Burner makes you feel as nauseous as if you had worked 40 minutes with heavy weights.

IRON CLAD MONEY-BACK GUARANTEE
Use the Bulgin' Belly Burner just 10

minutes a day for 5 years. If you're not 100% delighted with the new "you," try using it 20 minutes a day for the next 10 years. If you're still not in better shape than our professional models shown above, return the unit for a full refund. (Must be in brand-new condition, in original package, to qualify. Please include a $15 restocking charge.)

ONLY ONE BELLY BURNER PER PERSON!
Only one unit per customer may be purchased. But we won't insult your intelligence by checking to see if you sent in multiple orders, so feel free to do so!
To order, mail this original ad together with $10 for each Bulgin' Belly Burner, plus $19.95 postage and handling and $12.76 insurance, and an additional $7.95 for the translated-from-Japanese instruction sheet. Allow 6 to 8 months for us to ship it and for you to forget that you ordered it.

Bulgin' Belly Burner, Cockamamie Products, Dept. Y-U, Gullibility, TX.

MAD #279
June 1988
Artist: Irving Schild
Writer: Dick DeBartolo

Dick DeBartolo was a natural to write this ad for a horribly low-rent exercise device since, when not writing for *MAD*, he did a recurring segment on *LIVE with Regis and Kathie Lee* exposing rip-offs and scams. Dick still appears on TV as the Giz Wiz to review the latest off-beat gadgets and gizmos.

The, ahem, *well-rounded* gentlemen in this photo are three mavericks of publishing: *Screw*'s Al Goldstein, *The Anarchist Cookbook* publisher Lyle Stuart, and *MAD*'s own William M. Gaines. The three were longtime friends, bonded in part by the various First Amendment battles each had fought over the years and, apparently, in part by their mutual need for a D-cup bra.

BONUS TRIVIA: This may be the only known photo of Gaines engaged in a physical activity other than eating.

MAD #281
September 1988
Artist: Sam Viviano
Writer: Staff

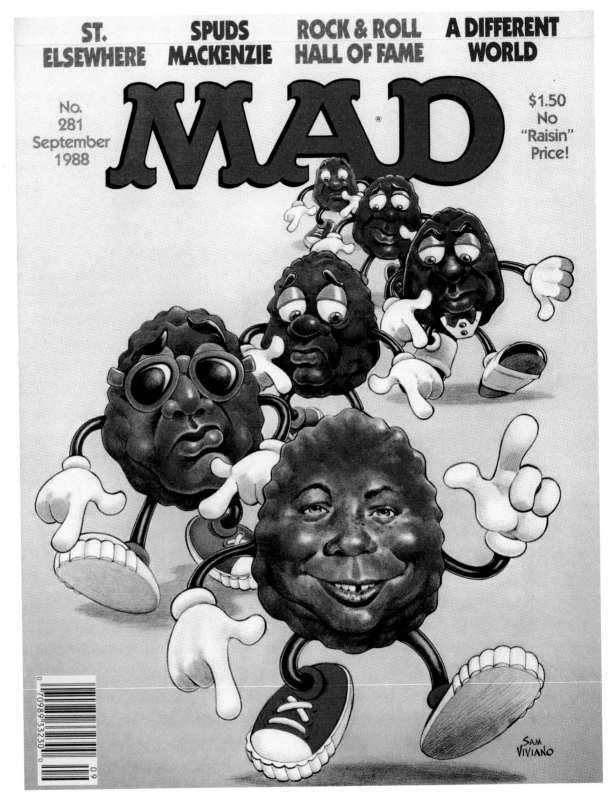

The Jolly Green Giant. The Pillsbury Doughboy. Spuds MacKenzie. The California Raisins. The list is endless! All of them the products of an ad executive's limited imagination, and all of them rammed down our throats until they become the beloved symbols of the goods they were created to huckster for! We've always found something phony about these characters, though. We just don't think they truly represent what their respective companies are like! Besides truth in advertising, we'd like to see some truth in advertising *characters!* We'd like some...

ADVERTISING CHARACTERS & CORPORATE MASCOTS
THAT BETTER REFLECT THE MISERABLE COMPANIES THEY WORK FOR

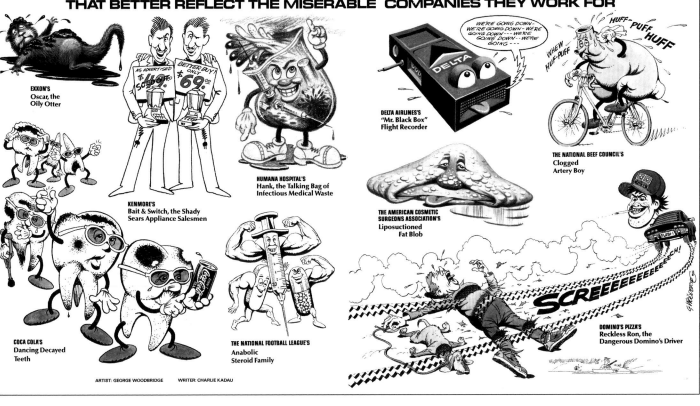

EXXON'S
Oscar, the
Oily Otter

KENMORE'S
Bait & Switch, the Shady
Sears Appliance Salesmen

HUMANA HOSPITAL'S
Hank, the Talking Bag of
Infectious Medical Waste

COCA COLA'S
Dancing Decayed
Teeth

THE NATIONAL FOOTBALL LEAGUE'S
Anabolic
Steroid Family

DELTA AIRLINES'S
"Mr. Black Box"
Flight Recorder

THE NATIONAL BEEF COUNCIL'S
Clogged
Artery Boy

**THE AMERICAN COSMETIC
SURGEONS ASSOCIATION'S**
Liposuctioned
Fat Blob

DOMINO'S PIZZA'S
Reckless Ron, the
Dangerous Domino's Driver

ARTIST: GEORGE WOODBRIDGE   WRITER: CHARLIE KADAU

MAD #302
March 1991
Artist: George Woodbridge
Writer: Charlie Kadau

OUR PLEDGE TO YOU:

If your parents don't buy you what you want, start kicking and screaming at the top of your lungs. Then they'll buy you anything. We promise!!

Iggy The Iguana

TOYS "Я" U

THE WORLD'S GREEDIEST TOY STORE

Sizzling Hot Toy Savings!

OUR PRICES AREN'T AS HIGH AS USUAL!

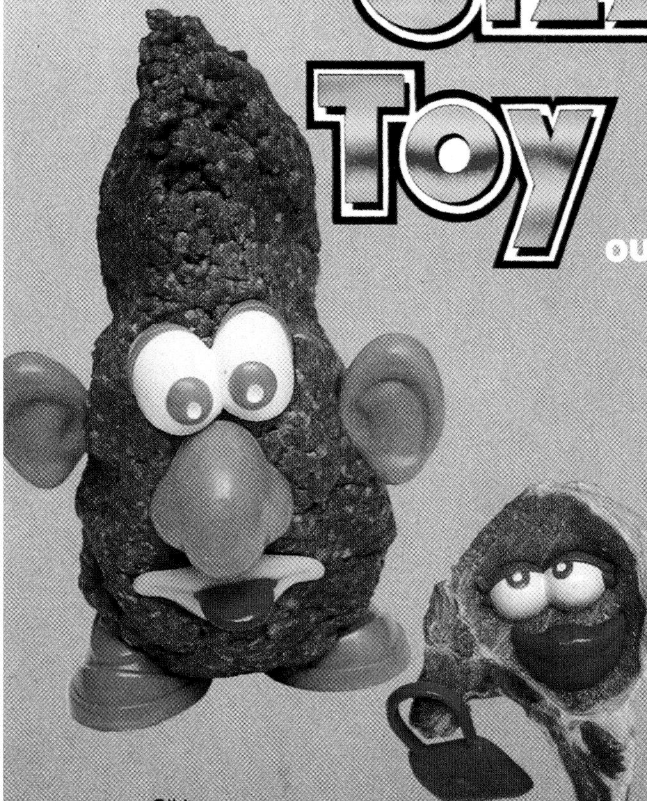

Sikko
MR. MEATHEAD
Use your favorite cuts of beef, pork and lamb to make clever, funny figures! Ages 1–up.
(Seven AAAAAAA batteries not included)

10.99

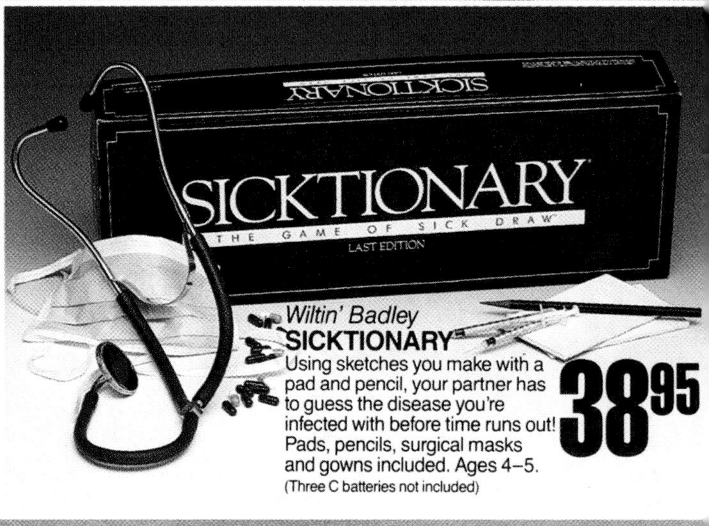

SICKTIONARY
SICKTIONARY
THE GAME OF SICK DRAW
LAST EDITION

Wiltin' Badley
SICKTIONARY
Using sketches you make with a pad and pencil, your partner has to guess the disease you're infected with before time runs out! Pads, pencils, surgical masks and gowns included. Ages 4–5.
(Three C batteries not included)

38.95

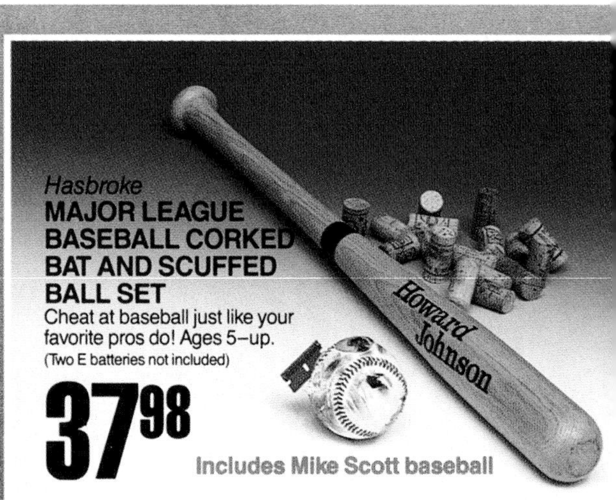

Howard Johnson

Hasbroke
MAJOR LEAGUE BASEBALL CORKED BAT AND SCUFFED BALL SET
Cheat at baseball just like your favorite pros do! Ages 5–up.
(Two E batteries not included)

37.98

Includes Mike Scott baseball

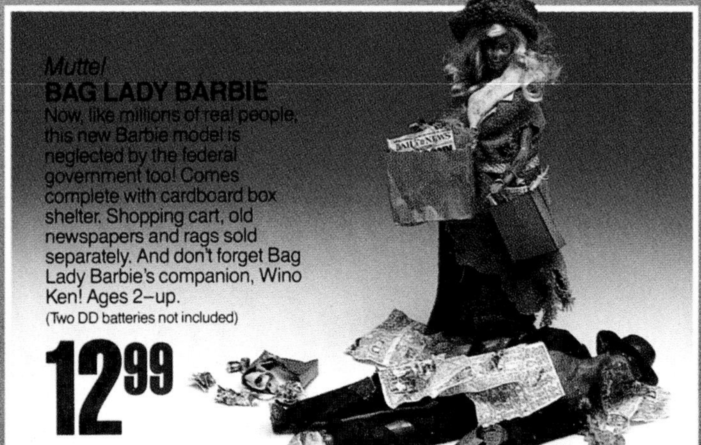

Muttel
BAG LADY BARBIE
Now, like millions of real people, this new Barbie model is neglected by the federal government too! Comes complete with cardboard box shelter. Shopping cart, old newspapers and rags sold separately. And don't forget Bag Lady Barbie's companion, Wino Ken! Ages 2–up.
(Two DD batteries not included)

12.99

WE ACCEPT:

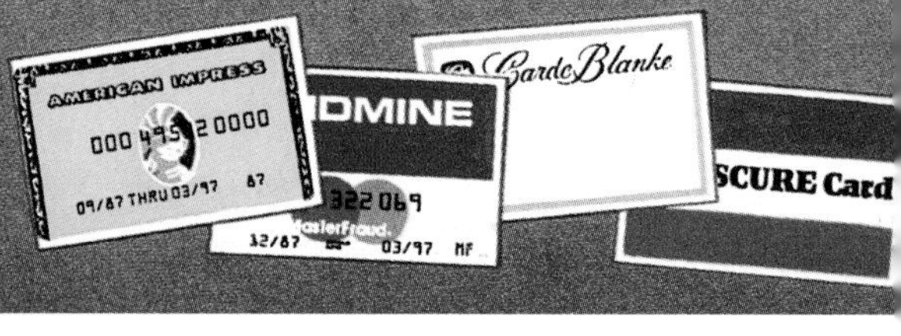

AMERICAN IMPRESS
000 495 2 0000
09/87 THRU 03/97
MasterFraud
CardeBlanke
SCURE Card

FOR MORE TOY BARGAINS TURN TO PAGE 24!

MAD #285
March 1989
Artist: George Woodbridge
Photographer: Irving Schild
Writers: Joe Raiola and
Charlie Kadau

Senior editor Charlie Kadau pulled triple duty on this piece. Not only did he co-write "Toys 'R' U" with Joe Raiola, but he helped direct the all-day photo shoot at Irving Schild's studio and even served as prop man, sculpting Mr. Meathead and dressing Bag Lady Barbie.

MAD #308

January 1992

Photographer: Irving Schild

Writers: Joe Raiola and
Charlie Kadau

WHITETAIL DEER: 4 years old. Forest creature and a member of the Nature's Revenge Association.

"Every year my peaceful woodland home is invaded by thousands of hunters who shoot at me with rifles and guns with absolutely no provocation on my part. Usually I'm just walking around, minding my own business or chewing on some berries when BANG! A bullet goes flying past my head. Now don't get me wrong. I have nothing against sportsmen, but I don't like being the target of some accountant from Scarsdale out for a weekend with his buddies. All of the bears, rabbits, racoons and other forest creatures I've spoken to feel pretty much the same way.

"That's why we formed the NRA—Nature's Revenge Association. We've learned that a hunter will have a new appreciation and respect for an animal that's armed as heavily as he is. We know that guns aren't toys... Believe me, we know. So we teach our members gun safety and train them not to shoot unless they've been shot at first... a lesson most hunters haven't learned yet.

"So this year we're ready. We've been practicing for months. We've got our permits. And we're determined to have a safe hunting season for all involved. If you want to visit our home and take our pictures, fine. But keep your guns in the cities where they belong.

No one wants to be the deer-ly departed." **I'm the NRA.®**

The NRA Animal Firearms Program provides law abiding beasts with basic instruction in the safe handling of guns with their paws. If you are an endangered species and want more information, write to Nature's Revenge Association, Yellowstone Ntl. Park, Wyoming, 00118.

A MAD AD PARODY

STRICTLY LOW CALIBER

Note: The editors of American Rifleman magazine (the mouthpiece of the National Rifle Association) recently expressed its outrage over several jokes in MAD satirizing the NRA. After whipping up their readers with some paranoid rantings about media conspiracies and threats to their children, they encouraged their readers to write to us. The following letter represents the gist of what we received.

The National Rifle Association did not miss the stupid, biased and liberal cartoon in your magazine about heavily armed wildlife and assault weapons. I used to read your magazine as a teenager and sometimes still do—but never again. I will boycott and write any and all advertisers that support your garbage magazine.

James Maass
Lima, OH

Boycott our advertisers!? Oh no, God, please, anything but THAT, Jimbo! You've got us quaking and trembling with fear! Now we know how the deer and other cute and furry woodland animals feel before hunters pump them full of lead to give themselves a cheap testosterone rush! Thanks for writing!—Ed.

Turnabout is fair play—Since they asked their readers to write to us, we're asking you to write to them! Do you think anyone (and we mean anyone—John Hinckley wannabes/disgruntled former postal workers/your weird cousin!) should be permitted to purchase any firearm, no matter how powerful it is, for whatever reason, whenever they want? Let those editors know by writing to them at: American Rifleman, 470 Spring Park Place, Suite 1000, Herndon, VA 22070!

It was easy for photographer Irving Schild to find someone to portray the hunter's body for this spoof of a National Rifle Association image campaign; he asked his next door neighbor in Pennsylvania who was an actual hunter. Getting the shot of the deer's head proved to be a much tougher challenge. Irving paid several visits to a private zoo with camera in hand, but never seemed to get what he needed.

"It was tough to get a deer to do exactly what I wanted him to do," explains Schild, proving the old Hollywood axiom "Never work with children or animals." Three trips later, Irving finally had the shot of the deer giving the expression he was looking for, and with lighting that would match the photo of the hunter's body. Irving then used Photoshop, a computer design program which at the time was relatively new to the market—but has since become a staple of the *MAD* art department—to meld the two images together.

This back cover prompted a swift and angry response, with the NRA organizing a letter-writing campaign in which its members threatened a boycott of *MAD*'s advertisers. Someone probably should've told them that a boycott wouldn't do much good since *MAD* didn't take ads, but then, who wants to correct a bunch of pissed-off gun owners?

Writer Charlie Kadau says this back cover came together pretty easily because "the best pieces come out of a seething anger that the writer lets bubble up . . . and a lot of advertising makes me angry." In the case of Metropolitan Life, Kadau wondered how sweet, innocent Snoopy had been corrupted into the mascot for a major insurance company. To Kadau, using a Peanuts character to sell insurance was as if "Dow Chemical had used My Little Pony as its spokesperson."

Coincidentally, at the time he wrote this piece, Kadau had not one, but two policies with Met Life, which he soon cancelled in a dispute with the company that was (we're pretty sure) unrelated to this spoof.

MAD #306
October 1991
Artist: Angelo Torres
Writers: Charlie Kadau and
Joe Raiola

CRASHING SYMBOLS DEPT.

Not too long ago, we confirmed the deaths of Mr. Clean, Charlie the Starkist Tuna and several other merchandising characters. It seems, however, that our list wasn't complete, and for MAD this won't do at all! Here, therefore, are *more*

OBITUARIES
FOR MERCHANDISING CHARACTERS

ARTIST: BOB CLARKE   WRITER: FRANK JACOBS

Noid Dies After Plot Fails to Pan Out

The Noid, longtime Domino's nemesis, died today after a failed attempt to sabotage the company's pizzas with tainted anchovies.

"It was clearly an act of revenge by a desperate creature," said a Domino's executive. "After we dropped him from our advertising campaigns, he vowed to get even. I guess he still wanted a slice of the pie."

It is believed that the Noid infiltrated an unheated oven, then was baked to death after it was turned on. He tried to escape, but was held fast by the melting cheese.

Funeral arrangements are being handled by Domino's, who promise to deliver him to his grave in less than 30 minutes.

NBC Peacock Dies

The NBC Peacock, 47, died today of poor exposure after failing to fight off an epidemic of cable-TV programs and video-cassette releases.

He will be replaced by a turkey.

Famed Party Animal Spuds MacKenzie Dies

Spuds MacKenzie, who electrified the nation with his beer drinking, carousing and gorgeous women, died today after being run over by a truck he was chasing. The Budweiser party animal had just turned six.

"He spotted a Miller Lite truck and went crazy," explained a Budweiser spokesman. "He was growling and snapping, determined to chase off the competition, but he got too close to the wheels. It's a great loss and we're as crushed as he is."

MacKenzie was hired by Budweiser as spokespooch in 1988, but not after some controversy. Several company executives feared he was giving the firm a black eye, and rumors persisted that he refused to be housebroken.

"Let's be fair to Spuds," the spokesman said. "Sure, he occasionally couldn't control himself at parties, but it's not easy holding all that beer."

MacKenzie will be buried on the company grounds, along with his leash, muzzle and diamond-studded collar. Pallbearers include Mighty Dog, Pluto, Snoopy, Marmaduke and McGruff, the Crime Dog.

Suicide Claims Life Of Exxon Tiger, 27

Suicide has claimed the life of the Exxon Tiger. He was 27.

The great cat, who inspired the slogan, "Put a tiger in your tank," was found in his locked garage with his motor running, a victim of carbon monoxide poisoning.

"I guess you could say it was a case of putting the tank in the tiger," joked an Exxon official.

According to friends, the Tiger had been extremely depressed ever since the Exxon oil spill in Alaska. As an endangered species, he was saddened by the loss of wildlife and felt ashamed of being the Exxon symbol.

"We'll probably stuff him and keep him as a trophy," said the Exxon executive, "or maybe use his hide as a slipcover."

The company has no plans to acquire another tiger. "Most likely, we'll come up with another animal as a symbol—like a snake or a vulture," the executive said. He is survived by a brother, Tony the Tiger.

Mr. Zip Dies at 36

According to a press release postmarked March 25, 1987, but received only today, Mr. Zip is dead after collapsing beneath several tons of junk mail. He was 36.

Energizer Rabbit Dies Of Digestive Disorder

The Energizer Rabbit died today of a digestive ailment, brought on by eating the burritos while interrupting a Taco Bell commercial.

"He couldn't resist the Mexican food," an Energizer spokesman said. "Within hours he was going and going and going. It wasn't a pretty sight! We tried to rush him into a Kaopectate commercial, but by then it was too late. He was going, going, gone!"

Mr. Peanut, 72, Dies In Mental Hospital

Mr. Peanut, longtime Planters employee, died yesterday at 72. He had been confined to a mental hospital, suffering from a severe identity crisis.

"He tried to put on rich, fancy airs with his top hat and monocle," said a company psychiatrist, "but deep down he knew he was only working for peanuts. He became terribly depressed, and despite years of therapy, we couldn't get him out of his shell. In the end, he was a certifiable nut case."

As of today, company officials had not decided whether to give him a funeral or a posthumous roast.

MAD #311
June 1992
Artist: Bob Clarke
Writer: Frank Jacobs

Smooth Character Dies After Missile Attack

Smooth Character, the humped symbol of Camel Cigarettes, has died of injuries suffered during a missile attack. He was 11.

According to a close friend, the Marlboro Man, the Smooth Character had been visiting relatives in Kuwait during Operation Desert Storm. He was struck by fragments of a Patriot Missile that had intercepted an incoming Scud.

"Actually his death is good for us," a Camel spokesman said today. "It proves beyond all doubt that smoking doesn't kill you, but missiles do."

Uncle Ben, 84, Dies In Racial Incident

Uncle Ben, 84, died today from injuries suffered in a racially motivated incident.

According to witnesses, he was stopped by Los Angeles police officers for no apparent reason. Though normally mild-mannered, Uncle Ben became stirred up and boiled over at the unlawful detainment, and a pressure-cooker situation quickly developed.

"We told him to put a lid on it," said one of the officers, "but he was in hot water from the start."

"No way," said Aunt Jemima, a neighbor. "Sure, he got steamed, but what they did to him goes against the grain."

Funeral arrangements are not complete, due to no one knowing Uncle Ben's religious preference. It is believed he was recently converted.

Bluebonnet Girl, 41, Dies

The Bluebonnet Girl, 41, died today of exhaustion. Company officials blamed her death on an ever-increasing workload.

"It was clear she was spreading herself too thin," said a spokesman.

In accordance with her will, she will be cremated with her ashes scattered over all 50 states. "After all," she said recently, "everything's better with Bluebonnet on it."

California Raisins Die of Old Age

The California Raisins, who sang and danced their way to national acclaim, have died of old age, according to news heard through the grapevine.

"It's not all that surprising," said Sun Maid, a close friend. "They were all dried up and wrinkled and feeling boxed in with age."

The group made their show-business debut as youngsters, calling themselves The Grapettes. Though green newcomers, they soon displayed the seeds of greatness. "A most pleasing bunch," said a local critic, who lauded them for their good taste.

As the years passed, however, the group appeared to run out of juice, forcing a major career change. "When they hung us out to dry, we gave our routine a new wrinkle," said one of the raisins last year, "and the fruit of our efforts paid off."

MAD #321
September 1993
Writer: Frank
Santopadre

Show You Care. Save A Child Star.

HERE'S WHAT YOU WILL RECEIVE:

✳ An 8 x 10 glossy photo of the Former Child Star you are helping!

✳ A letter of thanks from your Former Child Star's Parole Board!

✳ A complete copy of your Former Child Star's case history, including criminal and court records, mug shots, fingerprints and a detailed report on the Rehab Center your contribution is helping to support!

ALL THIS FOR ONLY $175 A DAY!

<u>Your monthly donation will provide so much:</u>

✳ Legal fees and bail money!

✳ Counseling, psychotherapy and substance abuse treatment!

✳ Acting and singing classes in the hope of getting their stalled career back on track!

✳ A new press agent or public relations firm to help restore their tarnished image!

✳ Cosmetic surgery, including facelifts, breast enlargement (or reduction), liposuction and shin implants to increase height!

Won't You Help Rescue A Former Child Star?

Here's how you can become a sponsor:

In most places around the world, $175 a day will pay for quite a few necessities: three meals, a comfortable place to live and much more. But in Hollywood, it's barely enough to cover the cost of new head shots or dinner in one of the trendy eateries frequented by high-powered agents, producers and other show business executives. Even so, for once-beloved child stars, that same $175 can make the difference between "prime time" and "doing time."

For example, take a look at the former child stars shown on this page. **They were once stars of hit TV sitcoms and millionaires** before they hit puberty. Their adorable faces graced fan magazine covers and posters on thousands of teenagers' bedroom walls. Now it's a constant struggle to keep those same faces off *post office* walls. Their savings squandered by selfish parents and greedy managers, their only real exposure now comes in the monologues of cruel standup comics or in an occasional supermarket tabloid story. They desperately need a renewed career and a chance to regain some of their former glory. **Won't you help?**

WRITER: FRANK SANTOPADRE

- -

☐ **Yes, I wish to sponsor a former child star. Enclosed is my first payment of $175.**

Child Star Preference (if any):
☐ Trouble with the law
☐ Victim of bad investments by managers and/ or parents
☐ Substance abuse problems

☐ I.R.S. woes
☐ No residual money from reruns
☐ No longer cute
☐ Reduced to appearing at nostalgia conventions and car shows.

NAME_____

ADDRESS_____ CITY_____
STATE _____ ZIP _____

☐ I don't wish to sponsor a former child star now, but notify me as soon as the kids on *Full House* reach drinking age.

Save A Child Star

MAD #313
September 1992
Artist: C. F. Payne
Writer: Dick DeBartolo

A TV AD WE'D LIKE TO SEE

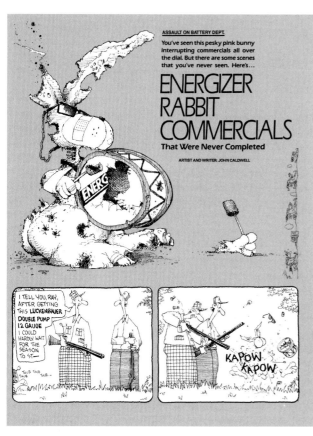

MAD #317
March 1993
Artist and Writer: John Caldwell

MAD prides itself on never doing victim humor, the kind of mean-spirited writing where the joke is on the victim—rather than the perpetrator or the surrounding press frenzy—of a major tragedy. In other words, you don't do gags about the late Nicole Brown Simpson; you hit O. J., the trial, Lance Ito, etc.

In this case, the target left itself wide open, as writer Dick DeBartolo savagely mocks those pandering, face-saving *mea culpa* open letters airlines always publish after one of their planes goes down in a fatal crash. This particular incident was the loss of USAir #427 outside of Pittsburgh in the fall of 1994. It should come as no surprise that of all the ad spoofs DeBartolo has written, this biting piece is among his favorites.

MAD #334
May 1995
Writer: Dick DeBartolo

USscAir

Dear Travelers:

Safety is our highest priority — right after making sure each seat pocket has a barf bag. This is validated each and every day by the tens of thousands of people who fly our planes and leave our flights shaken, but alive.

Before a flight leaves the ground, mechanics in neat looking overalls using sophisticated tools like metric hammers inspect each plane for the tiniest defect. Do we need to replace that missing wing? Can we get four more landings out of those bald tires? Will that hole in the tail affect flying ability? These may seem like small questions to you, but they're important to us. We may not know the answers, but the questions are still important!

To prove that we ARE safe, we are investing an unprecedented $20 million in running these ads! Another $10,000 will go toward inspecting our fleet. For added safety a lucky four-leaf clover is now mandatory in every USscAir cockpit — even though FAA regulations don't require it!

Furthermore, we have asked a former commander in the U.S. Air Force to oversee our safety operations. He'll be arriving on the very next Amtrak train.

In closing, let me say that our timetables, fare charts and petty cash receipts are open for public inspection, along with every other company document, except of course, our maintenance records.

I would not hesitate to let any of my in-laws fly on USscAir, and I would proudly be there — to wave good-bye.

Sincerely,

E. Death Scorchfield
Chairman and CEO

MAD #325
February 1994
Artist: James Warhola
Writers: Joe Raiola and
Charlie Kadau

Finally, A Cure for the Common Coffin!

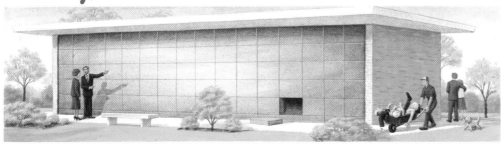

Special Savings Offered As Swindle Gardens Hopes To Fill New Mausoleum—And Fast!

Graves and drab headstones have been the choice of dead people for centuries. But now, through this exclusive offer that's running in 117 daily newspapers, Swindle Gardens invites you to consider the advantages and convenience of mausoleum entombment. It's not as creepy as you might think! Mausoleums were once considered a "rich man's" resting place. Today, since most of the rich men who felt that way are long dead, we're forced to offer our mausoleums to poor schmucks like you!

PEACE OF MIND: Unlike some of the "budget" mausoleums you see ads for, you won't find any dried blood caked on our walls! Also, our professional and conscientious staff MAKES SURE your loved one is deceased before interring them—if they aren't, we finish them off at no extra cost! And if by chance we do entomb someone who's still alive, you may skip a month's payment and incur no finance charge!

Yes, each mausoleum is a timeless tribute to your inability to think rationally when confronted with a fast-talking crypt salesman! Remember, your skin will decay and your body will decompose, but at Swindle Gardens, we'll never mention that, because if we did, we know there's no way you'd spring for $19,000 for a slab of hollow concrete!

TOP NOTCH CONSTRUCTION. Unlike the remains that decay inside of them, Swindle Garden Mausoleums are built to last. Our new mausoleums may look like hastily constructed, prefabricated sheet metal tool sheds, but don't be fooled… they were NOT hastily constructed!

We personally guarantee that each mausoleum resting place is permanently sheltered and will not be damaged by any of nature's destructive forces!*

SERENE ENVIRONMENT. Gone are the rodent infestation problems of last year! And the gypsy carnival has moved south for the winter! When strolling through Swindle Gardens you'll take comfort in the tranquil surroundings… towering Norway maples, babbling brooks…you'll completely forget we're located next to a livestock slaughterhouse (Between 12 and 3 you can hardly hear the sounds of the animals!)

Our ample parking lot has spaces for over 75 hearses, so there's never a wait! Special group rates are available for jet or bus accident victims!

PAY WHILE YOU'RE STILL BREATHING. With our revolutionary monthly pay-in-advance plan, you can purchase a sepulcher the same way you'd finance a rug at K-Mart! We don't charge you separately for administrative and processing costs since they're already hidden in your monthly bill!

Each day families are discovering the wisdom of buying memorial property in advance. They say, "It's the mature decision. Rather than suffer the distress and pressure when a loved one finally dies, we decided to suffer the distress and pressure NOW by making large and frequent payments to a mortuary!"

Cost-conscious families can save even more! At your request, we'll cram as many relatives as we can into each space, using our new compacting technology, previously available only to the auto salvage industry!

Questions often asked in our ads:

Q: Will my loved one be treated with dignity?
A. *Yes. At Swindle Gardens, your loved one will be treated with the same dignity and respect he or she received at such places as the Department of Motor Vehicles while alive.*

Q: Is vandalism a problem at Swindle Gardens?
A: *No. Our employees make it a point to remove all valuables from your loved one BEFORE internment, including rings, jewelry and even gold teeth—so there's nothing to steal when vandals pry the lid open!*

Swindle Gardens
85 Stiff Street
Rigor Mortis, RI 02921
Sure, I'm alive now, but who knows for how long? Before I take my terminal breath, please rush me more information about Swindle Gardens Mausoleums.
Name _____
Address _____
City _____
State/Zip _____
Order today and receive a free animated cartoon of the deceased!

*Except earthquakes, hurricanes, tornadoes, blizzards, wind, rain, humidity and sunrise.

Inspired by an ad in the local paper selling spaces in a new mausoleum, writers Joe Raiola and Charlie Kadau managed to create a line-by-line spoof of the original, putting a joke in every sentence. They wrote so much, in fact, that they actually had to cut lines, yet still managed to cover almost the entire back cover with copy, a rarity in a magazine that is so visually driven.

There is a disadvantage to all of this writing—a *MAD* writer gets paid by the page, not by the word, so even though writing a piece like "Swindle Gardens" was far more labor-intensive than most, Kadau and Raiola were still paid for authoring a single *MAD* page (which, as a writing team, they had to split).

MAD #343
March 1996
Artist: Richard Williams
Writer: House

IN THIS ISSUE WE

| SOUR ON | DUNK | CREAM | MILK |
| RACE RELATIONS | CLINTON & DOLE | BILL GATES | EVERY GAG |

No. 343 March 1996

MAD IND ®

Our Price $2.50 Cheap? $3.50 Canada

SCHMUCK
Not a surprise!

Bozell Worldwide, the agency behind the "Got Milk" and "Milk—What a Surprise!" campaigns, claims that its ads helped reverse a thirty-year downward trend in milk sales. We have no idea if that's true, but the ads have stuck around long enough to give *MAD* several opportunities to poke fun at them.

Apparently no one at Bozell or the Fluid Processing Board was too upset—when they collected the Milk ads into a book a few years ago, they included this *MAD* cover featuring Alfred with *Friends* stars Jennifer Aniston and Lisa Kudrow.

MAD #384
August 1999
Writer: J. Prete

I'm a beautiful, scantily-clad model standing in Times Square posing for this ad. Typical of Madison Avenue, they'll use sex to try and sell *anything*! Even something as wholesome as milk. Only one problem. Most readers are so busy checking out my fabulous body that they never really pay attention to the product being advertised. Could it be that everyone connected with this ad...

forgot milk?

A MAD
Ad
Parody

http://www.whatmilk?.com   REBECCA WHOMARRIEDTHATGUYFROMFULLHOUSE © NATIONAL FLUIDS PROMOTION BOARD THAT GOT MILKED

MAD #352
December 1996
Writer: Andrew J.
Schwartzberg

Tired Of Blending In With The Crowd?

Then Just Blend Some JUST FOR RODMAN® Into Your Hair And You'll Have People Gawking At You In No Time!

WASH AWAY HEALTHY LOOKING HAIR
If you've had enough of your boring brown, black or blonde hair, **JUST FOR RODMAN®** is just for you! Simply lather in a generous amount of **JUST FOR RODMAN®** before you shampoo and say sayonara to your natural hair color. It's not messy. It's not drippy. It's just offensive to those around you!

KISS CONFORMITY GOOD-BYE
Our specially-designed formula won't wash out—ever! The only way to change your hair color once you've used **JUST FOR RODMAN®** is to buy another shade of **JUST FOR RODMAN®**! And since it comes in seven different colors, you can have a new look every day of the week! Plus, there's enough variety to match ANY of your tattoos! You'll never look natural again!

FRIGHTEN ANIMALS AND CHILDREN
Whether you use **JUST FOR RODMAN®** to intimidate your neighbors, frighten children or sleep with Madonna, there's no denying that **JUST FOR RODMAN®** will get you the attention you crave! It's perfect for both rebounders and guys on the rebound! And hey, you may not get that mortgage loan, but you'll certainly be remembered at the bank!

JUST FOR RODMAN
Shampoo-In Haircolor
FLUORESCENT Conditioning Formula
Leprechaun Green

AS SEEN ON THE COVER OF MAD MAGAZINE!

Destroy Your Natural Looking Haircolor

From the World Leader In Technical Fouls

JUST FOR RODMAN®
Shampoo-In Haircolor
Leprechaun Green

ALSO AVAILABLE IN THESE BLINDING COLORS:

BASKETBALL ORANGE | BATMAN BLUE | BANANA YELLOW | CHALKY WHITE | CADILLAC PINK | FIRE TRUCK RED

A MAD AD

Sometimes an ad parody suggests itself from nothing more than a good pun, like this take on Just for Men hair-coloring products, featuring then-Chicago Bull Dennis Rodman, who had become famous for both his outrageous play and outrageous hairstyles. (He was also famous for bedding Madonna, but "Just for Man Whores" didn't seem like a strong enough play on words.)

MAD #353
January 1997
Artist: Bob Clarke
Writer: Butch D'Ambrosio

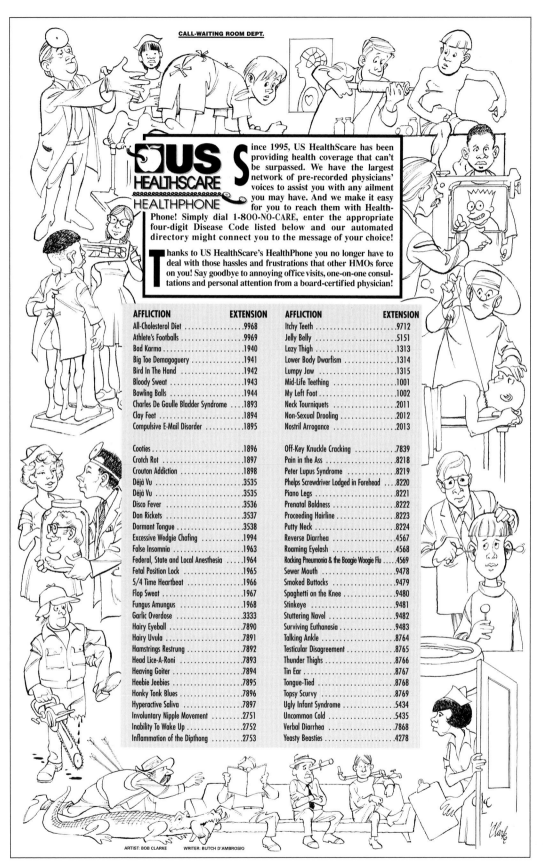

CALL-WAITING ROOM DEPT.

US HEALTHSCARE — HEALTHPHONE

Since 1995, US HealthScare has been providing health coverage that can't be surpassed. We have the largest network of pre-recorded physicians' voices to assist you with any ailment you may have. And we make it easy for you to reach them with Health-Phone! Simply dial 1-800-NO-CARE, enter the appropriate four-digit Disease Code listed below and our automated directory might connect you to the message of your choice!

Thanks to US HealthScare's HealthPhone you no longer have to deal with those hassles and frustrations that other HMOs force on you! Say goodbye to annoying office visits, one-on-one consultations and personal attention from a board-certified physician!

AFFLICTION	EXTENSION	AFFLICTION	EXTENSION
All-Cholesterol Diet	.9968	Itchy Teeth	.9712
Athlete's Footballs	.9969	Jelly Belly	.5151
Bad Karma	.1940	Lazy Thigh	.1313
Big Toe Demagoguery	.1941	Lower Body Dwarfism	.1314
Bird In The Hand	.1942	Lumpy Jaw	.1315
Bloody Sweat	.1943	Mid-Life Teething	.1001
Bowling Balls	.1944	My Left Foot	.1002
Charles De Gaulle Bladder Syndrome	.1893	Neck Tourniquets	.2011
Clay Feet	.1894	Non-Sexual Drooling	.2012
Compulsive E-Mail Disorder	.1895	Nostril Arrogance	.2013
Cooties	.1896	Off-Key Knuckle Cracking	.7839
Crotch Rot	.1897	Pain in the Ass	.8218
Crouton Addiction	.1898	Peter Lupus Syndrome	.8219
Déjà Vu	.3535	Phelps Screwdriver Lodged in Forehead	.8220
Déjà Vu	.3535	Piano Legs	.8221
Disco Fever	.3536	Prenatal Baldness	.8222
Don Rickets	.3537	Proceeding Hairline	.8223
Dormant Tongue	.3538	Putty Neck	.8224
Excessive Wedgie Chafing	.1994	Reverse Diarrhea	.4567
False Insomnia	.1963	Roaming Eyelash	.4568
Federal, State and Local Anesthesia	.1964	Rocking Pneumonia & the Boogie Woogie Flu	.4569
Fetal Position Lock	.1965	Sewer Mouth	.9478
5/4 Time Heartbeat	.1966	Smoked Buttocks	.9479
Flop Sweat	.1967	Spaghetti on the Knee	.9480
Fungus Amungus	.1968	Stinkeye	.9481
Garlic Overdose	.3333	Stuttering Navel	.9482
Hairy Eyeball	.7890	Surviving Euthanasia	.9483
Hairy Uvula	.7891	Talking Ankle	.8764
Hamstrings Restrung	.7892	Testicular Disagreement	.8765
Head Lice-A-Roni	.7893	Thunder Thighs	.8766
Heaving Goiter	.7894	Tin Ear	.8767
Heebie Jeebies	.7895	Tongue-Tied	.8768
Honky Tonk Blues	.7896	Topsy Scurvy	.8769
Hyperactive Saliva	.7897	Ugly Infant Syndrome	.5434
Involuntary Nipple Movement	.2751	Uncommon Cold	.5435
Inability To Wake Up	.2752	Verbal Diarrhea	.7868
Inflammation of the Dipthong	.2753	Yeasty Beasties	.4278

ARTIST: BOB CLARKE   WRITER: BUTCH D'AMBROSIO

MAD #354
February 1997
Photographer: Irving Schild
Writer: Dick DeBartolo

I CAN'T BREATHE!!

THANK YOU,
STOPPA-DA-SNEEZIN'® !

STOPPA-DA-SNEEZIN'®: *WHAT IT DOES*

*__*Stoppa-Da-Sneezin'*__® stops wheezing, coughing, snoring, crying, chafing, itching, burning, scratching, and, in some cases, breathing. It has not proven to be an effective remedy for sneezing.

*__*Stoppa-Da-Sneezin'*__® should not be used to treat ACUTE symptoms. It is mildly effective on very mild symptoms, and 100% effective on no symptoms.

***Success Rate:** More than 90% of the 2% that survived till the end of the controlled clinical study reported that they experienced something.

*42 patients were given __*Stoppa-Da-Sneezin'*__® and 42 patients were given a placebo. Some felt better and some didn't. Tests would have been more conclusive if we had kept track of who got the real pills and who got the placebo.

TOPPA-DA-SNEEZIN'®: *WHAT YOU NEED TO KNOW*

Before use: Check with your doctor and your pharmacist. Also, your pharmacist's doctor and your doctor's pharmacist. Boy, you'll be busy!

24-Hour Relief: Should occur over a 30-day period, averaging about 49 minutes of relief a day.

Drug Use and Dependence: There is no indication that ***Stoppa-Da-Sneezin'®*** is addictive or habit forming. Scientists in our marketing department are now working to try to correct that.

Stoppa-Da-Sneezin'® is not a substitute for other drugs. It IS however a substitute for MOP & GLO, Heavy Duty Lysol, WD-40 and Lo-Cal Cool Whip Topping.

This product is available ONLY by prescription. However some unscrupulous pharmacies have been known to sell it under the counter. For a list of unscrupulous pharmacies, please contact us.

STOPPA-DA-SNEEZIN'®: *IS IT RIGHT FOR YOU?*

Ask your doctor. If your doctor recommends ***Stoppa-Da-Sneezin'®***, begin immediately. If your doctor does not recommend our product, tell him to call our Doctor's Gift Incentive Program immediately.

This drug has been approved by the FDA (Fiendish Drug Administration).

Are there any side effects?

There are no known side effects, but your entire body may become numb, hot, cold, lukewarm and insensitive to pain. If you are able to drive nails into a cement wall with your forehead and not feel a stinging sensation, you might consider reducing the number of pills you're taking. **Body Shrinkage:** Fingernails and toenails may shrink and fall off. At the very least, they will become soft and may melt. Wear cheap socks while taking this drug. **Impairment of Fertility:** Studies with laboratory mice indicate no reduced sexual drive, therefore the patient should not experience any adverse reaction if he/she is sexually attracted to laboratory mice. **Adverse Reactions:** Nasal burning, bruising, irritation, redness, soreness, infection, and, in very few cases (less than 71%), complete blockage of oxygen to the brain. **Cardiovascular:** May cause heart to slow down, speed up, stop, reverse direction, palpitate, skip or relocate. In rare cases, heart will start to operate as a second liver. **Vision:** Blurry vision, watery eyes, conjunctivitis, peripheral edema and glaucoma can occur. If you experience temporary blindness while driving, pull over to the side of the road for a few minutes. If blindness persists, re-read product dosage instructions carefully. **Nervous System:** Paresthesia, confusion, hyperkinesia, hypertonia, vertigo and the desire to burrow underground and live in a hole are other possible side effects. Also Axolotl may occur. **Gastrointestinal:** Hysopedsia, abdominal pain, diarrhea, flatulence, constipation, vomiting, ulcerative stomatitis, aggravated tooth caries, gastritis, rectal hemorrhaging, hemorrhoids and melanoma may occur in "cry baby type" patients. **Hair:** May turn gray, curl, loosen, fall out, move, thicken, thin, recede or start growing on the inside of the scalp. Hair growing on the inside is not particularly harmful, but it will make shaving and haircuts slightly more difficult. **RHINITIS** and **IDIOPATHIC URTICARIA** can occur, but only people who know what these words mean need be concerned. **Blood Pressure:** This drug should not be taken by patients with high blood pressure or low blood pressure. Or normal blood pressure. There are no adverse effects for people with no blood pressure. **Dosage:** Two pills every four hours. If symptoms persist, try four pills every two hours. Don't take more than 48 pills in 181 hours 20 minutes, or at one time, unless of course ***Stoppa-Da-Sneezin'®*** is near the end of its shelf life and you have to use it up quickly. **Interaction with Food and Other Drugs:** For best results we recommend you do not eat 24 hours before, or 24 hours after taking ***Stoppa-Da-Sneezin'®***. If you are taking other drugs, triple the recommended dosage of ***Stoppa-Da-Sneezin'®*** so your body knows it's in there! **Explosion Hazard:** While recommended dosages are nonvolatile (in general), excessive use in a confined area near an open flame can result in a small explosion, estimated to be less than the equivalent of five sticks of dynamite, or 200 cherry bombs.

This is a brief copy of the side effects. For a copy of ALL the side effects, call 1-800-212-ACHOO and ask for publication SDS-a7, volumes 1 through 26.

STOPPA-DA-SNEEZIN'®

PHOTO: IRVING SCHILD   WRITER: DICK DEBARTOLO

MAD #355
March 1997
Writer: Dick DeBartolo

HERE'S EXCITING NEWS!!!

PSYCHIC FIENDS NETWORK®, the original psychic line that has helped more than 10 million obtain higher phone bills, is introducing the

SPECIAL PSYCHIC FIENDS PHONE HOTLINE

The Psychic Fiends Network® is a worldwide legend. By far the most successful and acclaimed psychic line not yet shut down by a government agency! More Americans turn

NOW YOU CAN SPEAK TO THE WORLD'S MOST TALKATIVE PSYCHICS...AND IT'S FREE!*

to the Psychic Fiends Network® than all other psychic, guidance or astrology lines combined. Every day we receive thousands of calls from everyday people — government workers, teachers, office workers — virtually anyone whose employer hasn't blocked their access to 1-900 numbers!

The second you call us, we'll start telling you things about yourself. Personal things, such as how gullible you are and how you need to get a life!

As we build your confidence and keep you on the phone longer and longer, we'll tell you life-shattering things, such as if you have an incurable disease, whether your mate is cheating on you, who might want to see you dead and when and if you'll be totally disfigured in a car crash. Of course, all of our life-shattering predictions are for AMUSEMENT PURPOSES ONLY!

WE'RE ALWAYS AS CLOSE AS YOUR TELEPHONE

We know you have concerns day and night, so we're here 24 hours a day, 7 days a week. You can call us as often as your credit card or long distance carrier allows!

"The ff-ff—irst t—ttt-hing ttthe psychic tt—tttold me, wwwaasssss ttthaatt I-I-I s-s-stuttered...a-and sshee ddddoesn't eeven k-k-know mmm-me! AA-AAA-Amazzing!"

NEED PROOF? READ ON!

Famous paid celebrities boast about our services. Our own spokespeople will tell you how wonderful Psychic Fiends Network® is! And Ms. Dionne Wartlick, our founder and single largest stockholder, is our biggest supporter! This respected recording artist is making more money with us than she ever did with her old, saccharine-sweet records.

Dozens of other successful celebrities have had their careers really take off since using the Psychics Fiends Hotline, including former stars of *The Love Boat* and *What's Happening!!* Of course, to mention

Washed-up recording star Ms. Dionne Wartlick had no future until she stumbled into the Psychic Fiends Network business.

them by name would mean we'd have to compensate them, and you don't have to be psychic to know we don't want to do that!

WHAT CAN I ASK ABOUT?

Ask about love, romance, career, job, health, money — hell, we don't even care if you ask about recipe shortcuts, lawn care tips or how to get that ugly stain out of your carpet. At $3.99 per minute, no subject is too difficult or trivial for our Master Psychics.

HOW DO I KNOW THE ADVICE I GET IS GOOD?

Because our Master Psychics don't make snap judgments or decisions! After you ask us something, we think, we mull, we confer, we contemplate, we ponder, we deliberate. Often our Master Psychics go into deep trances, which could last 10, 20, 30 minutes or longer. While attaining this higher plane of consciousness, it may sound like you are being put on hold, or that they are taking another call from someone else or have simply gone out on a lunch break. But don't be fooled and above all DON'T

CALL US NOW TOLL-FREE AT
1-800-FIENDS!

Be amazed at how fast we can switch you to our high toll 1-900 number!

HANG UP! We want to be sure you get the right information, and we don't care how long it takes.

(In order to call, you must be 18 years or older, or have access to a valid credit card that belongs to someone 18 years or older. Under 18, please pretend you are over 18 and we'll pretend we're not psychic and don't know your real age!)

Remember, this is a **FREE READING!** We'll read to you from the newspaper, *TV Guide*, maybe a phone book. But if you want psychic predictions, now you're talking money! **Call today!**

(*you pay just for the call, the words spoken are FREE!)

A MAD AD PARODY

MAD #359
July 1997
Writer: Dick DeBartolo

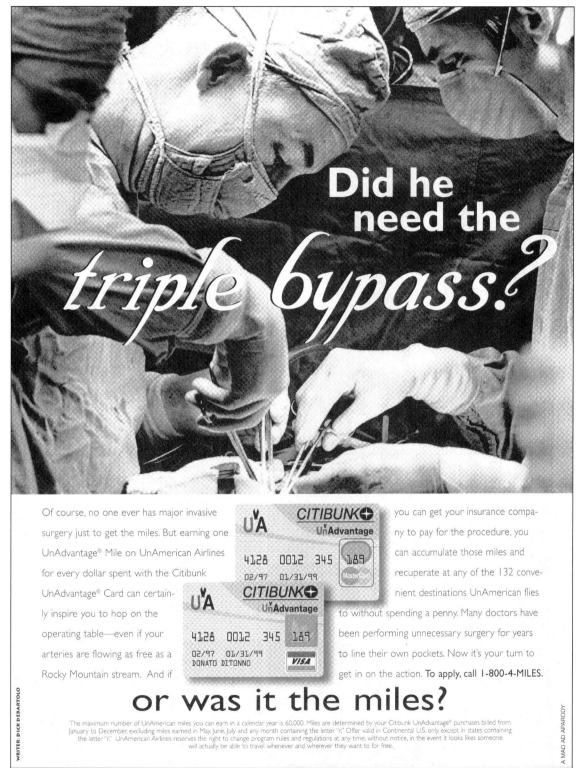

Did he need the *triple bypass?*

Of course, no one ever has major invasive surgery just to get the miles. But earning one UnAdvantage® Mile on UnAmerican Airlines for every dollar spent with the Citibunk UnAdvantage® Card can certainly inspire you to hop on the operating table—even if your arteries are flowing as free as a Rocky Mountain stream. And if you can get your insurance company to pay for the procedure, you can accumulate those miles and recuperate at any of the 132 convenient destinations UnAmerican flies to without spending a penny. Many doctors have been performing unnecessary surgery for years to line their own pockets. Now it's your turn to get in on the action. **To apply, call 1-800-4-MILES.**

or was it the miles?

The maximum number of UnAmerican miles you can earn in a calendar year is 60,000. Miles are determined by your Citibunk UnAdvantage® purchases billed from January to December, excluding miles earned in May, June, July and any month containing the letter "r." Offer valid in Continental U.S. only, except in states containing the letter "r." UnAmerican Airlines reserves the right to change program rules and regulations at any time, without notice, in the event it looks likes someone will actually be able to travel whenever and wherever they want to for free.

WRITER: DICK DEBARTOLO

A MAD AD APARODY

Once again, Dick DeBartolo followed the old writer's adage, "Write what you know," as Dick D is a notorious collector of airline frequent-flier miles. No word on whether or not Dick actually had elective surgery just to earn enough for a free first-class upgrade, but we wouldn't put it past him.

MAD #360
August 1997
Photographer: Albert
Crudo/ACA Studios
Writer: Scott Maiko

IKRAPPA®
CATALOGUE

SHÄRDDS
drinking glasses,
assorted
.... $3.00

TÖCSIK bowls,
set of four
.... $9.00

LEEKS vase
.... $17.00

TIPP
half-rocker
.... $119.00

**275 pages
of shoddy
merchandise
to give any
tastefully-
decorated
home the
look of
a rundown
college dorm**

IKRAPPA

1997

KÖLLAPPS table
.... $32.00

DÜNG incense,
assorted scents
(pig, goat, dog, ox)
.... $4.00

DÜNG INCENSE — Dog

DÜNG INCENSE — Ox — Goat

You don't have to sacrifice value for quality at IKRAPPA®.

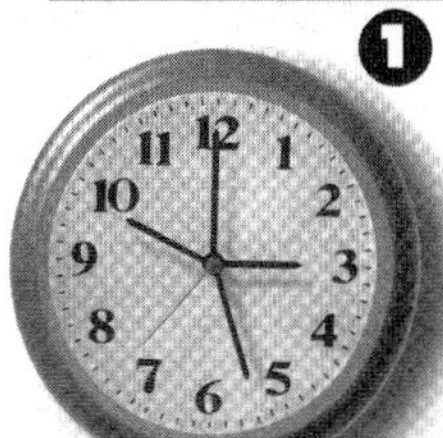

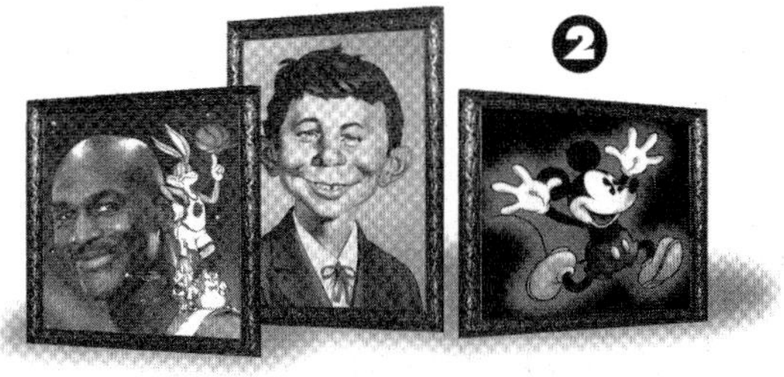

You don't have to sacrifice quality for value, either.

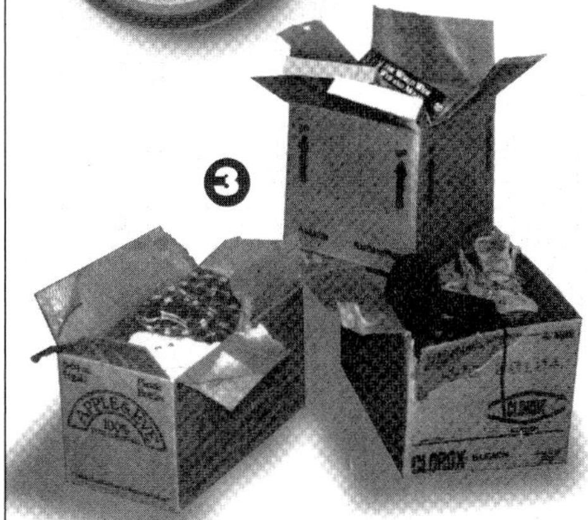

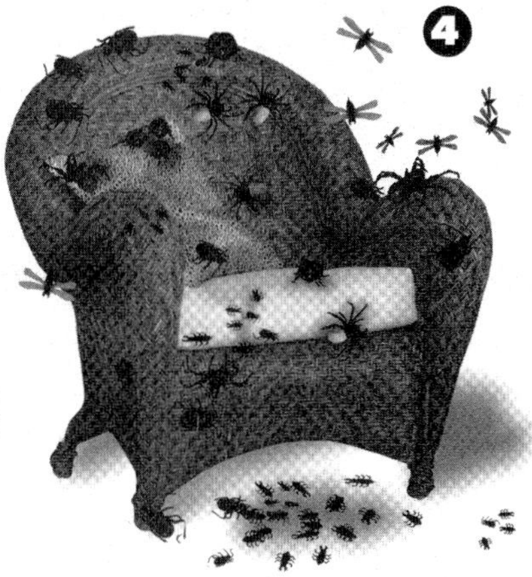

1. RÖNG clock, **$14**
Telling time is an exciting challenge, thanks to the exclusive four-hand design of our unique wall clock!

2. ÜNLYSINSD framed posters, assorted designs, **$12**
Velvet painters from around the world have created these handsome, mass-produced prints that just might remind you of your favorite artist.

3. DÜMSTIR boxes, assorted sizes, **$7**
Organizing is a cinch with these storage boxes gathered from Sweden's famous alleyways. They're not used — they're "broken in."

4. NESST chair, **$32**
Casual Swedish design meets imported South American wicker in these fantastic chairs. Perfect for indoor or outdoor use!

Because we've already sacrificed them both — and slaughtered elegance, durability, and style as well.

Satisfy your non-conforming tastes with something unique – designs available only at **IKRAPPA**®! We made them just for you...

...and the thousands of other people who can't afford to shop at a *real* furniture store, either.

IKRAPPA

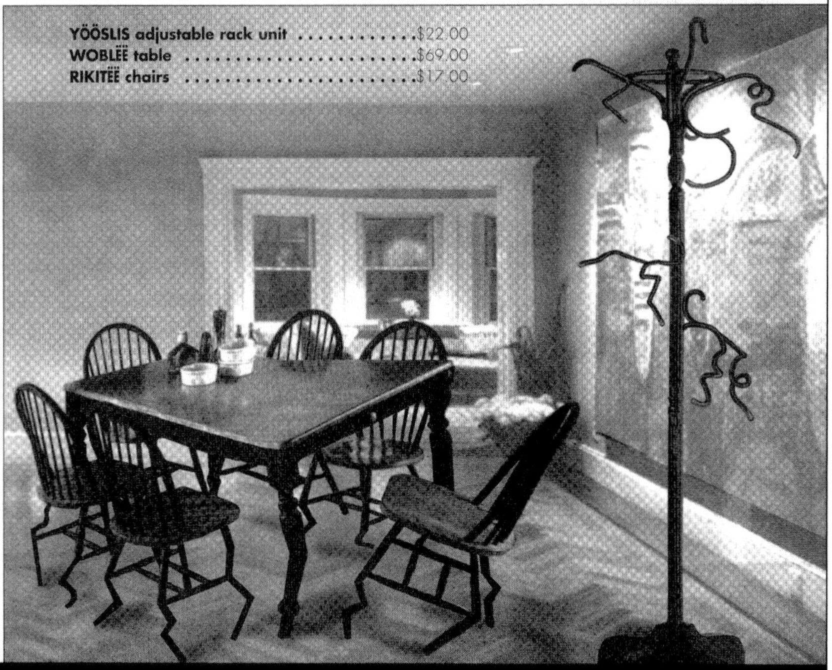

YÖÖSLIS adjustable rack unit $22.00
WOBLËË table $69.00
RIKITËË chairs $17.00

MAD #363
November 1997
Photographer: Irving Schild
Writers: David Shayne and
Joe Raiola

Just as it was promoting its new line of sweat-wicking clothing, Nike was doing a little perspiring of its own after media reports surfaced that the company used low-paid child workers in overseas factories to manufacture its apparel.

Somehow, photographer Irving Schild and senior editor Joe Raiola convinced a small Chinatown "factory" (read: sweatshop) to allow them to bring in a camera and a child model (who, given *MAD*'s penchant for cheapness, probably wasn't paid all that well, either) for this photo shoot.

The Day Sports Endorsements Went Too Far
TIGER WOODS AT THE PGA CHAMPIONSHIP

ARTIST: MORT DRUCKER WRITER: JOHN CALDWELL

MAD #361
September 1997
Artist: Mort Drucker
Writer: John Caldwell

NEW!!! FROM NORDIC TRAP!!!

THE TOTALLY AMAZING
AB TERRORIZER!!!™

You can have incredible ABS with JUST ONE REP PER DAY!!!
You read that right! Just one rep per day! That's because the patented granite headrest on each and every AB Terrorizer weighs an incredible 786 pounds!

What makes this incredible progress possible?

The AB Terrorizer is a phenomenal combination of weights, pulleys, leverage and advertising hype!

Isn't it difficult to do even one rep with a 786 pound headrest?

Normally, it would be very difficult. But because of the precision tooling and geometrically sound leverage pivot points of the AB Terrorizer, the 786 pounds is no more difficult to lift than a small Buick of equal weight!

Does the AB Terrorizer come with any guarantee?

Absolutely! We guarantee that the AB Terrorizer is the last piece of exercise equipment you will ever buy! That's because once you receive and examine firsthand this phenomenal piece of engineering, we're sure you will have learned your lesson to never again fall prey to the phenomenally ridiculous claims made by mail-order exercise equipment manufacturers!

The complete AB Terrorizer is only $249.95! There are no hidden extras! Your AB Terrorizer is available for pickup at either of our two convenient warehouse locations in Kowloon Peninsula, Hong Kong or Krakow, Poland. Should you wish delivery to your home, the AB Terrorizer is still only $249.95, plus $2,374.85 freight, handling and bubble wrap. For even faster service call 1-800-HERNIA!

"I went from this... ...to this — in seven — yes, just seven reps!!!" *

*Seven reps, done in conjunction with a daily regimen of running, rollerblading, wrestling, mountain climbing, liquid diet, yoga, aerobics, swimming, hiking, cross country skiing, sit ups, push ups, liposuction, chin ups, vitamins, food supplements, a round-the-clock personal trainer and a professional air brush artist.

USE THIS MONEY SPENDING COUPON RIGHT NOW!!!

Yes! Rush me my AB Terrorizer right away! I understand that if for any reason I am unhappy or not completely satisfied, Nordic Trap guarantees to feel phenomenally sympathetic for my disappointment without being required to refund the purchase price or assume any other responsibility whatsoever. This same sympathy clause applies to Nordic Trap's exclusive iron-clad warranty should my AB Terrorizer ever break down or malfunction in any way.

Name:
Address:
City/State:
ZIP

Mail to: Ab Terrorizer
T Reps Drive
Dubious Claims, Nebraska
68504

Before you start any exercise program, consult a doctor. Before bringing an AB Terrorizer into your home, consult a structural engineer.

PHOTOGRAPHER: IRVING SCHILD   WRITER: DICK DEBARTOLO

MAD #363
November 1997
Photographer: Irving Schild
Writer: Dick DeBartolo

MAD #365
January 1998
Photographer: Irving Schild
Writer: Dick DeBartolo

FORGET FOUL-TASTING GUM!
FORGET EXPENSIVE HYPNOSIS!
NIC-O-STOP® IS THE ONLY PRODUCT THAT GUARANTEES YOU'LL STOP SMOKING IMMEDIATELY!
NO IFS, ANDS OR BUTTS!

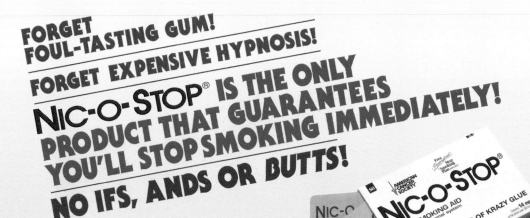

Stop Your Nicotine Cravings…Permanently!

The Nic-O-Stop® Patch is all you need to insure that a cigarette never touches your hopelessly-addicted, nicotine-craving lips again! Unlike inconvenient arm and ear patches which require repeated use and often fail, you apply the revolutionary Nic-O-Stop® Patch only once — over your entire mouth! And thanks to its unique combination of space age kevlar and hi-tech adhesives, you won't be removing the Nic-O-Stop® Patch any time soon!

"Mmmmph mmffmp! Fmmphfm mmmmph!" — Sylvia Mangojello
Translation: *"Thanks to Nic-O-Stop® I don't smoke anymore! Now please get this thing off me, I'm having trouble breathing."*

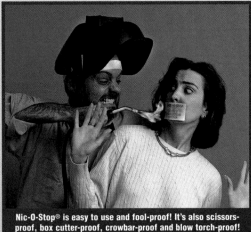

Nic-O-Stop® is easy to use and fool-proof! It's also scissors-proof, box cutter-proof, crowbar-proof and blow torch-proof!

Clinically Tested And Proven To:

- Stop Smoking!
- Stop Nail-Biting!
- Stop Bad Breath!
- Stop Flossing!
- Stop Talking!
- Stop Eating!

Even this sword, which is the logo of the

AMERICAN CANCER SOCIETY

can't remove the Nic-O-Stop® Patch.

Finally, an effective way to stop smoking without gaining weight!

By just wearing the Nic-O-Stop® Patch you could easily drop 50, 60, even 70 pounds! And believe us, you won't have the time or energy to worry about your stupid little tobacco cravings after you've gone a few weeks without eating!

NIC-O-STOP®
The power to **Calm.**
The power to **Comfort.**
The power to **Kill.**

A MAD AD PARODY

This tiny type is to inform you that any wild claims printed above in big type are hereby disclaimed! Furthermore, you should be aware that Smyth-Clam-Reachem is a drug company with deep pockets and a huge team of high-powered, highly-paid lawyers who could drain your bank account dry should you even THINK about taking us to court for any reason! So there.

MAD #366
February 1998
Photographer: Irving Schild
Writer: J. Prete

HOW TO TALK TO YOUR KIDS ABOUT DRUGS.

Talking to your kids about drugs. It's probably one of the most difficult tasks that parents face today. But it's a job that must be done.

The best thing about the subject is that you don't have to do it well. You simply have to try. Your kids probably don't expect much from you anyway, given how badly your talk about sex with them went. But that's another matter and it's in the past. This is your chance to gain back a shred of the trust and respect you lost in their eyes after that debacle.

ACCEPT REBELLION.

At the heart of it, drugs, alcohol, wild hairstyles, ear-splitting music and the like is teenage rebellion – your child's way of telling you that they hate you, your lifestyle, your friends and all the values that you hold in high esteem and have worked your entire life to achieve. This is a good thing. If teenagers are to develop any sense of self worth and superiority, there is no one better or more convenient for them to look upon with disdain and contempt than their parents.

You rebelled. They're rebelling. Problem is, you did it much more intensely and recklessly than your kids would ever dream of doing it. Which is why you have no credibility discussing topics like drugs with your kids and why they hate you so, frequently laughing at you and mocking you behind your back.

But, like we said, you have to have this talk with them about drugs so you might as well just get on with it.

DON'T GET DISCOURAGED.

When you talk to your kids about drugs, you may think nothing is getting through to them. And you're probably right. But keep at it anyway. Nag incessantly if you have to. Your parents did it to you and now's your chance to do it to your kids and to continue this disturbing family tradition.

Sometimes it can be very awkward getting started. Most parents rarely talk to their children, and when they do it's usually about something very superficial and unimportant, like what time the mall closes or missing money from a wallet or pocketbook. To get the ball rolling, try rehearsing the conversation with your spouse beforehand. Many parents have written to tell us they found this technique very helpful. Many more parents have written to say they found a tequila shot or two right before confronting the child to be even more helpful.

START ANYWHERE.

However you get started is up to you. But what you say and how you say it is extremely important if your conversation with your child is to be effective.

"Do you know about any of your friends or classmates doing drugs?"

"What kind of drugs?"

"Do you know where they usually buy them and how much the dealer charges?"

"How could mommy or daddy get in touch with this dealer?"

SOME DO'S AND DON'TS.

Most psychologists say what's most important when speaking to your child is that you speak from the heart. That's crap. Society's been listening to these eggheads for years and things haven't gotten one bit better. And besides, if most parents told their kid what's really in their hearts, the kid would run out of the room screaming and be horribly, emotionally scarred for the rest of their life. Where do you think serial killers and ax murderers come from, anyway?

No, it's better if you do as little talking as possible. There's less chance to screw up and it puts more of the burden on the defensive child.

The dialogue should be open and frank. Ask your child his or her opinion about drugs. Express to your child your fears and concerns. Share with your child what it was like when you were a teen growing up, though here it's probably best if you leave out or deny any experimenting you may have had with marijuana, cocaine, hallucinogenic mushrooms, LSD and heroin.

Also, consider leaving out or denying any stories about your being expelled from school, any Grateful Dead concerts you may have gone to, waking up in a bus terminal in a pool of your own vomit, drug-related traffic accidents in which one or more of your classmates or friends were killed with you behind the wheel and that whole seven-year Colombian "vacation" you took.

Above all, be honest.

We know it isn't easy, especially with your short-term memory problem. But it's important that you try. That your child knows how you feel.

And it's probably best if, when you speak to your child, you don't do it when you're stoned.

For more information about how to talk to your kids about drugs, ask for our free book, "Do As I Say, Don't Do As I Did." Call 1-800-HIPPOCRIT.

PARTNERSHIP FOR A DRUGGED-OUT AMERICA

A MAD AD PARODY

Get 11 CDs for 1¢

when you buy 10 more at club prices! it's like getting 21 albums for the price of 57!

Jewelio
GREATEST HITS

(Columpia) 137.463

Here's How to Join: First, lock yourself in your room. That way no one will be able to tell you how bad CD clubs are and talk you out of becoming a member. Next, choose any 11 selections from the list of forgettable albums on this page and send us a check or money order for one measly penny (Do NOT send cash). In exchange, we will force you to buy 10 more bad-selling CDs at regular club prices which are currently $20.98 to $99.98★ – plus shipping and handling.

Convenient Home Shopping: Every month we choose a CD which no one has ordered in the last few years to be our "selection of the month." If you want the "selection of the month," do nothing. It will be sent to you automatically. If you don't want the "selection of the month," too bad! We'll send it to you anyway and you'll have to go through the trouble and expense of returning it. When we receive it back we'll make it our *next* "selection of the month" and send it to you again– and we'll keep doing this until you finally break down and buy it!

Dionne Warwick–That's What Psychic Friends Are For (Lowtown) 108.787

Bruce Springsteen–Poor Selling Acoustic Album (Columpia) 257.279

PAUL SIMON
SONGS THAT HAVE SINCE BEEN CUT FROM THE CAPEMAN

Paul Simon–Songs That Have Since Been Cut From The Capeman (Reekodisc) 121.178

Children Of A Joe Besser God –Orig. Sndtrk. (Epicch) 487.249

LeAnn Rimes–Country Jailbait (Polydork) 139.774

The Allman Brothers–Best of the Heroin Years (1969-1972) (Polydork) 430.439

The Allman Brothers–Best of the Methadone Years (1972-1976) (Polydork) 430.440

Sarah McLachlan–Fumbling Towards Obscurity (Goofen) 384.636

Bob Dylan–Positively Incoherent (Columpia) 126.037

The Black Crowes, Counting Crows And Sheryl Crow–Crow Your Own Way (Crowlumbia) 462.192

Michael Jackson–The White Album (Epicch) 132.126

Nirvana–Smells Like Kurt's Decaying Remains (Goofen) 127.050

Willie Nelson–Old And Scuzzy (A&P) 460.972

Puff Daddy–Songs I've Stolen (Def Ham) 110.650

The Go-Go's–Gone Gone (Reekodisc) 485.755

Snoop Doggy Dogg–Neutered (Death Roast) 465.955

Whitney Houston–I Will Always Irritate You (Lowtown) 136.028

Various Artists–Musicians For The Destruction Of Walden Pond (Warper Bros.) 141.267

Barbra Streisand and Sting–Dueling Egos (A&P) 113.555

Styx–Sux (Swill) 152.124

Tupac Shakur–Dead Man Rapping (Death Roast) 121.871

Kathie Lee Gifford–Sweatshop Favorites (Goofen) 139.774

Not Quite As Good As Ezra (Swill) 122.960

Alex Trebek–Sings That Song They Play During Final Jeopardy (Crapitol) 134.932

Tom Petty and Johnny Cash –The Petty Cash Tour (Warper Bros.) 110.155

ABBA–Live at the Palindrome Theater (Epicch) 139.113

Luciano Pavarotti
The Songs of Dom Deluise

Luciano Pavarotti–The Songs of Dom Deluise (Fatlantic) 136.010

The Notorious R.I.P. (Death Roast) 112.714

Van Halen–Who The Hell Is Their Singer Now?? (Warper Bros.) 110.866

Elton John–Don't Shoot Me I'm Not Gianni Versace (Polydork) 122.184

Barney
Sings Marilyn Manson
WARNING! Explicit Kiddie Lyrics

Barney–Sings Marilyn Manson (Maverecch) 129.486

–The Artist Formerly Known as Prince (Warper Bros.) 136.846

–The Artist Formerly Known as (Warper Bros.) 337.857

–The Artist Formerly Known as (Warper Bros.) 290.916

Free Magazine: **Join now and we'll send you ou exclusive full-color magazine jam packed wit threats of the legal action we'll take should yo fail to fulfill your enrollment agreement. You' also get these other exciting benefits: Hassle with the post office...Years of aggravation an inconvenience... Bewilderment as to why yo ever became a music fan!**

Special bonus: No matter what you've read in this ad so far, you'll be required to buy at least 8 more CDs than we've led you to believe. 8 CDs!

Free 10-day no-risk offer: Actually, there is no free 10-day no-risk offer, but we wanted those words to appear in this ad somewhere.

Just imagine: CDs you could buy much cheaper in any store, shipped right to your front door in damaged condition. What could be more convenient? **Join today!**

A FREE T-SHIRT WITH MEMBERSHIP!
COLUMPIA HOUSE

T-Shirt shown actual

RUSH ME THESE 11 CDs RIGHT NOW!

Yes! I'm a glutton for punishment. Please accept my membership in the Columpia House CD Club. I agree to the confusing terms outlined in this ad and will buy as many CDs as you want me to for as long as I live. I am fully aware that I am trapped and will never get out of this club. I am your slave.

THE MUSIC I LIKE MOST IS: (CHECK ONLY ONE)

❑ Danish Funeral Marches ❑ Midget Hip Hop ❑ Songs Heard When You're On Hold

❑ Mr. ❑ Mrs. ❑ Ms.________________________
(PLEASE PRINT) First Last

Address________________________

City____________ State______ Zip______

Do you have a telephone? (Don't lie and say no.) YES____ NO____

Write in your number so we may sell it to aggressive and rude telemarketers. (_____)_____-______

★CDs that are playable on audio equipment sold in the United States may cost more. We hope you don't read this. That's why it's in such small print at the bottom of the page.

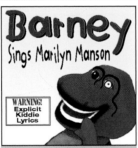

MAD #368
April 1998
Photographer: Irving Schild
Writer: David Shayne

MAD #368
April 1998
Photographer: Irving Schild
Writer: Scott Brooks

◀ *MAD* **Pop-Off Videos**
May 1998
Writers: Charlie Kadau
and Joe Raiola

MAD #370
June 1998
Writer: J.Prete

A MAN'S GUIDE *to not buying into* DIAMONDS

ARE YOU *one of the* TWO MILLION victims of ENGAGEMENT RING AD anxiety?

1. Relax. Most guys don't know about this stuff and that's exactly what the diamond industry is counting on when they run "friendly" ads like this one.

2. But you could be easily duped, so read on.

3. Spend wisely. It's tricky because, just like no two diamonds are alike, no two appraisals for the same diamond are alike. DeBores has over 100 years' experience in over-valuing diamonds and then mining the wallets of unsuspecting customers. They sort rough diamonds into over 5,000 grades before they go on to be cut, polished and endlessly marked up. So you're never quite sure exactly what you're buying.

4. Learn the jargon. Not that 4*C's "Cut, Color, Clarity* and *Carat weight."* That's *Crap.* Before stepping into any jewelry store, learn the 4*H's. How much? How come* you keep showing me rings I told you I can't afford? *How come*, if the ring is "appraised" at $5,000, you're willing to sell it to me for half that amount? *How much* will you give me for the ring if this engagement blows up in my face and I want to resell it back to you?

5. Determine your price range. Most industry-sponsored ads suggest the *two months' salary guideline.* Spend less, they say, and the relatives will talk. Spend more, and they'll rave. Spend the next ten years of your life paying off the damn thing and you'll be miserable, broke and resentful.

6. Watch her as you browse. But whatever you do, don't take your fiancée with you when you're prepared to buy! Women have been thinking, dreaming and scheming about a diamond from the first moment they drew breath on God's green Earth. What they want and what you can afford are always miles apart. In the months leading up to the purchase, continually cry poverty to her. That way she will be surprised and cherish the fact that you sprung for any ring at all.

7. Find a reputable jeweler. Good luck! And while you're at it, maybe you can help O.J. find the "real killer"! Once you've found a jeweler, ask questions like, "If you say you make 'almost nothing' on a ring sale, how can you afford to wear $3,000 Armani suits and drive a Mercedes?"

8. *Learn more.* Ask whether any of your wiseass friends have an uncle in the business who can get you "the exact same ring, GUAR-UN-TEED, for half of what you paid," *before* you buy.

9. Finally, think romance. Chances are if you don't break down and give her a ring, she's going to cut you off. So buying a diamond is an important occasion in your relationship. No ring, no sex. *Besides, it's not like you had anything important to do with two months' salary!*

Diamond Misinformation Center
Sponsored by DeBores Conspiring Mines, Ltd.,

A diamond is an error.
DeBores

HEAR THE RADIO THAT WOKE UP AN ENTIRE INDUSTRY*

*To the fact that there are idiots out there willing to spend hundreds of dollars just for a radio!

Popular Audio wrote that it is "a sonic masterpiece." *Radio Magazine* wrote that it is "simply amazing...a genuine break-through in sound quality!" And *High Fidelity* wrote, "Sorry, but you'll have to take thousands of dollars in advertising in *our* magazine like you did in *Popular Audio* and *Radio Magazine* before we'll write hyped-up copy about how great your radio is." What radio are they all talking about? The Boose® Wavy radio.

HALF A MILLION PEOPLE ALREADY OWN THE BOOSE® WAVY RADIO.

In just over three years, the Wavy radio has changed the way half a million people listen to music — people like Stanley Karpinski of Staten Island, NY, who said, "It's changed the way I listen to music. I stopped listening to CDs and audiocassettes! I had to! The Wavy won't play them. It's just a damn radio!"

OUR EXCLUSIVE, AWARD-WINNING DESIGN

The secret to the Wavy radio's remark-able success lies in an exclusive, award-winning design. Our experts spent countless hours designing sleek, elegant ads for the Wavy radio, resulting in a remarkably suc-cessful ad cam-paign that has won numerous awards for its design. The actual design of the radio itself

Open up a Wavy radio and you'll see our exclusive acoustic wavyguide speaker technology. You'll also immediately void our 30-day money back guarantee.

was a piece of cake, using the same technology found in a $9 K-Mart clock radio. The Wavy radio measures just 4 1/2" x 14" x 8 1/4" x 10"x 22 1/8" x 9". It comes with a credit card-sized remote control that will easily slip between the tightest of sofa cush-ions never to be seen again, six AM/FM pre-set buttons that have been perma-nently set at the factory to our favorite stations for your convenience, and dual alarms which can be heard up to five miles away. Is it any wonder that people who weren't smart enough to buy a stereo system with a CD player, AM/FM radio, dual cassette deck, graphic equalizer and detachable speakers (for half the price that our product costs) are now stuck using the Boose® Wavy as their primary stereo system?

This miniature remote control was last forever right after this photo was taken.

EVEN OUR IN-HOME TRIAL SOUNDS GREAT.

Order a Wavy radio today and take advantage of our risk-free, in-home trial. If after 30 days, you aren't con-vinced that this is the best sounding radio you've ever heard, simply return the radio to us in its original unopened carton for a full refund. No questions asked! That's right! You have our 100% guarantee that our in-home trial sounds great, providing you don't go back and reread this last paragraph for finely-crafted legal loopholes.

CALL TODAY AND MAKE SIX INTEREST-FREE PAYMENTS.

The Wavy radio is available for $349 direct from Boose®, one of the leading names in high fidelity equipment manu-facturers when listed alphabetically. And now our six-month installment payment plan lets you make six monthly payments interest free when you agree to our exclusive seventh payment of all interest! Call today and hear more about the product that has consumer groups and state attorneys general talking.

CALL BY NOVEMBER 1, 1998
and ask our operators about
FREE SHIPPING
and why we don't offer it.

CALL 1-800-BAMBOOZLED EXT. R2D2

When you call, ask about our six-month installment payment plan. (Qualifications based on a sworn affidavit that you own a valid credit card and that your call is not being traced or recorded by law enforcement officials.) Also ask about FedEx® delivery service and how it differs from the third rate carrier we'll be using to ship your radio.

Please specify your color choice:
☐ Barry White ☐ Earl Gray

Mr./Mrs./Ms.

Name _____ (Please Do Not Print)

Address

City _____ State _____ Zip

Morning Phone

Afternoon Phone

Late Afternoon Phone

Evening Phone

(No Salesman will call.)

Mail to Boose® Corporation, Dept. NOCD-RU-NUTS
The Compound on The Mountain, FramedAgain, MA 00019

BOOSE®
Better sounding ads through research®

A MAD AD PARODY

True story: Writer J. Prete was so incensed by the thought of a radio costing $349 that when he received his paycheck for writing this piece, he promptly went out and bought one.

MAD #371
July 1998
Writer: Dick DeBartolo

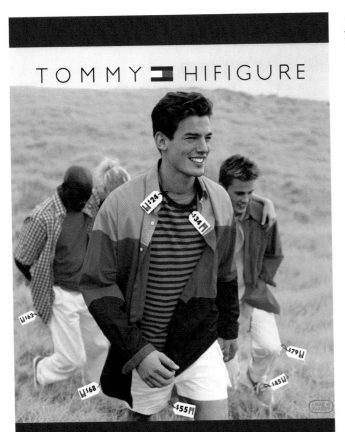

When Dick DeBartolo pitched his idea for a "Tommy Hifigure" ad, he figured they would have to restage the original ad. But co-editor John Ficarra had a better idea—put the price tags right on the actual Tommy Hilfiger photo, which *MAD*'s lawyers determined would be legal under fair-use laws.

MAD #372
August 1998
Artist: James Kirkland
Writers: Joe Raiola and
David Shayne

Believe it or not, as of press time some guy in Westbury, NY, has since registered the address *www.badcrash.com*. We're not sure we want to know what he wants to use it for.

Call toll free **1-800-WESUCK** ext.R2D2

☐ Yes, I want a home clean of all clutter and debris. Despite this, I'm mailing in this coupon asking you to deluge me with Orwreck sales literature. I understand you will keep sending me stacks of misleading brochures until I can't take it anymore and agree to buy an Orwreck XL. I also understand you will include details of Orwreck's exorbitant 12-MONTH PAYMENT PLAN, in which I have NO INTEREST WHATSOEVER!

☐ No! Forget the stupid sales literature! I've already bought the Orwreck XL and completely destroyed my home and all of my possessions. Please send me information immediately on how I can shut the damn thing off!

Name_____ Address_____

City_____ State_____ Zip_____

Phone (_____)_____ Most Inconvenient Time for Salesman to Call_____

ORWRECK

Nothing sucks more than an Orwreck.
1000 Attachments Road, New Orleans, MA 10301

SAND, CAT HAIRS, EVEN A FIVE-PIECE SECTIONAL SOFA— NOTHING ESCAPES MY 8-POUND ORWRECK XL.

The world's most powerful vacuum. With its brushes revolving at 65,000,000 rpm, the Orwreck XL is the most uncontrollable machine to have ever skated by the Product Safety Commission. It will dislodge embedded dirt, sand hardwood floors, gouge concrete surfaces, rip up an asphalt driveway and remove tattoos and facial hair — whether you want it to or not!

Our exclusive Filter System. If you're an allergy sufferer, say goodbye to cat and dog hairs. In fact, say goodbye to your cat and dog! Golden Retrievers, Pit Bulls, even a Shetland Pony, no living creature is too big or fast for the Orwreck XL.

It's the lightest full-size vacuum available. The Orwreck XL weighs just 8 pounds, so lugging it to the repair shop every month or so is a breeze! Best of all, every Orwreck XL comes with a Universal Attachment Nozzle which fits many of those novelty suction devices usually advertised in the back of men's magazines.

The choice of professionals everywhere. The Orwreck XL is already the favorite vacuum of mortuary attendants, unlicensed asbestos removers and illegally hired hotel maids who fear loss of their job if they don't say what we tell them to say. Now this same vacuum can be yours, thanks to this amazing offer and the circumventing of Federal laws banning the sale of highly dangerous and untested machinery.

Free Super Compact Canister. The same 4-pound Suck-Master you've seen on TV for a split second before hitting the remote! It's so powerful, it will lift a bowling ball!* And the Suck-Master is yours free when you purchase the Orwreck XL and completely suspend all notion of hidden costs and good consumer common sense.

Take the Orwreck Challenge. Try the Orwreck XL risk free. If after 15 days, your floors are not completely free of all dirt, carpeting, pets, and toddlers, just return it. Simply pay us what we say you owe us and you'll never hear from us again!

TAKE THE **ORWRECK** CHALLENGE ™

FREE GIFT

*Individual bowling scores may vary. Manufacturer assumes no responsibility for 7-10 splits. Consult your local bowling league for rules and restrictions. Bowling shoes not included.

ARTIST: HERMANN MEJIA   WRITER: J. PRETE

A MAD AD PARODY

MAD #377
January 1999
Photographer: Irving Schild
Writer: J. Prete

You're a group of Christian-based, conservative organizations with several million dollars to spend. Do you: feed the hungry? Clothe the poor? Don't be so naive! You blow the millions on a series of slickly-worded, logic-bending ads espousing a widely-discredited theory that one can be "cured" of homosexuality through counseling and prayer. What we pray is that somebody would spend millions to run *this* ad.

A NEWSPAPER AD WE'D LIKE TO SEE

I'm living proof that Untruths can win you votes.

"Recently, several prominent right-wing politicians like Gary Bauer and Trent Lott have spoken out against homosexuality...likening it to kleptomania and calling it a sin. When I was a homophobe, I liked hearing stuff like that...until I realized that homosexuals are God's children too...and that politicians were just playing on my fears and ignorance to trick me into voting for them."

One boy's joke and the making of a homophobe.

"I was nine years old when a teenage boy first made a joke about someone who was gay. Something about a gay waiter and rice pudding. I didn't get it, but I laughed anyway. It made me feel cool, like one of the guys. And as I grew, I continued to laugh at these jokes, even though I suspected they were wrong. Saddest of all, I heard my parents and their friends making the same kind of dumb jokes, usually about some guy named Liberace."

Being a decent man became a mystery.

"By the time I hit my teens I was macho...my heart cold, my brain dead. I believed being "macho" meant picking on the sensitive and vulnerable...so mistreating gays felt right. I had so thoroughly rejected my own decency that I found myself hanging out on street corners with other guys, looking to taunt and beat up anyone we suspected of being a homosexual. On nights when we couldn't find any, we took turns acting gay and beating up each other."

There's a phallic-shaped hole in many people's head.

"My homophobia really blossomed in college, and I quickly joined a campus anti-gay/lesbian group. But it was in the course of those meetings that I realized I was morally bankrupt — and not just because we had beer and hookers at the meetings. While I longed to be "one of the guys," I knew gay bashing just wasn't right. That's when I went home and prayed, *"God, please help me to understand why I keep acting like a freakin' moron."*

Knock and He'll answer. (Unless you're an Amway salesman.)

"Change didn't come overnight. Within six months I'd made a firm decision to forsake homophobia, though I still had a strong desire to laugh at jokes and snickering references about Richard Simmons. Even though I filled my days with Christian activity, I fell back into hanging around with the same old homophobic crowd. Only now the Richard Simmons jokes were replaced with George Michael jokes. The pain inside me was intense as I spiraled down an

Thousands of people like these paid models have been repulsed by extremist ads which bash gays and attempt to impose "morality" on others. Throughout the U.S., many people are working to combat this intolerance. Most, however, are typical Americans and don't give a damn one way or the other.

ugly, dark road of mental and emotional instability, culminating in the Fall elections when I voted Republican — *straight* Republican, if you know what I mean."

Once God answers He never hangs up. Though He may put you on hold.

"I knew I was running from God, and one day I just put it to Him: 'Lord, I don't want to be an A-hole my whole life. I need you to help me.' Shortly after that prayer, I met an enlightened man, a *former homophobe*, who listened to my story and led me to a group of average American people. People who understand that we must have tolerance and understanding of others, despite what all the pandering politicians were saying on TV and in slick newspaper ads. This is what America is all about. A homophobe no more, I was finally on the road to sanity."

Changing hearts. Changing political parties.

"Leaving homophobia was the hardest thing I've ever had to do. I finally saw the perverse patterns of my insensitivity and came to understand the underlying fears that had sparked my stupid behavior. As my knowledge grew, I knew I was changed forever. Gone were the words *faggot, homo, queer* and *rump-wrangler* from my vocabulary. More importantly, gone was my tolerance for those who claim to speak in the name of God for their own personal wealth and gain.

There is another way out. Trent, Newt, are you listening?

"Please, if you, a friend or politician you know is struggling with homophobia, show them this story. Remind them that God made man in His image — gays included! Are we now saying that He goofed? People should be judged by their actions and deeds, not their sexual preference. And that's a truth you'll never hear from a sleazy politician bottom-fishing for votes or a self-appointed political opportunist masquerading under the pretense of doing God's work.

If you really love your fellow man, it doesn't matter if he's gay. And that's the truth.

In the public interest, this message was paid for by the following organizations, representing millions of average Americans.

- Citizens Who Think Trent Lott and Company are Full of Crap
- The Council of Americans Who Have Actually Read the Constitution
- Federation of Clergymen Against Using God's Name to Further a Political Agenda
- Alliance Against Gary Bauer and Other Intolerant Little Twerps
- Organization of NFL Fans Who Think Reggie White Suffered Some Sort of Head Injury or Why Else Would He Be Acting Like That, Inc.

WRITER: J. PRETE
PHOTOGRAPHER: IRVING SCHILD

Since 1999 *MAD* has run the *MAD* 20, a special section in its January issue honoring the dumbest people, events, and things of the prior year. When a coalition of conservative organizations released a series of ads suggesting that homosexuality could be "cured" through religion, writer J. Prete knew he had comedic gold.

This "Newspaper Ad We'd Like to See" takes the original ad's text and flips it on its head word for word, with headlines like, "Once God answers He never hangs up," becoming "Once God answers He never hangs up. Though he may put you on hold."

The group shot of the *MAD* staff and their families (above) was taken by Irving Schild during a gathering at John Ficarra's house for managing editor Annie Gaines's baby shower. Ironically, Annie, the widow of publisher Bill Gaines, wasn't there because she had prematurely gone into labor just hours before the party began.

Since we only have 224 pages in this book, we won't list everyone in the photo, but you can write the author in care of the publisher to request a complete list. (You won't get one, but you can still write.)

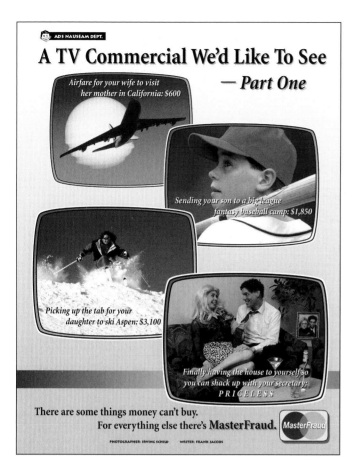

MAD #384
August 1999
Photographer: Irving Schild
Writer: Frank Jacobs

MAD #384
August 1999
Photographer: Irving Schild
Writer: Frank Jacobs

MAD #385
September 1999
Photographer: AP/Wide
World Photos
Writer: David Shayne

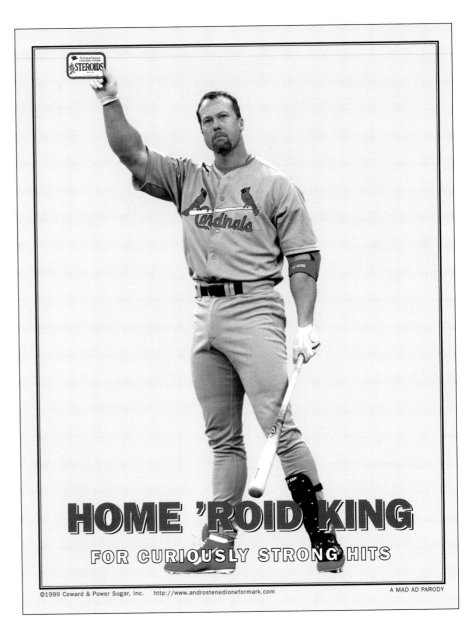

HOME 'ROID KING
FOR CURIOUSLY STRONG HITS

©1999 Coward & Power Sugar, Inc.   http://www.androstenedioneformark.com   A MAD AD PARODY

MAD ran this Altoids spoof as a comment on reports that St. Louis Cardinal Mark McGwire was using the controversial supplement adrostenedione when he broke Roger Maris's single-season home run record.

One of the toughest aspects of pulling off this parody was getting just the right color of green for the background. After all, Altoids uses a very specific color, but it's not like you could call them up and ask which one. And, as art director Sam Viviano explains it, you can't simply scan the original, because in the four-color printing process you'd just wind up with dots of yellow, black, cyan, and magenta. So Viviano had to painstakingly sample hundreds of shades until he got just the right hue.

Meanwhile, Altoids was in the process of signing a deal to use *MAD*'s *Spy vs. Spy* characters in a national campaign just as this back cover appeared on the stands. We're still not sure if they know about this, so if you could keep it quiet, we'd appreciate it.

MAD #386
October 1999
Artist: Robert Tanenbaum
Writers: Frank Santopadre
and Michael Patrick Dobkins

"George was very curious... The little white capsules smelled funny... different...like sour apples. Suddenly, his head began to turn! Then, he felt as if he were flying! Then everything went dark, and George was at peace."

DR. KEVORKIAN'S CHILDREN'S BOOK CLUB

We Put the "Youth" in "Euthanasia"!

Let's face it, parents — your kids are going to learn about the harsh realities of our fleeting existence sooner or later, no matter how much you try to protect them. But with these easy-to-read books personally recommended by "Dr. Death" himself, your child will learn all about severely traumatizing subjects like terminal illness, prolonged bed-ridden suffering and doctor-assisted suicide in a fun, lighthearted way!

JOIN TODAY!
Because after all, childhood can't last forever.

Book cover titles:
- If You Give a Mouse a Cyanide-Laced Cookie
- "It's Inoperable, Charlie Brown!"
- CLIFFORD the Big Red Dog's Very Last Trip to the Vet
- WHERE THE DEAD THINGS ARE
- THE CAT IN THE CASKET
- WHERE'S WALDO'S CORPSE?

Order now, and TAKE 5 BOOKS FOR ONLY $1!

Choose any of the following titles from Dr. K's personal library:

- ☐ Goodnight Forever, Moon
- ☐ Green Eggs and Hemlock
- ☐ Fox in Pine Box
- ☐ Madeline Takes the Gas Pipe
- ☐ The Hardy Boys Take Dad Off Life Support
- ☐ The Little Engine That Couldn't Take It Anymore!

- ☐ 101 Dalmations Are Put to Sleep
- ☐ Mr. Wizard's Build Your Own Suicide Machine from Neat Stuff Found Around the House
- ☐ The Berenstain Bears Lose the Will to Live
- ☐ Dr. Kevorkian's "Right-to-Die" Coloring & Activity Book

- ☐ A Collection of Kids' Suicide Notes to Santa
- ☐ James and the Giant Tumor
- ☐ Yertle the Turtle Gets Flushed Away!

- ☐ The Indian in the Cupboard Drinks Drano
- ☐ My Little Pony and the Glue Factory
- ☐ Junior Kroll Buys the farm

- ☐ The Five Chinese Brothers and the Group Suicide Pact
- ☐ If You Give a Pig a Cyanide-Laced Pancake

DR. KEVORKIAN'S CHILDREN'S BOOK CLUB
"Teaching Youngsters to Accept Reality for Over a Decade"

YES! I believe it's never too early to make my children morose. Please enroll me in Dr. Kevorkian's Children's Book Club according to the risk-free membership plan. Send me the 5 BOOKS I've indicated and bill me just $1*

Name _____
Address _____
City_____ State_____ Zip _____

MAIL TO: Dr. Kevorkian's Children's Book Club
c/o Oaks Correctional Facilty
East Lake, MI 49726

EXTRA BONUS
Order now and receive your choice of Dr. Kevorkian's 365 Reasons to Commit Suicide Page-a-Day Calendar or Dr. Kevorkian's Guide to Overdosing on Over-the-Counter Medications in Chewable Kids Tablets as our gift! (Offer not valid in Michigan or non-"Right-to-Die" states.)

*Plus $275 shipping and handling. All proceeds will be forwarded to the Dr. Jack Kevorkian Legal Defense Fund.

STOP WORRYING ABOUT THE HIGH COST OF CABLE TV
And *Start* Worrying About The High Cost Of A Satellite Dish Antenna!

SLIMEDISH
DIGITAL TELEVISION

WHAT A DEAL!

You'll receive all of the nation's top channels - unless you consider ABC, NBC, CBS or FOX "top channels"! Other super programming values include movie multi-channels like *Turnip Classic Movies, Greek HBO* and *Costner Movie Classics!* Call now to get more details from our Customer Service Representative — just as soon as we hire one.

So look to the leader in the industry for the best all-digital television value, but after you do, sign up with SlimeDish!

ONLY
$39⁹⁵ PER MONTH!

Plus a convenient one-time installation fee of $12,449.

> You Can't Get Any Lower Than This!*
> *We're talking about program content, not price.
>
> Sign Up Now And Get Two Free Months!*
> *July 2079 and February 2102 only.

What if you have service problems after installation?
Just call our toll free number and we'll tell you about our exciting plans to create a service department!
(Note: toll free from Guam only)

30-Day Money Back Guarantee!
If for any reason we are not satisfied with you as a customer, we will return your money, no questions asked!

A MAD AD PARODY

All prices, channel packages and programs subject to change without notice. Local, state and federal taxes you never heard of apply. There is an additional charge for extra services such as hooking your satellite dish to your converter box and your converter box to your TV set. Plugging it into the wall also costs more. There is also an additional charge if you want sound with your picture. Double that amount if you want stereo sound. Triple that amount if you want the sound to match the picture. WARNING: Some unscrupulous servicemen will illegally provide you with unauthorized satellite dish service. But there's no need to do business with them when you can deal with us directly!

WRITER: DICK DEBARTOLO

MAD #388
December 1999
Writer: Dick DeBartolo

MAD #392
April 2000
Writer: Dick DeBartolo

MAD #394
June 2000
Writer: Peter Kuper

Artist Peter Kuper tweaked a familiar Microsoft icon to make a comment about the company's unstoppable dominance in the computer software market.

The explosion of Home Depot stores across the country has made competition a thing of the past, driving mom and pop retail stores out of business faster than a guy selling John Rocker t-shirts in Queens! That's why their recent ad campaign showing how much they have helped small business was about as believable as a commitment to quality from Adam Sandler! Here's...

A MORE FACTUAL VERSION OF THAT DECEPTIVE HOME DEPOT AD

WE CAME INTO HER TOWN. THEN WE TOOK HER BUSINESS.

Thanks for making my small business impossible!

Me at Home Repo next Tuesday!

Me

TNT

FREE "HOW-TO" CLINICS

DUMPSTER DINING: Get the choice morsels ahead of those pesky racoons! Every Monday at 7 pm

SHAVING YOUR LEGS with BROKEN GLASS Every Tuesday at 8 pm

ASKING STRANGERS for a PLACE to STAY Every Wednesday at 8 pm

HOW to MAKE SHOES OUT of DUCT TAPE and TRASH Every Thursday at 7 pm

Doing what I have to do

FOR SALE

Dear Home Repo:

It all started innocently enough. A few months ago, I owned a thriving decorative ceramic tile business. Everything was going okay until you opened up down the road and pretty soon, things got out of control.

Here's what I mean...

After watching my business dry up in a matter of weeks, I decided that I couldn't possibly compete with such a bloated, faceless corporation. My bank account was getting smaller and smaller, so finally I came to you and bought my own hammer, nails and plywood — I'd already sold off all of mine in my "Going Out of Business" sale. Once I'd invested in that, I went back to my store and thought, "Well, I'd better board the place up!"

So I did. Thanks to Home Repo, I've gone from successful entrepreneur to full-time welfare recipient. Lighting fixtures and linoleum, sure, but who knew you guys were into destroying lives too? So thanks for helping me make the move into the local YWCA. They've given me my very own cot and towel and a really shiny Members Only jacket from the Lost and Found. Thanks Home Repo — none of this would have been possible without you.

Sincerely,

Debbie Nohaus

Debbie Nohaus

FOR LEASE COMMERCIAL OFFICE & RETAIL SPACE 555-6555

BANKRUPTCY ALL CHAPTERS Mark Lewis, Esq. FREE CONSULT 9699 Boodlegger Road, Bronx 718-555-9988

Service To DEBORAH NOHAUS **GAS BILL** Next Meter Reading JAN 20 2000 PAST DUE

Service To DEBORAH NOHAUS **ELECTRIC BILL** Next Meter Reading JAN 20 2000 PAST DUE

THE HOME REPO

OPPONENT'S NAME *Debbie's Ceramic Tile Supply* LOCATION *Red Bank, NJ* PROJECT *Eradicate* EMPLOYEE NAME *Joe Jeffandgeorge* DATE *3/3/00* VICTORY NO. 973

PHOTOGRAPHER: IRVING SCHILD   WRITER: JACOB LAMBERT

MAD #396
August 2000
Photographer: Irving Schild
Writer: Jacob Lambert

In the late '90s, the arrival of big box stores like Wal-Mart, Barnes and Noble, and, in this spoof, Home Depot meant that smaller, independently owned businesses were being systematically squeezed out.

That's Irving Schild's wife Regina as the once-successful, now-bankrupt businesswoman.

MAD #395
July 2000
Artist: Hermann Mejia
Writers: Joe Raiola and
David Shayne

Name Your Own Price For Airline Tickets With hypeline.con And Save BIG...

Assuming We Can Find An Airline Desperate Enough To Accept Your Lowball Offer, You Cheap Bastard!

"I saved $11 and all I had to do was change planes seven times between New York and Hartford. Thanks, hypeline!"
—*Norm Ovum, Boonton Falls, MD*

"It was a real thrill flying a no-name, non-FAA approved carrier and I never would have done it without hypeline!"
— *Celeste Crampy, Decay, IN*

"Okay, okay, I'll use hypeline. Anything to get that idiot Shatner to stop singing on those lame TV commercials!"
— *Moira Gonzalez, Scaramendo, CA*

IT'S EASY! Now you can save time and money by naming your own price for airline tickets! Just follow these 6 convenient steps:

1) Try logging on to hypeline.con through AOL without getting a busy signal. Keep trying every 90 seconds for the next three hours.*

2) Finally get through only to discover that your 56kbps modem isn't fast enough to handle our graphics-intensive, slow-loading home page.

3) Rewire your entire house with an ultra-fast, ultra expensive T-1 line.

4) Try logging on to hypeline.con through AOL without getting a busy signal again. Keep trying every 90 seconds for the next four hours.

5) Finally log on and spend two hours trying to figure out our patented EZ-Use® Interface.

6) Start saving BIG on airline tickets, choosing from such quality carriers as TWA (Tim Watson's Airline), Err Canada, UScair, Incontinental, Chechneya Air, The Black Box Shuttle and Ocean Floor Express.

* Sorry, but if you don't have a computer you'll have to buy your tickets the old-fashioned, inconvenient way by spending a few minutes on the phone with an airline and having the tickets mailed to you.

"When it comes to wasting time, I told you hypeline was gonna be big, REALLY BIG!"

NOW YOU CAN NAME YOUR OWN PRICE FOR GROCERIES!

It's great, especially if you're the kind of person who doesn't mind spending six hours online to save three cents on a 64-ounce jar of generic salsa (that may not be in stock once you get to the store)!

PRODUCT	SAVINGS
Guldens Mustard (38 lb family size only)	14¢
Oy Gevalt™ Brand Kosher Tongue (Grade B)	16¢
Swanson's Frozen Swiss Chard (after manufacturer's rebate)	6¢
I Can't Believe It's Not Lard™ Luncheon Spread	1¢
NEW! Mr. Clean Lemon-Ammonia Vinaigrette Salad Dressing	2¢
Lays Unsalted Crushed Potato Chips (8 oz bag)	4¢
Pepto-Bismol Ice Cream Sandwiches (4 pack)	5¢
Maalox Onion Flavored Antacid Liqui-Gels	2¢

ARTIST: HERMANN MEJIA   WRITERS: JOE RAIOLA AND DAVID SHAYNE

waldbum's

The Fool Emporium

 SHOP WRONG

BLAND UNION   TRAVESTINOS

A MAD AD PARODY

Coming Soon! Christline.con – name your own price for personal salvation!

MAD #397
September 2000
Artist: Roberto Parada
Writer: Staff

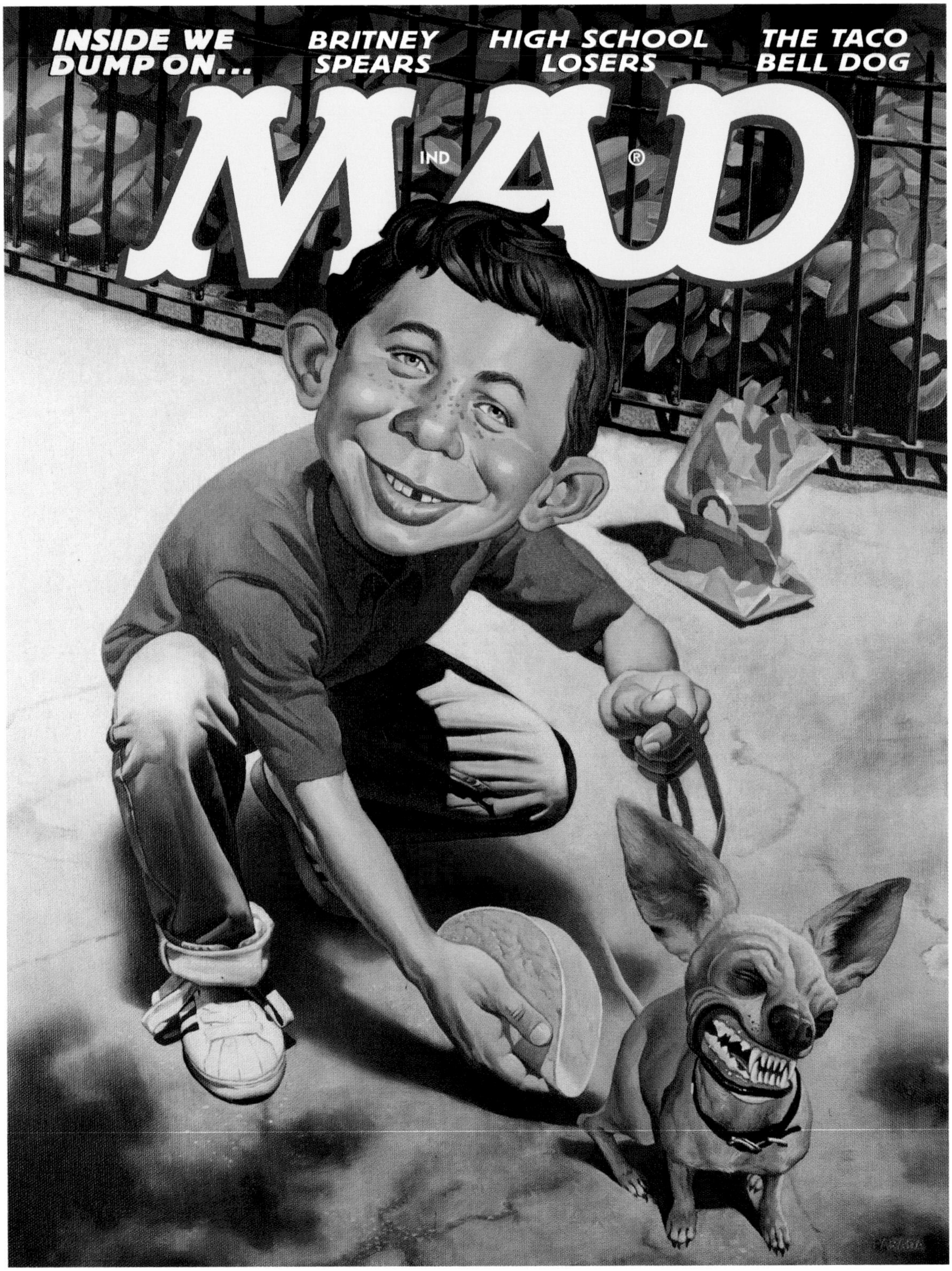
INSIDE WE DUMP ON...
BRITNEY SPEARS
HIGH SCHOOL LOSERS
THE TACO BELL DOG
MAD
IND
®

MAD #399
November 2000
Artist and Writer: Al Jaffee

The hot catchphrase sweeping America is "Whassup?" When you hear it, it means it's time for parties, good times and beer, beer, beer! Yep, whether you're home, at a sports bar or over a friend's place, when someone says "Whassup?" it's time to crack open some tall, frosty brews. But that's not all "Whassup?" stands for. To really find out "Whassup?" fold page in as shown.

A ◄► FOLD PAGE OVER LEFT   **B** FOLD BACK SO THAT "A" MEETS "B"

SHOUTS OF "WHASSUP?" BRINGS
COLLECTIONS OF HAPPY PARTYING PALS OUT TO STAGE
BIBULOUS BEER BASHES. THESE DUDES SEEM STRANGE
TO SOME, BUT THEIR LOUD "WHASSUPS?"
DRAW MILLIONS OF FANS TO JOIN THEIR WAY OF THINKING

A ◄►   ARTIST AND WRITER: AL JAFFEE   **B**

FOLD PAGE OVER LIKE THIS!

A ◄► **B** FOLD BACK SO THAT "A" MEETS "B"

COLLEGE
BINGE

DRINKING
A ◄► **B**

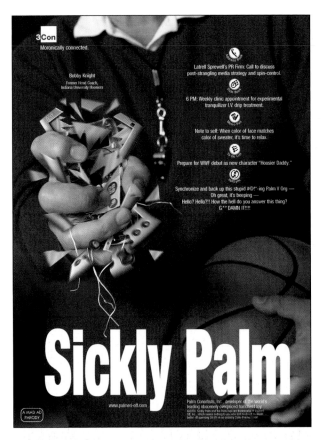

MAD #400

December 2000

Photographer: Irving Schild

Writer: Arie Kaplan

When writer Arie Kaplan submitted a piece to *MAD* spoofing Palm PDAs, he was working for a New York-based movie producer who used his Palm for everything. Arie's first draft wasn't an ad parody, just a general article commenting on both the Palm and, as Arie describes it, "The sleazy, glamorous life of a Hollywood producer." In talking it over with the editors, though, the decision was made to go after the "Simply Palm" campaign that had just started running nationally.

Arie had hoped his "Simply Palm" spoofs would become a recurring series (he even wrote a few more, including one hitting director Tim Burton), but alas, the real campaign was discontinued shortly after these one-pagers appeared in *MAD* #400. Who knows? Maybe the folks at Palm had simply had enough of *MAD*'s teasing.

From the Makers of Cherry Garcia and Phish Food Come...

NEW
"ROCK & RAP INSPIRED"
BEN & JERRY'S FLAVORS

Also available! Sour McLachlan and Alanis 'SmoresSette!

Sample the world's first "sampled" ice cream! A'ight!

Try it and help topple the corporate whore ass-kissing Praline agenda!

The favorite of convicted felons with refrigerator privileges!

A MAD AD PARODY

®

Our Guarantee
If You Find a Lower Price Anywhere Else, So What?

$9
Box of 100

Pre-Bent Nails
Why pay extra for straight nails when you've botched every hammer job you've tried since 1987? Bent at a variety of angles for your convenience, these light-weight, aluminum nails are ideal for gluing onto cardboard and paper. (Not recommended for use with wood.)

$9

Murderous-Gro Fertilizer
Perfect for making homemade bombs and other explosive devices. The choice of terrorists around the globe!
Not recommended for tomato plants.

$12

The Ultimate EZ-Lock™
You'll never forget your combination again with the new Ultimate EZ-Lock™ from Crapperco! With the advanced one-turn-in-any-direction-to-any-number method, opening your lock is now a snap, both for you and everyone else. (Please Note: Manufacturer not responsible for stolen property.)

$103,000
Deluxe Storage Shed
Store your tools and more in this super-sized backyard shed. Comes complete with adjustable shelving, handyman's workbench, Jacuzzi, banquet hall, ballroom and optional walk-in wine cellar. (Some assembly required.)

$59
Rickety-Rak 3-Person Swing
Spend an afternoon putting it together, then weeks wondering if this is the night those chains snap

ARTIST: GEORGE WOODBRIDGE   WRITERS: JEFF KRUSE AND RUSS COOPER

MAD #403
March 2001
Artist: George Woodbridge
Writers: Jeff Kruse and
Russ Cooper

Supplies For the Stubborn Handyman of the House Who Just Refuses to Acknowledge He Doesn't Know What He's Doing!

THE HOME DESPOT ®

$4
Work Area Signs

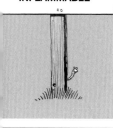

DANGER!
STOPPING TO READ THIS SIGN INCREASES THE CHANCE OF A STEEL BEAM FALLING ON YOU BY 87%

WARNING!
WOMEN PASSING HERE MAY BE SUBJECT TO OBSCENE GESTURES, VULGAR LIP SMACKING AND RUDE COMMENTS ABOUT THE SIZE OF THEIR BUTTOCKS

THINK!
ABOUT HOW WEIRD IT IS THAT "FLAMMABLE" MEANS THE SAME THING AS "INFLAMMABLE"

$12
Jangly Utility Belt
Holds plenty of heavy tools, guaranteed to pull your pants down for maximum butt-crack exposure, like real fix-it guys.

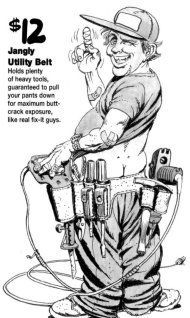

$6 /PAIR
Work Gloves
You name the number of remaining fingers — we have the glove for you! Available in Medium, Large and Stumpy.

$47
Annoy-A-Lot Leaf Blower
Notice it's called a "leaf blower" and not a "leaf remover" or a "leaf picker-upper." Three-speed option allows you to spray leaves, dirt and branches in 132 different directions. 486 decibel level guarantees you'll disturb everyone within a 30-mile radius. (Protective ear-wear sold separately.)

$17
Cordless Hammer
How many times have you wished you could hammer a nail without having that annoying cord get in the way? Well, here's your answer! From the makers of the cordless extension cord.

$9
Tin-Tuff Fake Toolbox
Realistic-looking "toolbox" is actually a cooler. You can appear to be hard at work when, in fact, you are drinking the day away! Holds approx. 24 cans.

$144
Pocket Lawnmower
Now you can trim your lawn blade-by-blade with Swiss Army precision-cutting just like the professionals! Starts without the strenuous yanking required in conventional mowers. No gasoline required.

FREE!
Thumb-Operated Forward/Reverse Handle

MASTERFRAUD
AMERICAN EXCESS

WE ACCEPT

LIBRARY CARD

GET OUT OF JAIL FREE CARD

The MAD Bulletin Board

POLKA BAND SEEKS HIP-HOP SINGER
Must be able to freestyle rap, kick it old school and bust a move. Knowledge of Ol' Dirty Bastard songs a plus. 555-8373

NEED HELP GETTING PREGNANT?
Man with van will drive to your house and have sex with you 24 hrs a day!
555-BABY

RESEARCH VOLUNTEERS EARN UP TO $12!
Painful bone grafts, followed by unnecessary bowel surgery. Will pay for first week of two-month long hospital stay!
Institute of Unpleasant Circumstances 555-3902

PROBLEMS BINGE EATING?
PLEASE don't come to our restaurant!
**Ben's All-You-Can-Eat-Café
Rte. 1, Edison, NJ.**

BETH
We met at a singles party on Friday night and I thought I was getting somewhere until I spit corn chips and guacamole with salsa on your sweater. Please call me, it was an accident.
Phil 555-2727

UGLY OLD STRIPPERS
Twice The Experience, Half The Price!
555-9202

CHEAP MARIJUANA!!!!!
Instructional video shows you how to fake glaucoma symptoms so you can purchase top-quality pot at bargain prices from sympathetic medical marijuana collectives in California!
555-1818

DO-IT-YOURSELF ANGIOPLASTY
Save time and money! No gate-keeper physician approval required or pesky insurance forms to fill out! Send for kit and easy instructions!
(artery balloons included)
The Center For Clogged Plaque Advancement 555-0918

RESEARCH STUDY
Having deja-vu? We can help.
555-4987

JEWISH MYSTIC
Out of work since 1994, looking for career suggestions. 555-6722

PENIS ENLARGEMENT
Sure, our patented **Pinch-An-Inch™** procedure hurts like hell, but we guarantee you'll see and feel the results or we'll cut you back down to size FOR FREE!
**The Penile Enlargement Warehouse
555-1019**

TIRED OF PROFESSIONAL LOOKING PRINT JOBS?
Let me design your fliers, brochures, newsletters, etc. Extensive expertise using Zapf Chancery, Goofy Goofs and other hard to read fonts!
555-3453

CURE DIARRHEA OVER THE PHONE!
Please call from toilet.
555-3838

THE STARBUCKS COLONIC!
Only at the Energetic Enema Center
energeticenema.com

DEAR JILL
Or was it Jody? Anyway, remember me? We met at the lounge at LAX. You were the sexy 25-year-old blonde in the short little skirt reading Proust. I was the overweight conventioneer with the mustard on his lapel. You asked me to "f*** off."
I thought there was a spark between us.
Call me. I'm at my mom's house.
Stan 555-6542

RESEARCH RESEARCH STUDY STUDY
Are Are you you seeing seeing double double? Call Call us us. **The The Northern Northern New New England England Research Research Institute Institute**
555555--99887733

TIRED OF FUNNY STATE-OF-THE-ART WEBSITES?
Visit **www.madmag.com** now!

RESEARCH STUDY
Having deja-vu? We can help.
555-4987

ALICE, I LOVE YOU. CALL ME.

ALICE, WHY HAVEN'T YOU CALLED ME?

SERIOUSLY, ALICE, WAS IT SOMETHING I DID? CALL ME!

YOU'RE A BITCH, ALICE. GO TO HELL! (CALL ME FIRST, THOUGH.)

ALICE, SORRY ABOUT THE "BITCH" INCIDENT. CALL ME.

NEED CREDIT?
New Jersey loan shark, just minutes from Manhattan, will lend you cash regardless of credit rating. Late payments strongly discouraged.
Little Pussy 555-9288

ACTORS
Needed for independent film. No experience or talent required. No Pay. Poor opportunity.
555-3344

NEED A WEDDING BAND?
We only know one song (*Who Let the Dogs Out*) but we work cheap! Baha Men 555-8302

SEE 'N Sync AT THE GARDEN!
From behind a line of wooden police barricades, an hour after the show's over as they run quickly into their limousines. $1100
Gouge Ticket Agency 555-0292

PREVENT HEAD COLDS IN PARROTS
With **Parrot Bath Therapy***, breakthrough preventive treatment created by renowned alternative-ornithologist from Mexico City.
Not available in stores! 555-1811

PSORIASIS. ECZEMA. WRINKLES.
Dermatology clinic wants to give you all these skin conditions and have a good laugh at your expense.
555-1247

THE EXTREMELY COLD, DAMP, DARK DUNGEON
Where "Mistress Eva" Makes A Living By Putting On An Uncomfortable Red Rubber Suit And Pretends To Get Aroused As She Spanks Paunchy, Bald, Bare-Assed, Middle-Aged Men With A Ping-Pong Paddle.
555-0191

FEELING TOO COMFORTABLE?
Man with van will come to your house and push you into a bush of stinging nettles.
555-3344

LRN 2 WRT GD & FST WTHT VWLS (XCPT TH LTTR "Y")
555-1652

SEE *HOLLOW MAN* 100 TIMES IN 1 MONTH!
Plus *Karate Kid 3* and *Adventures in Babysitting!*
Subscribe to HBO now!
555-HBOO

SEE "THE PRODUCERS" ON *BROADWAY*
Great tix available for June 2007, starring Troy Aikman and the guy who played Cameron in *Ferris Bueller!*
Gouge Ticket Agency 555-0292

THE EXTREMELY COLD, DAMP, DARK DUNGEON
Where **"Mistress Eva"** Makes A Living By Putting On An Uncomfortable Red Rubber Suit And Pretends To Get Aroused As She Spanks Paunchy, Bald, Bare-assed, Middle-Aged Men With A Ping Pong Paddle Is Now Hiring. 555-0191

RESEARCH STUDY
Having deja-vu? We can help.
555-4987

INFANT BREAST ENHANCEMENT!
Why wait? Boys welcomed!
infantbreast.com

NUDE PLUMBER
No pipes too big or small.
555-2828

Lose Cash Now!
Ask me how! Drop $300 in thirty days Guaranteed! 555-7983

FORMER MAD WRITERS
Seek employment after writing this lame "Bulletin Board" drivel. Joe Raiola and David Shayne, PO Box 64, High Falls, NY, 12440

◄ *MAD* #418
June 2002
Writers: Joe Raiola
and David Shayne

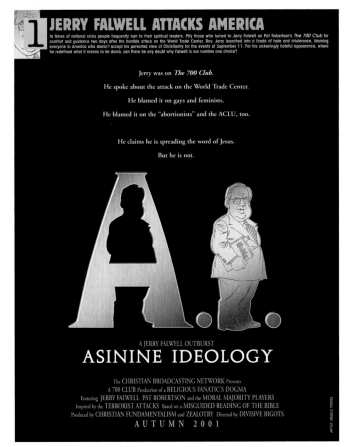

MAD #413
January 2002
Artist: Angelo Torres
Writer: House

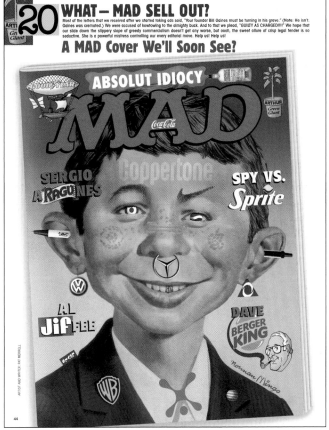

MAD #413
January 2002
Writer: Pat Merrell
Artist: Norman Mingo
altered by Pat Merrell

The Usual Gang of Idiots will make fun of anyone and anything, including (or, perhaps, *especially*) themselves. So in 2001, the year the magazine added color and began accepting advertising, the *MAD*men included themselves in their annual round-up of the year's 20 dumbest.

It is telling that in spite of the rigged jury, *MAD still* couldn't make number one!

MAD #423
November 2002
Photographer: Irving Schild
Writer: Scott Maiko

Cents-Less Coupons
Your money-saving circular

Surprise!
That's __NOT__ Meat!
It's Mulch, Mulch More.

Taste familiar? It should.
Your old comic books are in there. So's your baseball card collection. (Thanks, Mom!) Grass clippings, too. And so's the oak that came down in that storm last March and blocked the street until a road crew could get out with a chainsaw and a wood chipper! It's *all* in there, plus a lot more. With Fiber Burger, a meatless patty made from recycled materials isn't pulp fiction anymore.

Fiber Burger
85% Post-Consumer Content   100% Delicious

TRY ALL 4 VARIETIES!

Hickory Newsprint

Pepper Maché

Spicy Cardboard & Crabgrass

Kinko's™ Smokehouse

| MANUFACTURER'S COUPON | NOT REDEEMABLE |

Save $1.00
on any variety of *Fiber Burger*

TO THE CONSUMER: This coupon is good on any purchase of FIBER BURGER Recycled Meal Patties. Any other use constitutes fraud. It's a frickin' coupon! What else are you going to do with it?! Pay off a gambling debt? Re-paper the bedroom? Collect your dry-cleaning? Listen, pal, it's not worth it. You've worked too hard to get where you are to throw it all away like this. Think of your family, man! There's people out there who care about you! It doesn't have to end this way. C'mon, now, drop the coupon. That's it. Nice and slowly…Okay, Becker, MOVE IN NOW! GO GO GO!

PHOTOGRAPHER: IRVING SCHILD   WRITER: SCOTT MAIKO

To come up with this multi-part spoof of Sunday coupon supplements, writer Scott Maiko simply went on a shopping trip. "I was in the supermarket and saw these pointless products," he explains. "There's so much out there that people are blowing their money on."

Not that writing "Cents-Less Coupons" was easy. When stores really sell things like ice cream for dogs, it's tough to come up with items more ridiculous than what's already on the shelves. For example, the eight-bladed razor included here (page 186) was originally going to be only four . . . until an actual four-bladed razor hit the market.

Then there's the matter of the coupons. *MAD* has a long-standing tradition of getting as many gags onto the page as possible. With its tiny type, coupon copy is a great place for unbridled silliness in an ad spoof. "I just came up with random stuff," says Maiko. Since the editors wanted different jokes in every coupon, Maiko searched for anything text-driven and "crammed it into the little boxes at the bottom. That part drove me up the wall."

As a writer who also provides sketches when he writes a script, Scott said he was thrilled with how the art department executed his ideas, although he had lobbied for actual UPC codes on the coupons: "I had this vision of kids cutting them out and slipping them into their moms' coupon caddies."

Once again, various *MAD* staffers serve as models, but this time *MAD* editor John Ficarra's family also gets in on the act. That's his daughter Mary Emily in the ad for "FunClumps," joined by associate art director Nadina Simon.

MAD #427
March 2003
Photographer: Irving Schild
Artist: Scott Bricher
Writer: Scott Maiko

Cents-Less Coupons

Your money-saving circular

Announcing the arrival of new

Monthlies

THE EXPANDABLE DIAPER!

With new Monthlies, constant changing's a thing of the past! A patented reservoir fanny e - x - p - a - n - d - s to carry a month's worth of loads — as much as your little one can dish out! A super absorbent, quicklime lining locks in most odors while decomposing waste. Dated "Change Me" stickers remind you when it's time to replace diaper.

Dated "Change Me" stickers remind you when it's time to replace diaper!

CHANGE 11/30 ME

May cause severe chafing in some infants.

Monthlies
Jumbo
Monthlies
THE EXPANDABLE DIAPER!
38 Diapers Couches Pañales

Start Saving Now! HURRY! OFFER EXPIRES TODAY!

MANUFACTURER'S COUPON — WHO ELSE'S?

Save $1.50

when you buy any **Monthlies** expandable diapers

Monthlies Jumbo **Monthlies** THE EXPANDABLE DIAPER! 38

Consumer: Limit one coupon per purchase on product(s) indicated. Coupon not transferable. Consumer must pay any sales tax. Help me, Obi-Wan Kenobi! You're my only hope! Good only in the continental U.S.A., Alaska, Hawaii, and Puerto Rico.

WRITER: SCOTT MAIKO
ARTIST: SCOTT BRICHER
PHOTOGRAPHER: IRVING SCH

HURLIGAN'S BISTRO & CANTINAHAUS

The Mid-Priced Restaurant Chain Outside An Office Park Where Low-Income Families Come to Celebrate A Birthday

2 Summer Favorites! Your choice just $12.99 each for a limited time only!

Combo Platter
- Refried Burrito Toast
- Six Microwave Popcorn Shrimp
- Three Pluck 'N Chew Chicken Knots
- 8-oz. Batter-Dipped Golden-Fried Steak*
- Plus All-You-Can-Eat from our Bottomless Rice-Cooker!

*Weight before eating

Platter Feast Combo
- Steak & Cheese Zapata
- Chicken-Fried Potato
- Four Pry 'N Yank Crab Legs
- Four Sautéed Chicken Wads
- All this and unlimited visits to the Pudding Vat!

It's Back! Add our delicious Flamin' Egg™ to any entree for only $1.49

HURRY! EXPIRES WHEN YOU DIE!
Buy One Entree Get One Free!*

*of significantly lesser value when you order three additional meals, combos, party platters or catering service for 24 at regular price.

Call 1-800-555-HURL for the location of the Hurligan's nearest you

It's always summer! Don't forget anything on your backyard barbeque checklist!
☐ soda
☐ chips
☑ Blo-Dogs!™

Blo-Dogs Made With Real Gum! BUN SIZE BEEF FRANKS

AMERICA'S FAVORITE ALL-BEEF HOT DOG WITH THE CHEWY BUBBLE GUM FILLING!

The Unhealthier Alternative
For the One Food Your Kid Never Complains About Eating Even Without the Unnecessary Addition of Bubble Gum to Make It More 'Fun'!

MANUFACTURER'S COUPON MAY BE REFUSED WITHOUT REASON
50¢ OFF Blo-Dogs (any flavor)

Dry 'n Flush DISPOSABLE BATH TOWELS

Tired of drying off with the same towel you just used yesterday? Sick of paying high bed & bath store prices for bath linens that just end up costing even more with each washing?

It's easy as 1–2–3!
1. Tear off one single-use sheet
2. Dry thoroughly
3. Flush!*

MANUFACTURER'S COUPON VALID IN GREECE ONLY
Money-Saving Offer! **SAVE $1.00** Save $1.00 on any roll of Dry 'n Flush Disposable Bath Towels and receive a check by mail good for $99 off your next plumbing bill!

70 2-PLY TOWELS 2 FT. X 3 FT.

Tired of waiting... and waiting... and waiting... for the grill to heat up?

Food's ready faster when the charcoal starts itself!

3RD DEGREE SPONTANEOUS COMBUSTION CHARCOAL BRIQUETTES
8 LBS.
WARNING: NEVER STORE LOOSE BRIQUETTES IN BABY'S CRIB WITHOUT ADEQUATE VENTILATION.

MANUFACTURER'S COUPON EXPIRES WITHOUT LIFE SUPPORT
Save $1.00 when you buy any size bag of 3rd Degree Spontaneous Combustion Charcoal Briquettes and 3rd Degree Oily Rags.

In a forgotten corner of your local supermarket.

YARD SALE Sat 9/7 — Clothes, furniture, stereo & comp. equipment, collectibles. 1262 Bicknell. 8am to ???. Great bargains. Found boyfriend in bed with neighbor's wife; must sell all out of spite. NO EARLY BIRDS

"A delicious meal we can enjoy together!"

CAT & ELDERLY FOOD **Fixed Income Fixins** Tuna n' Cheese Tapioca

'Tuna n' Cheese Tapioca may contain traces of horsemeat.

MANUFACTURER'S COUPON EXPIRED JUST A FEW MINUTES AGO
50¢ OFF Three (3) cans of Fixed Income Fixins*

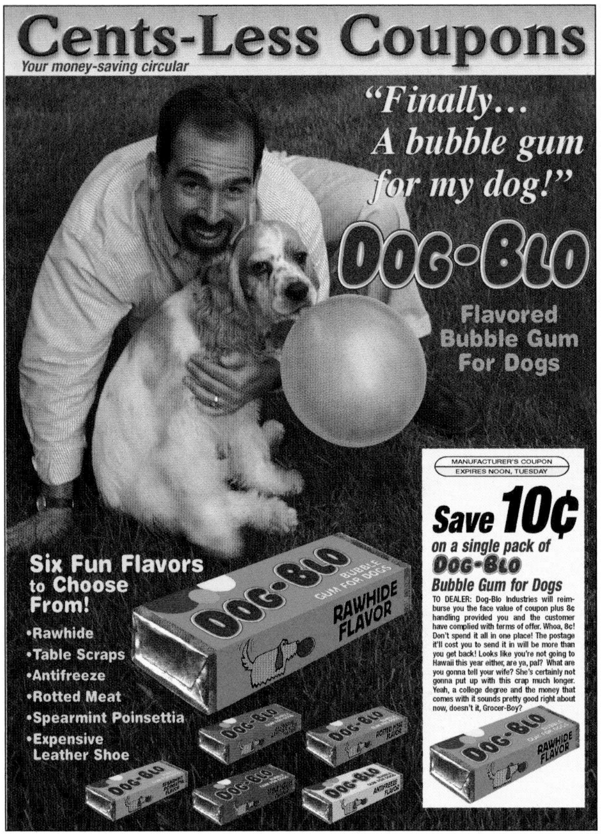

Cents-Less Coupons
Your money-saving circular
"Finally... A bubble gum for my dog!"
DOG-BLO
Flavored Bubble Gum For Dogs
Six Fun Flavors to Choose From!
•Rawhide
•Table Scraps
•Antifreeze
•Rotted Meat
•Spearmint Poinsettia
•Expensive Leather Shoe
MANUFACTURER'S COUPON
EXPIRES NOON, TUESDAY
Save 10¢
on a single pack of
DOG-BLO
Bubble Gum for Dogs
TO DEALER: Dog-Blo Industries will reimburse you the face value of coupon plus 8¢ handling provided you and the customer have complied with terms of offer. Whoa, 8¢! Don't spend it all in one place! The postage it'll cost you to send it in will be more than you get back! Looks like you're not going to Hawaii this year either, are ya, pal? What are you gonna tell your wife? She's certainly not gonna put up with this crap much longer. Yeah, a college degree and the money that comes with it sounds pretty good right about now, doesn't it, Grocer-Boy?
RAWHIDE FLAVOR

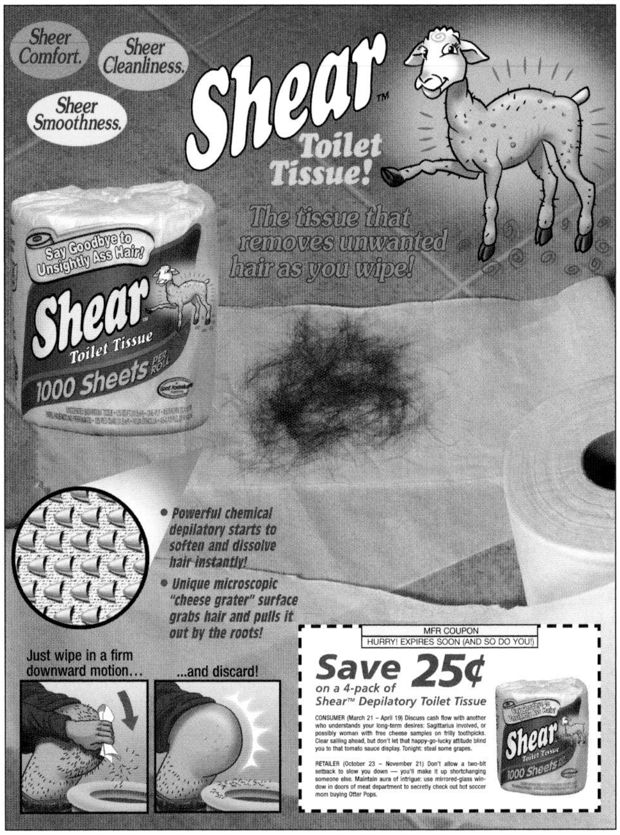

Sheer Comfort.
Sheer Cleanliness.
Sheer Smoothness.
Shear™ Toilet Tissue!
The tissue that removes unwanted hair as you wipe!
Say Goodbye to Unsightly Ass Hair!
Shear Toilet Tissue
1000 Sheets
• Powerful chemical depilatory starts to soften and dissolve hair instantly!
• Unique microscopic "cheese grater" surface grabs hair and pulls it out by the roots!
Just wipe in a firm downward motion...
...and discard!
MFR COUPON
HURRY! EXPIRES SOON (AND SO DO YOU!)
Save 25¢
on a 4-pack of
Shear™ Depilatory Toilet Tissue
CONSUMER (March 21 – April 19) Discuss cash flow with another who understands your long-term desires: Sagittarius involved, or possibly woman with free cheese samples on frilly toothpicks. Clear sailing ahead, but don't let that happy-go-lucky attitude blind you to that tomato sauce display. Tonight: steal some grapes.
RETAILER (October 23 – November 21) Don't allow a two-bit setback to slow you down — you'll make it up shortchanging someone else. Maintain aura of intrigue: use mirrored-glass window in doors of meat department to secretly check out hot soccer mom buying Otter Pops.

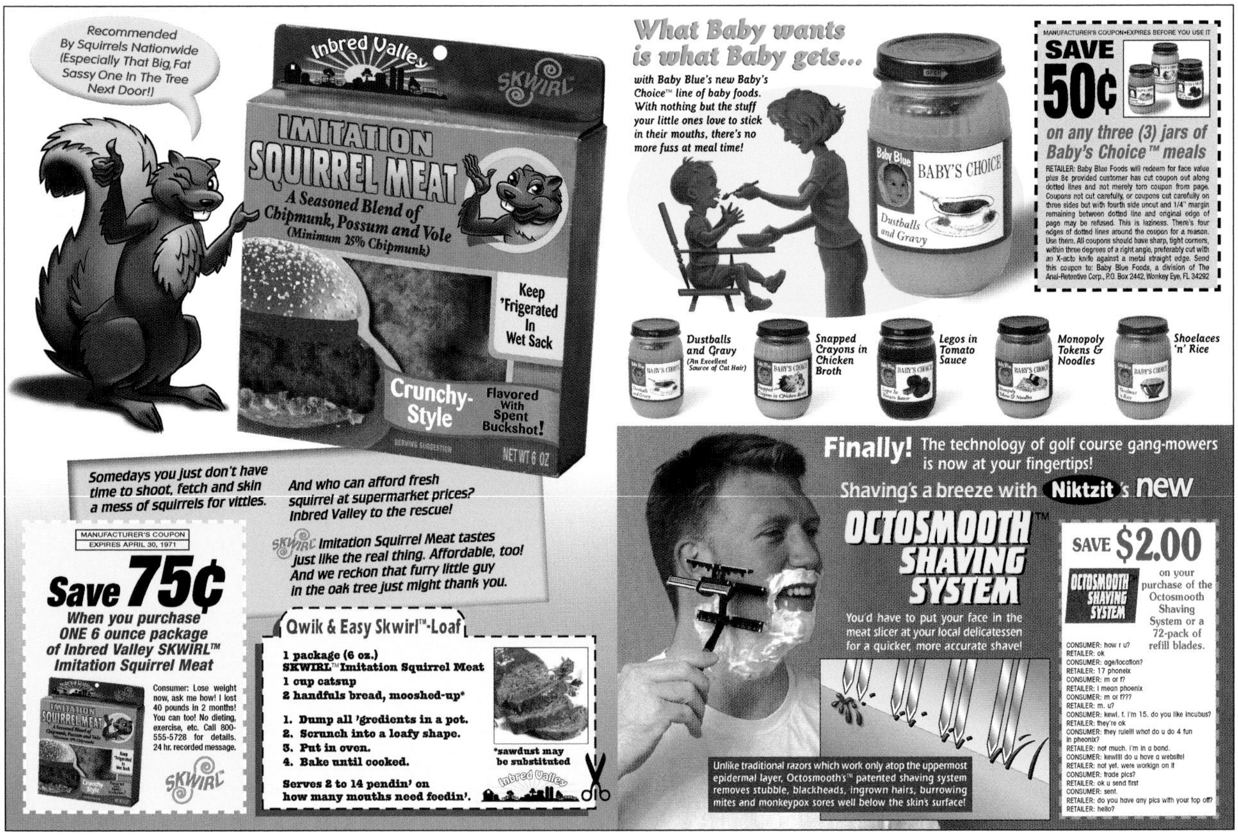

Recommended By Squirrels Nationwide (Especially That Big, Fat Sassy One In The Tree Next Door!)
Inbred Valley
SKWIRL
IMITATION SQUIRREL MEAT
A Seasoned Blend of Chipmunk, Possum and Vole (Minimum 25% Chipmunk)
Keep 'Frigerated In Wet Sack
Crunchy-Style
Flavored With Spent Buckshot!
NET WT 6 OZ
Somedays you just don't have time to shoot, fetch and skin a mess of squirrels for vittles.
And who can afford fresh squirrel at supermarket prices? Inbred Valley to the rescue!
SKWIRL Imitation Squirrel Meat tastes just like the real thing. Affordable, too! And we reckon that furry little guy in the oak tree just might thank you.
MANUFACTURER'S COUPON
EXPIRES APRIL 30, 1971
Save 75¢
When you purchase ONE 6 ounce package of Inbred Valley SKWIRL™ Imitation Squirrel Meat
Consumer: Lose weight now, ask me how! I lost 40 pounds in 2 months! You can too! No dieting, exercise, etc. Call 800-555-5728 for details. 24 hr. recorded message.
SKWIRL™
Qwik & Easy Skwirl™-Loaf
1 package (6 oz.)
SKWIRL™ Imitation Squirrel Meat
1 cup catsup
2 handfuls bread, mooshed-up*
1. Dump all 'gredients in a pot.
2. Scrunch into a loafy shape.
3. Put in oven.
4. Bake until cooked.
Serves 2 to 14 pendin' on how many mouths need feedin'.
*sawdust may be substituted
Inbred Valley
What Baby wants is what Baby gets...
with Baby Blue's new Baby's Choice™ line of baby foods. With nothing but the stuff your little ones love to stick in their mouths, there's no more fuss at meal time!
Baby Blue
BABY'S CHOICE
Dustballs and Gravy
MANUFACTURER'S COUPON•EXPIRES BEFORE YOU USE IT
SAVE 50¢
on any three (3) jars of Baby's Choice™ meals
RETAILER: Baby Blue Foods will redeem for face value plus 8¢ provided customer has cut coupon out along dotted lines and not merely torn coupon from page. Coupons not cut carefully, or coupons cut carefully on three sides but with fourth side uncut and 1/4" margin remaining between dotted line and original edge of page may be refused. This is laziness. There's four edges of dotted lines around the coupon for a reason. Use them. All coupons should have sharp, tight corners, within three degrees of a right angle, preferably cut with an X-acto knife against a metal straight edge. Send this coupon to: Baby Blue Foods, a division of The Anal-Retentive Corp., P.O. Box 2442, Wonkey Eye, FL 34292
Dustballs and Gravy (An Excellent Source of Cat Hair)
Snapped Crayons in Chicken Broth
Legos in Tomato Sauce
Monopoly Tokens & Noodles
Shoelaces 'n' Rice
Finally! The technology of golf course gang-mowers is now at your fingertips!
Shaving's a breeze with Niktzit's new
OCTOSMOOTH SHAVING SYSTEM™
You'd have to put your face in the meat slicer at your local delicatessen for a quicker, more accurate shave!
Unlike traditional razors which work only atop the uppermost epidermal layer, Octosmooth's™ patented shaving system removes stubble, blackheads, ingrown hairs, burrowing mites and monkeypox sores well below the skin's surface!
SAVE $2.00
OCTOSMOOTH™ SHAVING SYSTEM
on your purchase of the Octosmooth Shaving System or a 72-pack of refill blades.
CONSUMER: how r u?
RETAILER: ok
CONSUMER: age/location?
RETAILER: 17 phoneix
CONSUMER: m or f?
RETAILER: i mean phoenix
CONSUMER: m or f???
RETAILER: m. u?
CONSUMER: kewl. f. i'm 15. do you like incubus?
RETAILER: they're ok
CONSUMER: they rule!!! what do u do 4 fun in pheonix?
RETAILER: not much. i'm in a band.
CONSUMER: kewl!!! do u have a website!
RETAILER: not yet. were workign on it
CONSUMER: trade pics?
RETAILER: ok u send first
CONSUMER: sent.
RETAILER: do you have any pics with your top off?
RETAILER: hello?

MAD writers are always observing the world around them for sources of inspiration—television, movies, the Internet, and, in this case, the pages of *MAD* itself.

When I was flipping through my latest issue of *MAD*, I noticed that a lot of the real ads in the magazine were for video games, inspiring me to come up with an ad for the most boring driving game I could possibly imagine, influenced in part by the interminable hours I spent as a kid riding to school in a carpool.

Once again, the writer, art department, artist (or, in this case, two of them), and the editors teamed up to try to trick readers into thinking they were looking at a real ad for a new game. From the logos to the layout, we broke down every element of a typical video game ad and tried to recreate them in look, feel, and even placement on the page. Editor John Ficarra decided to run the piece where an ad would typically appear, and without a department head to tip the reader off.

We received reports that even some *MAD* staffers skipped right past this piece thinking it was real. Which means we were either very successful in pulling off the subterfuge or, like most *MAD* staffers, they skipped past everyone else's piece to find their own stuff.

MAD #435
November 2003
Artists: Scott Bricher and
Timothy Shamey
Writer: David Shayne

◀ *MAD* #433
September 2003
Photographer: Irving Schild
Artist: Scott Bricher
Writer: Scott Maiko

MAD #437
January 2004
Photographer: Irving Schild
Writer: Don Vaughn

12 KOBE GIFTS HIS WIFE: The Fraud Of The Ring

We can't say for sure whether Kobe Bryant is innocent or guilty of sexual assault — that's up to the cable news commentators — but what we *can* say is that he spent much of the year in a desperate frenzy to restore his wholesome, all-American family-man image. While his still-commercially-viable teammate Shaq made lame Radio Shack commercials, Kobe hunkered down with his "advisors," trying to figure out which necktie makes him look "most innocent." Everyone knows that Kobe's won three championship rings with the Lakers, but the most important ring of his career may turn out to be the one he had to pay for.

After you've disgraced her, buy back her affection with our exquisite $4 million classic-cut diamond ring, a symbol of your abiding love that she's sure to cherish forever, or at least until the next time you're accused of sexual assault.

The Kobe Diamond.
Just two months' salary.
If you're Kobe.

Remember the "4 Sees" when selecting a diamond: 1. See how badly I screwed up? 2. See how scared I am of your lawyers? 3. See how important you are in maintaining my public image? 4. See how much I'm willing to spend in the desperate hope that you'll forget about this?

A diamond bribes her forever.

PHOTOGRAPHER: IRVING SCHILD   WRITER: DON VAUGHN   BACKGROUND PHOTO: GETTY IMAGES

Shortly after admitting he had committed adultery and was being charged with sexual assault in Eagle County, Colorado, Los Angeles Laker Kobe Bryant was seen shopping for a $4 million, eight-carat diamond for his wife Vanessa, earning himself the 12th spot on the *MAD* 20 for 2003.

This parody doesn't spoof any single ad, but instead uses elements from both the De Beers diamonds print and TV campaigns to create a sort of hypothetical ad.

Creating it required combining literally dozens of images in Photoshop. Irving Schild photographed several different models to get photos of Kobe's body, Vanessa's hands, Vanessa's body, Vanessa's face, and Vanessa's hair. Meanwhile, elements like the courtroom and Kobe's head were procured from Internet photo services.

Art director Sam Viviano says creating the final product was like assembling "a jigsaw puzzle—putting all of those pieces together to look right."

Sam Vivano knew recreating Apple's iPod campaign would be trickier than it might appear at first blush, because although the figures may look like silhouettes, they are in fact "very high contrast shadow images, with a sense of shadows and highlights."

Artist Scott Bricher picked up on this subtlety and perfectly recreated Apple's look, giving the types of details and contrast you wouldn't find in a simple silhouette.

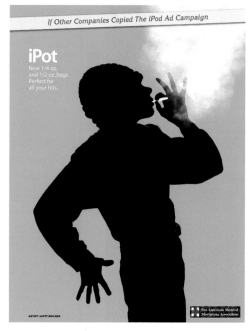

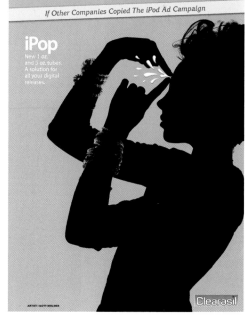

MAD #439
March 2004
Artist: Scott Bricher
Writer: House

THE CIGARETTE ADS

Among *MAD*'s proudest accomplishments (okay, *MAD*'s ONLY accomplishment) is the magazine's relentless pursuit of the tobacco industry.

Tobacco manufacturers have a rather unique dilemma: they market a product that will ultimately lead to an early death among their users, so they must constantly lure new buyers. To that end, they have spent billions on advertising over the years, trying to get people hooked on their addictive product as early as possible.

Although *MAD* has never had a political agenda, it was and is, as Al Feldstein describes it, "a socially conscious humor magazine." Sure, *MAD* has always featured simple inanity (and insanity), but there was also the goal of using laughter to teach its primarily young readers to be skeptical about the world around them. As Feldstein puts it, "We were trying to do it as humorously as we could, but in many instances we were communicating a very serious message."

MAD doesn't look for anyone's seal of approval, but the American Cancer Society and the American Heart Association are among those who have commended the magazine over the years for its anti-smoking pieces. In fact, *MAD* began warning of the dangers of smoking long before the Surgeon General did, and while many of these spoofs fall into the category of repeating the simple message "smoking is bad," if there was ever a message that bears repeating, this is probably it.

Here are most of *MAD*'s cigarette ad parodies from the last 50 years . . . .

MAD #27
April 1956
Artist: Will Elder
Writer: Harvey Kurtzman

MAD #32
April 1957
Artist: Mort Drucker
Writer: Allan Robin

"Rolly Cigarettes" is one of *MAD*'s earliest TV ad spoofs. While *MAD* has done many TV ad parodies over the years, few of them have hit the tobacco industry. Why? Because Congress banned cigarette ads from the airwaves in 1971, which was unfortunate only for the fact that it gave *MAD* one less thing to make fun of.

Fortunately, as you'll see throughout this section, cigarette manufacturers still provided plenty of fodder for the *MAD*men.

MAD #37
January 1958
Photographer: Larry
Maleman
Writer: House

This parody (above) marks the first use of photography in a *MAD* ad spoof. Nick Meglin and Jerry De Fuccio are the stars.

MAD #40
July 1958
Artist: Kelly Freas
Writer: House

MAD #41
September 1958
Artist: Kelly Freas
Writer: House

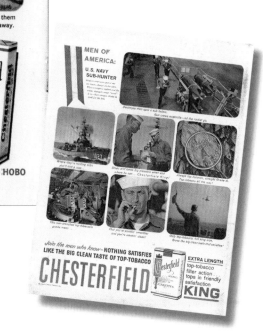

The Chesterfield campaign highlighted the "men of America" like jet pilots and law enforcement agents enjoying a smoke on the job. But what about the jobless? If anyone could use a nice, "relaxing" smoke, isn't it them?

MAD #86
April 1964
Photographer: Lester Krauss
Writer: House

Likely Strife separates the men from the boys...

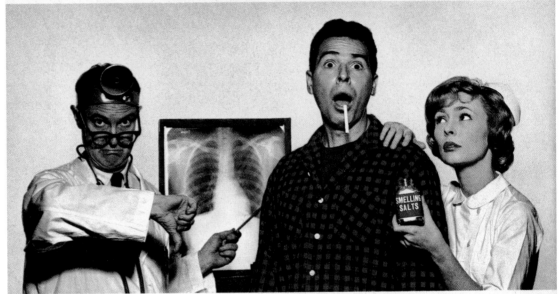

but not from the doctors.

LIKELY STRIFE "IT FIGURES"

CIGARETTES

Smoking is a habit we'd like to get all you kids hooked on.
Hey, kids! Wanna feel grown up? Wanna feel like a man?
Wanna be separated from the boys—but not from the girls?
Smoke Likely Strife—and you'll discover one other thing:
You'll also be separated from your health!

PHOTOGRAPHY BY LESTER (L.S./M.F.T.) KRAUSS

Even after *MAD* stopped using professional models, it has occasionally gone outside the office (but generally stayed within the *MAD* family) for its photo shoots. That's Nick Meglin in the flannel shirt, and playing the doctor is *MAD*'s art supplies dealer at the time, Stan Cohen.

MAD #88
June 1964
Photographer: Lester Krauss
Writer: House

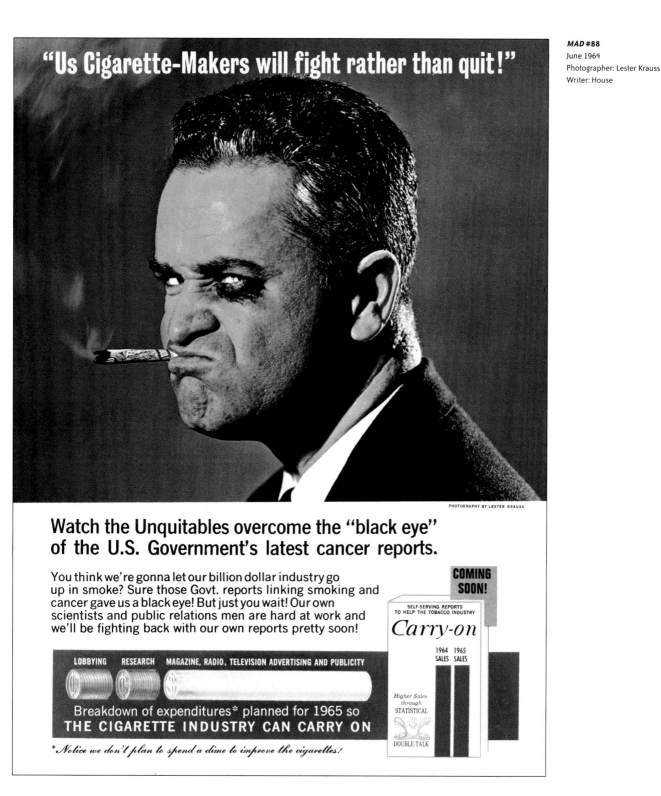

"Us Cigarette-Makers will fight rather than quit!"

PHOTOGRAPHY BY LESTER KRAUSS

Watch the Unquitables overcome the "black eye" of the U.S. Government's latest cancer reports.

You think we're gonna let our billion dollar industry go up in smoke? Sure those Govt. reports linking smoking and cancer gave us a black eye! But just you wait! Our own scientists and public relations men are hard at work and we'll be fighting back with our own reports pretty soon!

COMING SOON!

SELF-SERVING REPORTS TO HELP THE TOBACCO INDUSTRY

Carry-on

1964 SALES 1965 SALES

Higher Sales through STATISTICAL DOUBLE-TALK

LOBBYING   RESEARCH   MAGAZINE, RADIO, TELEVISION ADVERTISING AND PUBLICITY

Breakdown of expenditures* planned for 1965 so
THE CIGARETTE INDUSTRY CAN CARRY ON

Notice we don't plan to spend a dime to improve the cigarettes!

Tarryton cigarettes' campaign featured good-looking people with black eyes who declared, "We would rather fight than switch." Here, the slogan is twisted, as Al Feldstein represents all the cigarette manufacturers who would do everything in their power to make sure that their customers don't quit on them.

Feldstein (who at the time of this spoof was a smoker, but quit a few years later) says this spoof is his personal favorite.

1. Winsom tasted good like a cigarette should've.

2. You mean... *as* a cigarette should've.

3. What did you want, good grammar or good taste?

4. I wanted to live a lot longer than this!

Winsom

Winsom may not say it right, but they sure know how to put you right—six feet under with CANCER BLEND tobaccos

MAD #89
September 1964
Photographer: Irving Schild
Writer: House

Cigarette People:

They like their jobs, but none of them smoke. (They just want you to!)

Col. Kent "Lucky" Lark owns a Tobacco Plantation in Virginia

Winston Tareyton is President of a Tobacco Company in North Carolina

Paul Mall is a Cigarette Account Executive on Madison Avenue

Phil Morris is a Cigarette Wholesaler-Distributor in Illinois

These people depend on cigarette-smoking for their livelihoods, and all those cancer reports haven't made their lives any easier. Although they've kicked the smoking habit themselves, they wouldn't dare tell you to try. They want you to keep doing as they say, not as they do. Then, they'll be <u>satisfied</u>!

CIGARETTE FINKS say "Smoke! Smoke—till you have no Chest to feel!"

MAD #103
June 1966
Photographer: Irving Schild
Writer: House

Photography by Irving Schild

If ever you're on the outskirts of Laredo,
Or any such town like that here in the West,
You'll see all the places we've planted young cowboys
Who died from those cigarette slugs in the chest!

Famous Marble-Row Funereal Black

WE HANDLE EVERYTHING from headstones to our famous "flip-top box"

YOU GET A PLOT YOU LIKE

Marble-Row FUNERAL DIRECTORS
"A Complete Burial Service"

Send for this free catalogue today!

MAD #107
December 1966
Photographer: Irving Schild
Writer: House

Aside from his talents as a photographer, Irving Schild excels at stretching a dollar. As he explains it, "[former editor] Al Feldstein would direct these shoots like they were a $10,000 national campaign." Problem is, *MAD*'s budgets are nowhere near $10,000 for a photo shoot, which means Irving often finds himself coming up with creative ways to save a buck.

In the case of this Marlboro cigarette spoof, renting a horse would have been prohibitively expensive, since a stable would expect a pricey modeling fee. So Irving went out to Long Island with his camera and the fake grave he had built, and constructed his scene along a bridle path. He then walked to a nearby stable, rented a horse, and rode it over to his set-up. He removed his boots, placed them in the scene, and shot the photo.

Problem was, as soon as he was done the horse ran off, and a bootless Irving found himself chasing it down through the field.

In the end, he got his horse . . . and the shot.

MAD #104
July 1966
Photographer: Irving Schild
Writer: House

Photography by Irving Schild

MAD's Great Moments In Advertising

THE DAY A GENTLEMAN FINALLY OFFERED A LADY A TIPARILLO

THE LADY IS JO ANNE WORLEY, STARRING IN "THE MAD SHOW"

The lady receiving the Tiparillo is actress Jo Anne Worley, who was appearing at the time in *The* MAD *Show*, a successful off-Broadway revue written by *MAD*men Larry Siegel and Stan Hart. Worley went on to star in *Laugh-In*. Offering her the Tiparillo is Jerry De Fuccio, who went on to star in . . . well, this photo shoot.

MAD #114
October 1967
Photographer: Irving Schild
Writer: House

MAD's
Great Moments In Advertising

THE DAY THE "SHOW US YOUR 'LARK' PACK" CAMERA CREW
PASSED THE WRONG GROUP OF SMOKERS

MAD #109
March 1967
Artist: Bob Clarke
Writer: Vic Cowen

Irving Schild had this photo shoot, spoofing the Lark cigarettes "Show us your Lark pack" TV campaign, meticulously planned out. He would set up Lenny Brenner on top of a rental truck, park it on the corner of 28th and Park Avenue South, and recruit passersby to fill out the crowd scene. The one thing he didn't plan for was the cops showing up.

"What're you doing?" asked one of New York's Finest.

"What does it look like I'm doing?" Schild snapped back. "I'm taking a picture."

Irving didn't know that he needed a permit, something he had failed to acquire, and now his shoot was in jeopardy of being shut down before he snapped off a single photo. Thinking quickly, Irving did what any smart, reputable artist would do in that situation: He bribed the cop with 20 bucks.

MAD'S
Great Moments In Industry

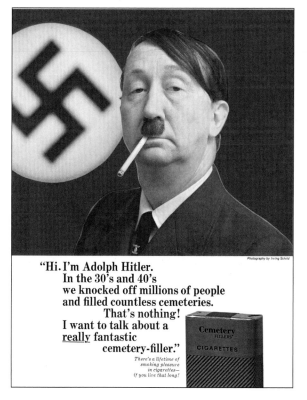

THE TOBACCO COMPANIES GO TO EVEN GREATER LENGTHS...WITH...

The 100 mm Cigarette
AND LONGER

MAD #118
April 1968
Photographer: Irving Schild
Writer: Harry Borgman

MAD #140
January 1971
Photographer: Irving Schild
Writer: House

If it wasn't for Winsom, I wouldn't smoke.

I also wouldn't cough. And my breath wouldn't smell. And my fingers wouldn't be stained yellow. And my hair and my clothes wouldn't stink from stale smoke. And my taste buds wouldn't be deadened. And my nose wouldn't run and my eyes wouldn't tear and—

The Surgeon General Is Amazed That Cancer, Emphysema, High Blood Pressure and Heart Disease Weren't Even Mentioned In This Ad

By the early '70s, with the women's rights movement in full swing, cigarette companies tried to sell their products using a feminist spin. After all, don't women deserve the same opportunity as men to get lung cancer and die an early death?

"Hi. I'm Adolph Hitler.
In the 30's and 40's
we knocked off millions of people
and filled countless cemeteries.
That's nothing!
I want to talk about a
really fantastic
cemetery-filler."

*There's a lifetime of
smoking pleasure
in cigarettes—
if you live that long!*

Cemetery
FILLERS'
CIGARETTES

MAD #125
March 1969
Photographer: Irving Schild
Writer: House

MAD #154
October 1972
Photographer: Irving Schild
Writer: Al Jaffee

Can you spot the former Cancel smoker?

In this picture, everybody has a compulsive hang-up ... well, almost everybody! Try finding the idiot who no longer has one.

1. Nope. This jerk is still wallowing in his compulsive hang-up. He's Gordon Focus, camera bug. He gets his kicks out of buying expensive cameras. Never takes any pictures. Just likes wearing them around his neck. **2.** Sorry. He's Ernie Yellowbelt, a self-defense freak. Likes chopping bricks and boards in half. Gets mugged regularly. Nobody ever holds him up with a brick or a board. **3.** No. She's Selma Wheatgerm, health food nut. She's so hung up eating nothing but health foods, she's dying of malnutrition. **4.** Wrong. Vinnie Gadrool, sexist pig. Compulsive hang-up: Digs looking at girls. Looks at them in magazines, in the movies, through his binoculars. Hasn't touched one yet. **5.** Right! This idiot no longer has his compulsive hang-up! He was once a heavy smoker. Now his friends, these other idiots, are lining up to buy newspapers so they can read his obituary. **6.** She's Tillie Telly, a TV addict. She'll watch anything on TV, even the test pattern. She's hoping they'll mention her recently deceased friend on "Sermonette."

CANCEL Cigarettes
They're not for anybody

CANCEL
CIGARETTES

Warning: The Surgeon General Has Determined That Cigarette Smoking Is Dangerous To Your Health. But This Compulsive Idiot Didn't Listen To Him.

MAD #163
December 1973
Photographer: Irving Schild
Writer: House

PHOTOGRAPHER: IRVIN

Warning: The S
ALL Cigarette S

MAD #242
October 1983
Photographer: Irving Schild
Writer: Billy Doherty

al Has Determined That
ngerous To Your Health.

You found out!

The Truth. That even smoking the one
enjoyable ultra low tar cigarette
doesn't make it any less deadly.

Any member of the Usual Gang of Idiots will tell you that his job is fraught with danger. Whether it's a painful hand cramp after hours of illustrating a movie satire, or debilitating brain freeze when trying to come up with yet ANOTHER way to say that Michael Jackson is a major-league weirdo, the *MAD*man puts life and limb at risk every time he goes to work.

In this case, Irving Schild was worried that one of the locals in the small Pennsylvania town where he took this photo might not take too kindly to a guy traipsing through their cemetery carrying a large-format camera and a shovel. Yet there was Irving, fake headstones and all, waiting for just the right light to capture this eerie photo. He even brought his own dirt.

And yes, he made it out of the graveyard alive.

MAD #259
December 1985
Writer: Billy Doherty

SMOKE GETS IN YOUR LIES DEPT.

Some straight Talk about selling cigarettes to a hostile public.

We're R.J. Riddles Tobacco, and we're trying to improve our image.

That's why you keep seeing these drab, black-and-white ads, full of long-winded copy, in which we wax informative on the subject of smoking and try to prove how well we understand and appreciate both sides of the smoking controversy.

We explain the pros and cons of smoking. We present both the smokers and non-smokers arguments. We tell kids that we don't want them smoking, like their parents. We say anything and everything we can think of, so you get the subliminal message that us "bad guys" are really "good guys" and that maybe our product isn't so bad, either.

This isn't as easy as you might think. New anti-smoking laws are popping up all across the nation. Non-smokers continue to argue that "passive" smoking is just as deadly as "active" smoking. The atmosphere is very unfriendly out there right now.

We want to replace this hostility with the trust and confidence the public once had in us—before the ax falls and we get legislated out of business. These double-talk ads were our P.R. firm's brilliant solution.

So, we may be keeping this up for awhile. It's a great way to advertise because—since we don't picture our product—we don't have to include that lousy Surgeon General's Warning.

R.J. Riddles Tobacco Company

WRITER: BILLY DOHERTY

MAD #294
April 1990
Artist: John Pound
Writer: Duck Edwing

MAD #392
April 2000
Artist: Scott Bricher
Writer: Darren Johnson

Perhaps no tobacco campaign was more nefarious than R. J. Reynolds's "Joe Camel" campaign, which targeted children and adolescents in the company's attempt to hook them on cigarettes.

A 1991 article in the *Journal of the American Medical Association* revealed that 91% of six-year-olds could identify Joe Camel, giving him about the same recognition as Mickey Mouse. By 1997, the Federal Trade Commission charged that the campaign was illegally selling to minors, prompting R. J. Reynolds to do something *MAD*'s ad parody had done symbolically seven years earlier—kill off Joe Camel.

GALLERY OF SIN # 2

THE BOOZE ADS

MAD has spoofed just about every brand of beer and liquor on the market, taking on the liquor industry from the earliest days of the magazine. One reason, says Nick Meglin, is that in the '50s and '60s, the liquor companies (along with the tobacco companies) frequently bought the most ads and ran them in the most prominent places, taking up not only the back covers of many of the nation's weekly magazines, but reinforcing their campaigns with billboards across the country.

Besides, given that booze ads all basically boil down to one ridiculous message—"Getting drunk is glamorous!"—they are an awfully easy target.

Speaking of getting drunk, this section would probably seem a lot more interesting if you poured yourself a stiff drink or two. . . .

MAD #25
September 1955
Artist: Will Elder
Writer: Harvey Kurtzman

MAD #26
November 1955
Artist: Will Elder
Writer: Harvey Kurtzman

it's HIGH ADVENTURE

When you bird watch for the Pipit!

1 "It is not without danger to birdwatch for the Meadow Pipit!" writes an American friend of Canadian Clubbed. "Many's the time one blunders and stumbles through the dense underbrush in pursuit of what he thinks to be the Meadow Pipit only to discover he has been following the Tree Pipit. We had been crashing through the dense underbrush of the Bronx Botanical Gardens all day on the trail of the wily Meadow Pipit. My host, Sir Covert Scapular who was in the lead of our party from the Concourse Manor was suddenly observed to stiffen, his eyes riveted directly ahead of him. With joyous cries, we all rushed forward to share his discovery . . . a Planter's Peanut wrapper you can send away for premiums."

2 "I acted quickly shouting 'half-ies!' before the others could gather wits. We resumed our birdwatch. It was here Sir Covert Scapular showed his birdwatch prowess indicating what seemed to be a daub of mud, or an insect construction, which was in reality *the nest of the Meadow Pipit!*"

3 "Joyously tootling our bird whistles we rushed forward. For there is nothing like delicious Pipit eggs. You can whip a Pipit egg or even dip it, or dip a whipped Pipit egg for the dipped whippit is pipped, or rather dipped whipped pip dippit, but I digress. So there we were, crashing towards the nest of the Meadow Pipit which looked like a daub of mud or an insect construction. Imagine our surprise when we found that it really was an insect construction."

4 "In no time flat we were back at the Manor sipping Canadian Clubbed to mainly kill pain of stings. After the 12th drink imagine my surprise to find my host, Sir Covert Scapular was in reality . . . a Meadow Pipit!"

5 **Which all goes to show** that whatever part of the world you visit, whether it be Timbuktu or the Bronx Botanical Gardens . . . you will always find that drink that has been a popular favorite amongst connoisseurs for generations, you will find that ever popular drink, Coca Cola.

Canadian Clubbed too, is famous all over because it is *light* as scotch, *rich* as rye, *satisfying* as bourbon with distinctive character and flavor and like that. And mainly you get tight.

IN 87 LANDS . . . THE BEST IN THE IGLOO

"Canadian Clubbed"

6 YEARS OLD
PLENTY PROOF

IMPORTED WHISKEY MADE BY JEETER LESTER

IMPORTED FROM CANADA. OUR MOTTO: DRINK ENOUGH CANADIAN CLUBBED AND YOU'LL DRINK CANADA DRY.

"This one has the urp!"

Unmistakable! The sound of that

Padst Red Ribbon Urp

There's an outstanding reaction that now distinguishes Padst Red Ribbon from America's ten or twelve other great beers. Try some and you're sure to experience that reaction. We call it the *Urp of Red Ribbon Padst* (URRP, for short.) Padst is the only major brewer to bottle its own distinguishing URRP. It makes the difference. You can hear it! Next time your friendly bartender asks that friendly question: "What'll you have?" Just say "URRP" and get ready for another kind of reaction when he punches you right in the eye!

Tradebark by Reginald Uspatoff
© Padst Brewing Company. Repeat. Often.

You can tell that this is an early *MAD* alcohol parody because, instead of commenting on one of the dangerous side effects of alcohol like liver damage, DWI, or hooking up with an ugly ho-bag, this piece, a spoof of Pabst Blue Ribbon's "This one has the *touch*" campaign, comments on the (gasp!) horrors of beer-induced belching.

MAD #27
April 1956
Artist: Will Elder
Writer: Harvey Kurtzman

While you are visiting—

What makes a glass of beer taste so good?

Malted barley—with important body minerals plus liquid matter. For thing that makes glass of beer taste so good is terrible thirst.

Tangy hops. Yes—visiting can be a series of tangy hops if you play your cards right. And you'd be surprised how good free beer tastes!

The way it "goes with everything"—makes beer this country's Beverage of Moderation—the way it fits into our friendly way of life—the way each glass makes us friendlier and friendlier and friendlier.

Beer Belongs—Enjoy It!

The Brewers Foundation had created an image campaign to convince Americans that beer should be the national drink. Harvey Kurtzman conceived of a world where their dream came true in this piece beautifully rendered by artist Will Elder.

Knuckleheaded people who drink Inferial and then go driving, end up as a case

MAD #45
March 1959
Artist: Kelly Freas
Writer: House

MAD #53
March 1960
Artist: Kelly Freas
Writer: House

MAD #56
July 1960
Artist: Kelly Freas
Writer: House

If You're A Midget...
FLEISCHMAN'S
makes you a BIG guy!
90 PROOF is why!

BET ALL ALONG YOU THOUGHT THIS WAS A PICTURE OF A REGULAR-SIZE GUY CARRYING AN OVER-SIZE BOTTLE OF BOOZE, TOO!

FROM THE RUMMIE WALKER COLLECTION

"Crocked" by FRANK KELLY FREAS

Artist·Illustrator·Drunk

When we commissioned Frank Kelly Freas to paint his hobby for our ad campaign, we hoped he would come up with something as interesting as Harold Von Schmidt and Peter Helck and Robert Riggs had done before him. Unfortunately, it looks like Mr. Freas went a little astray after painting our whiskey bottle. Mainly, he killed the contents and ended up stewed to the gills.
 Guess the laugh's really on us. We never figured Mr. Freas's hobby would turn out to be "drinking"!

RUMMIE WALKER · BLACK LABEL · SCOTCH WHISKEY
Blended Scotch 86.8 Proof. Imported by Canada Dry Gin 'n Ale, Inc., New York

RUMMIE WALKER
Took his first drink in 1820 still going strong

Another of artist Kelly Freas's personal favorites, "Rummie Walker" depicted what happens when an artist has a little too much to drink while trying to finish a piece on deadline. Notice the signature, drunkenly slurred as "Freash."

 Freas painted "Rummie Walker" around the time he was living in Guadalajara, Mexico. Working from Mexico was a little tricky, thanks to Mexico's strict laws about exporting national treasures (perhaps the only time *MAD* art has ever been declared a "national treasure"). Because the export tariffs were so high, Freas would've paid more in taxes than the paychecks he was receiving for his paintings, so he resorted to smuggling out his work in the luggage of friends and family.

Sadder...
But wiser
where there's **strife**...there's Beer

WHAT A HEAD!
Who said you can't
tie one on with beer?
Here's a guy who drinks
"The Beverage of Moderation,"
and he's been in a beer
stupor for a month!

*Dear John,
I've taken your drinking just about as long as I can. I've also taken the children, the car, and the bank book. You'll be hearing from my lawyer! Goodbye!*

MAD #63
June 1961
Artist: Kelly Freas
Writer: Al Jaffee

MAD #76
December 1962
Photographer: Lester Krauss
Artist: Bob Clarke
Writer: House

MAD #78
April 1963
Artist: Bob Clarke
Writer: House

Designer George Lois was one of the leaders of the Madison Avenue cultural revolution of the '60s and his firm, Papert Koenig Lois, became famous for playful ads, like the Wolfschmidt Vodka campaign that featured vodka bottles bantering with mixers.

Here, the *MAD*men ostensibly create a plug for one of Wolfschmidt's "competitors"—Alcoholics Anonymous.

▶ **MAD #94**
April 1965
Photographer: Lester Krauss
Artist: Bob Clarke
Writer: House

In the real campaign, Canadian Club tried to create an adventurous image by showing average guys engaged in dangerous activities like bullfighting in Spain and shark-riding in Ecuador. When you think about it, the boys at Canadian Club were onto something, since you'd have to be awfully drunk to do something as stupid as fly down to South America to ride on a shark.

MAD #131

December 1969
Photographer: Irving Schild
Writer: House

MAD #311

June 1992
Photographer: Irving Schild
Writers: Joe Raiola and
Charlie Kadau

"She's had three miscarriages in the last two years. <u>Still</u> she drinks Johnnie Warper."

Good taste is always in absenc

Ron Reagan. Isn't he the ex-movie star who wanted to be President?

Yep! And it's something most folks would like to forget! That things like this are happening here in America! That old-time movie stars who weren't even that good in the first place have become Senators and Governors and yes— even made bids for Presidential nominations. It's enough to drive a thinking person to drink!

RIGHT WING LABEL
RONREAGAN
PUERTO
REAGAN
RUM

Ronreagan. A rum to help forget.

Photography by Irving Schild and Wide World.

See the guy in the front? Looks pretty annoyed, doesn't he? That's because he's a friend of photographer Irving Schild who agreed to lend his fancy Manhattan apartment for a *MAD* photo shoot without knowing that all of his furniture would be rearranged and a model would be jumping up and down on his nice, clean sofa. And for his efforts, did he get the $3,000 rental fee Irving would've forked over if he'd rented the place on a big ad agency budget?

Not exactly.

"He didn't get paid," says Schild, "but he got to keep the bottle of whiskey."

That's *MAD* artist Rick Tulka on the sofa with Irving's pal.

MAD ESP, PART 4

It wouldn't be a stretch to suggest that this *MAD* ad—lampooning both Ronrico rum and then-California governor Ronald Reagan's failed presidential bid—predicted not only Reagan's eventual presidency, but the political aspirations of another movie star who wasn't "even that good in the first place," Arnold Schwarzenegger.

Actually, maybe it would be a stretch. Never mind.

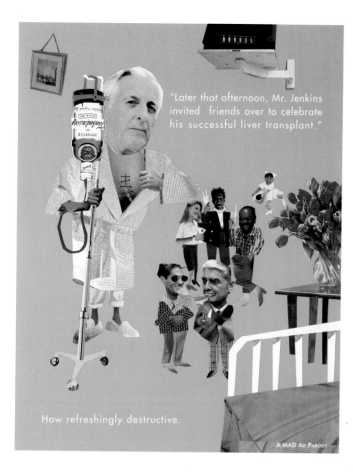

MAD #340
October 1995
Artist: Gerry Gersten
Writer: House

"Later that afternoon, Mr. Jenkins invited friends over to celebrate his successful liver transplant."
How refreshingly destructive.
A MAD Ad Parody

Sure, the scar may have been a little high for a liver transplant, but there's no doubt that this piece accurately portrayed what would have happened if Tanqueray's Mr. Jenkins—a suave, gin-guzzling gentleman who always appeared in photo collage ads with a drink in hand—kept up his empty life of heavy boozing and hanging out with pretentious yuppies and Gen-Xers.

MAD #343
March 1996
Artist: Bob Jones
Writer: J. Prete

A TV Ad We'd Like To See
I
I
D
I
D
I
W
W
D
W
I
D
W
I
CROAK!
ARTIST: BOB JONES WRITER: J. PRETE

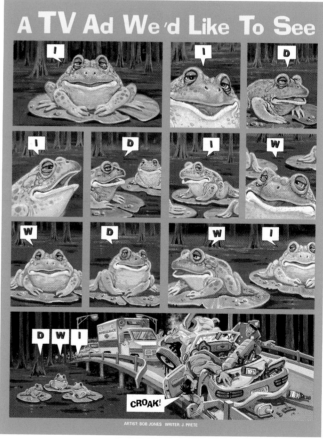

The Budweiser Frogs gained fame for their monosyllabic grunts of "Er," "Weis," and "Bud," which, by the end of the commercial, were croaked in the proper order to name their favorite brew. (If you can't figure out what that beer is, then you've probably had one too many yourself.)

MAD #298
October 1990
Photographer: Irving Schild
Computer Artist: Stephen
Hauslew/Premwdia, Inc.
Writer: Al Jaffee

For nearly a quarter of a century, Absolut has been using the shape of its bottle to create a series of visual puns that have become so popular, they've even spawned web sites devoted to collecting them.

MAD has visited the Absolut campaign several times, both to comment on the dangers of drinking and to use the ads as a vehicle to mock current events. And, in the case of "Absolut America West" (inspired by a news report that two of the airline's pilots were busted for drinking on the job), to do both at the same time.

MAD #356
April 1997
Artist: Greg Theakston
Writer: Al Jaffee

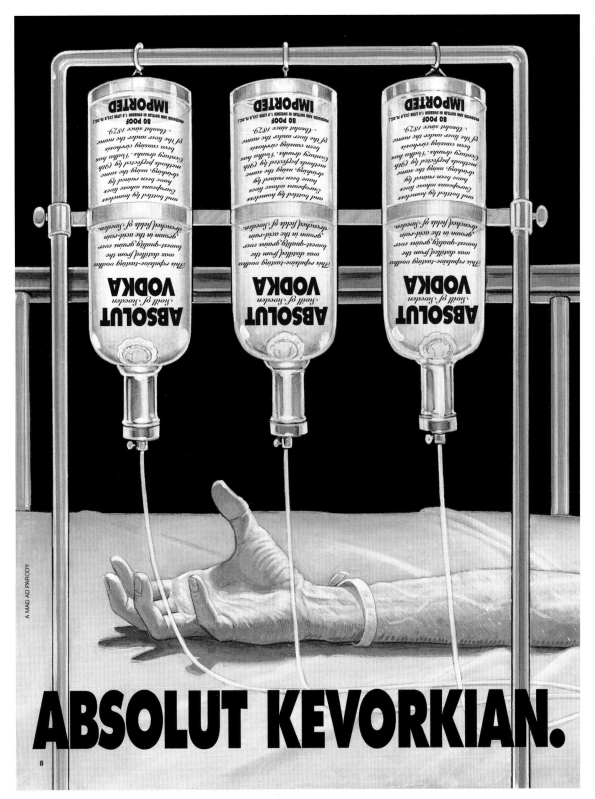

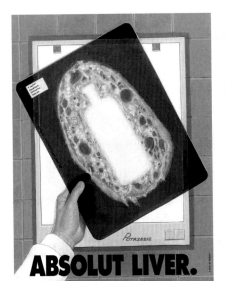

ABSOLUT LIVER.

ABSOLUT O.J.

MAD #356
April 1997
Artist: Greg Theakston
Writer: Al Jaffee

16 AMERICA WEST AIRLINES: HIGH IN THE SKY

May we have your attention readers, this is your editor speaking. Please fasten your seatbelts, as we will be going over the rocky, turbulent story of two America West Airlines pilots who, in July, made an unannounced layover at a local watering hole just hours before planning to fly 124 passengers from Miami to Phoenix. If you look carefully, you will notice the irresponsible flight attendants who didn't notify the authorities about the highly-fueled aviators. You might also observe the uncharacteristically vigilant airport security people reporting the soused pilots as they stumble aboard the plane. Guns in the cockpit? How about breathalyzers? Please notice that we have turned on the "No Fooling" sign. We ask you to remain seated until our satiric commentary comes to a complete stop.

ABSOLUT AMERICA WEST

▲ *MAD* #425
January 2003
Artist: Scott Bircher
Writer: Kenny Byerly

ABSOLUT WINTER.

A MAD AD PARODY

▶ *MAD* #369
May 1998
Artist: James Kirkland
Writer: J. Prete

A MAD AD PARODY

ABSOLUT SADDAM.

A MAD AD PARODY

Now that you've had a few, she's beginning to look pretty good, isn't she?

Dewar's

You just learned firsthand what "downsizing" means. Drink up.

Dewar's

Nice party trick. What do you call it— puking on yourself?

Dewar's

Listen, if you can handle, "Do you mind stepping out of the car, sir?" then you can handle this.

Dewar's

MAD #358
June 1997
Photographer: Irving Schild
Writer: David Shayne

In recent years, senior editor Joe Raiola has taken on the task of directing the models at many of the *MAD* photo shoots, relying on his experience as a theater director to get the best out of his actors. It can be tricky, especially since *MAD* now recruits employees not only from its own ranks, but from its sister company, DC Comics, to serve as models. Often they don't realize until it's too late that they have signed on to humiliate themselves in a national magazine. Joe has two tricks to get the best out of his subjects. First, he encourages them to make noises, as this process helps bring out the best facial expressions. Then, he gives them their prime motivation: "You're an a-hole."

Sometimes, though, *MAD* must hire a pro, as in the case of the model who specialized in "ugly" (her head shots included a lot of witches and ogres), since it can be a little awkward to tell a co-worker that she'd be perfect to play a nasty skank a guy drunkenly beer goggles in a bar.

On the other hand, some of us, like the author of this book, gleefully cover themselves and their favorite sport coat in fake vomit just for a chance to see their face in print. (That's associate editor Amy Vozeolas reacting in horror—she didn't need to dig too deep into her bag of acting tricks to come up with her look of disgust.)

REAL ADS BY *MADMEN*

Many of *MAD*'s artists—such as Bob Clarke, Jack Rickard and Norman Mingo—came to the magazine with a background in advertising, while others, like Mort Drucker and Jack Davis, were hired by advertisers on the basis of their work in *MAD*.

Here's a gallery of some "legitimate" ad work from the Usual Gang of Idiots.

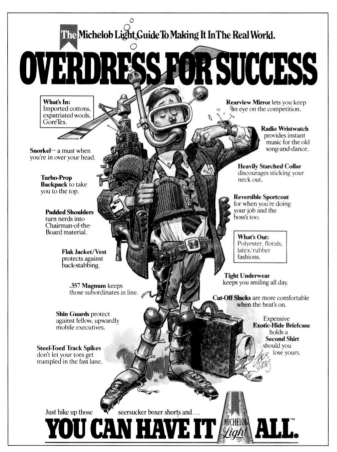

In addition to those shown here, **Jack Davis**' frenetic pen has illustrated everything from Harveys Bristol Cream ads to the poster for the movie *It's a Mad, Mad, Mad, Mad World* (which, title notwithstanding, had nothing to do with *MAD* Magazine).

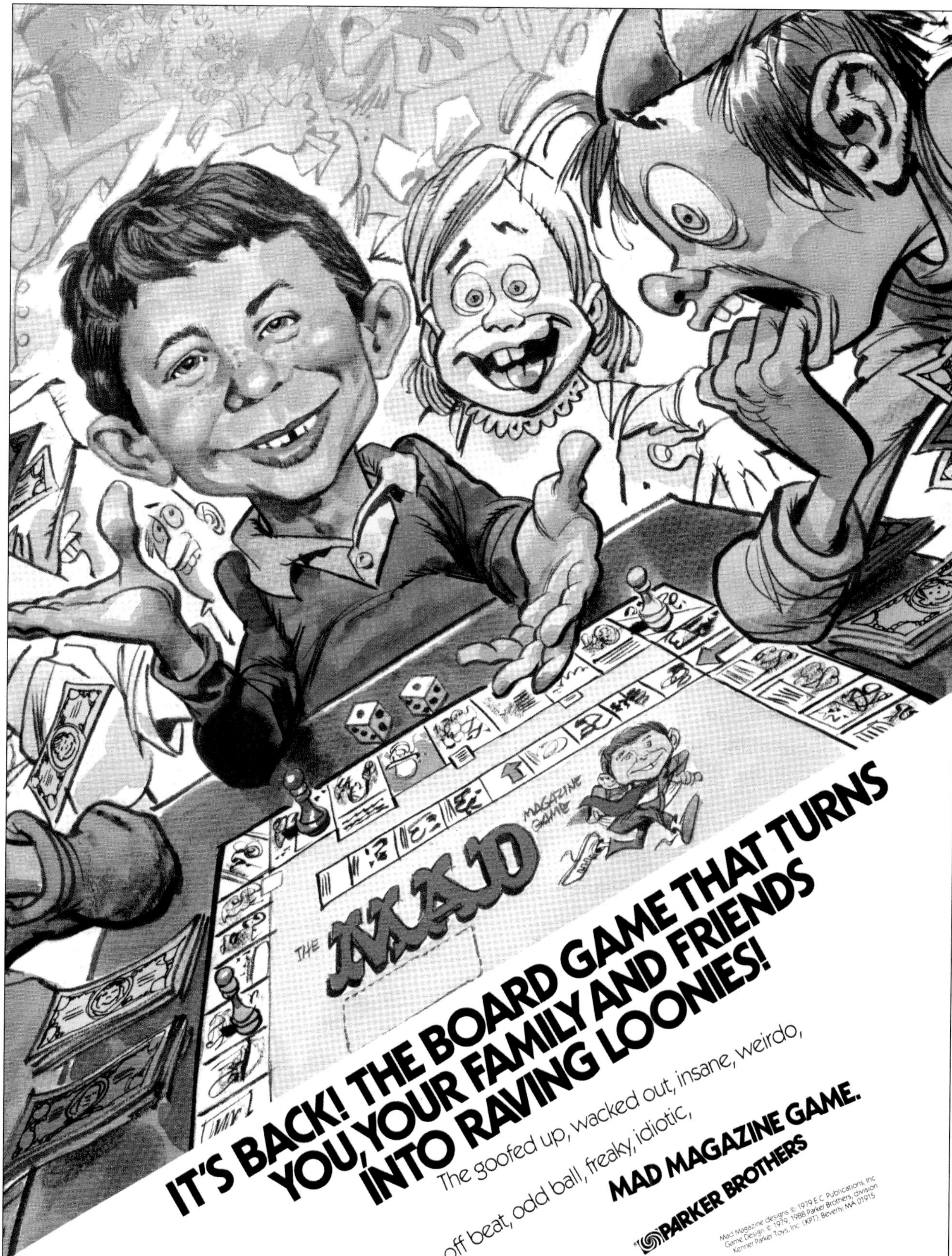
THE MAD MAGAZINE GAME
IT'S BACK! THE BOARD GAME THAT TURNS YOU, YOUR FAMILY AND FRIENDS INTO RAVING LOONIES!
The goofed up, wacked out, insane, weirdo, off beat, odd ball, freaky, idiotic,
MAD MAGAZINE GAME.
PARKER BROTHERS
Mad Magazine designs © 1979 E.C. Publications, Inc
Game Design © 1979, 1988 Parker Brothers, division
Kenner Parker Toys, Inc (KPT), Beverly, MA 01915

Tell us what you think-Call
1-800 "YES" 1-800

Your Comments Count!

As the man behind hundreds of *MAD* covers and TV and movie parodies, **Mort Drucker** has been recognized as one of the best caricaturists alive, making him a natural choice when a company wants to give one of its celebrities a comedic spin.

The Come As You Are Party Tyme.

Get your friends off the ski slope, out of the barber chair, out of the deep blue sea, and over to your place for a last minute crazy fun party.

To go with the dazzling array of outfits, a dazzling array of Party Tyme Cocktails.

Banana Daiquiris, rich with a sweet tropical banana flavor. Fruity Mai Tais, Whiskey Sours, Margaritas. 13 different Party Tyme Cocktail Mixes in all.

And they're all so easy to fix, they practically come as they are.

Party Tyme®
Cocktail Mixes
Anytime is Party Tyme.

Sam Viviano joined the Usual Gang of Idiots in 1981 when he illustrated the "Who Shot J.R." cover. The editors loved it so much, Sam didn't get another MAD job for four years, although he eventually went on to become the magazine's art director. In the meantime, Sam's caricatures and humorous illustrations continued to appear in several national ads.

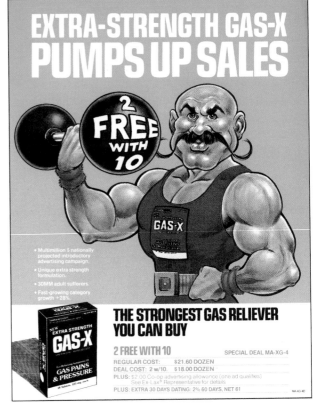

INDEX